End of the Line

End of the Line

The Failure of Amtrak Reform
and the Future of
America's Passenger Trains

Joseph Vranich

The AEI Press

Publisher for the American Enterprise Institute

WASHINGTON, D.C.

Available in the United States from the AEI Press, c/o Client Distribution Services, 193 Edwards Drive, Jackson, TN 38301. To order, call toll free: 1-800-343-4499. Distributed outside the United States by arrangement with Eurospan, 3 Henrietta Street, London WC2E 8LU, England.

NRI NATIONAL
RESEARCH
INITIATIVE

This publication is a project of the National Research Initiative, a program of the American Enterprise Institute that is designed to support, publish, and disseminate research by university-based scholars and other independent researchers who are engaged in the exploration of important public policy issues.

Library of Congress Cataloging-in-Publication Data
Vranich, Joseph
    End of the line : the failure of Amtrak reform and the future of America's
    passenger trains/ by Joseph Vranich.
       p. cm.
    Includes bibliographical references and index.
    ISBN 0-8447-4203-1 (cloth : alk. paper)
    1. Amtrak. 2. Railroads—United States—Passenger traffic. 3. Railroads—
Government policy—United States. I. Title.

  HE2791.A563V7 2004
  385'.22'065—dc22

                                      2004020641

10 09 08 07 06 05 04   1 2 3 4 5 6 7

Printed in the United States of America

To Peter Armstrong and the Rocky Mountaineer team—
may their Canadian privatized rail passenger service
be an inspiration to the United States.

Contents

Illustrations

Foreword

I was somewhat perplexed when my friend Robert Poole, founder of the Reason Foundation, asked me a few years ago to review a paper critical of Amtrak by Joe Vranich. Joe had worked hard on behalf of Amtrak for years and was the author of the seminal American work on high-speed rail, *Supertrains*. While I had never met Joe, I knew his work and didn't imagine we could agree on much of anything. While Joe had been promoting high-speed rail projects, I had expended considerable effort fighting them, and had played a role in the decent burial Governor Jeb Bush ultimately made of the Florida Overland Express boondoggle.

But I too had once been a railroad booster, and it turned out that Joe had embarked upon an intellectual pilgrimage not unlike my own just a few years before. When I was first appointed to the Los Angeles County Transportation Commission, I was an ardent supporter of urban rail. I was instrumental in providing the funding, in 1980, to build Los Angeles' first new light rail line in decades (Los Angeles to Long Beach), as well as much of the local funding for the subway line. I supported urban rail because I believed it would reduce traffic congestion—at least, that is what the consultants told us. It took more than a decade for us to learn that the consultants had misrepresented the outputs of their models. Now, even advocates generally acknowledge that the one thing new urban rail does not do is reduce traffic congestion.

When the evidence became clear, I believed it was important for policymakers to recognize that they were being misled. But much of the public policy community was only interested in one side of the debate. While the facts forced me to reassess my positions, many people who were friends and colleagues refused to reconsider. They held fast to their ideological commitment to publicly funded light rail and subways—a belief so fundamentalist I began to call it a "railigion."

Joe Vranich has made a similar intellectual journey and come to a parallel conclusion—that true support for an effective intercity passenger rail system requires opposing the counterproductive influence of the passenger rail bureaucracy, Amtrak. As a genuine advocate of intercity passenger railroads, Joe felt obliged to blow the whistle on Amtrak—to declare clearly that Amtrak had failed and had to be replaced. He first outlined these ideas in his previous book, *Derailed*. His "emperor has no clothes" analysis was unwelcome, to say the least, among Amtrak's many cheerleaders. Nor did Joe's message strike a positive chord among the special interests that benefit from Amtrak's considerable largess. But Joe has persisted in pursuing the true facts about Amtrak and the future of passenger rail service in America. *End of the Line* shows that the passage of time has only made it more indisputable that Amtrak must be replaced if Americans are to enjoy the passenger rail service that they deserve.

Beware: Amtrak may attempt to discredit this book by pointing to periodic financial and operational reports that are supposedly "favorable." This would be characteristic of Amtrak's behavior throughout most of its nearly thirty-five years of hemorrhaging losses, including the years of taxpayer-financed deception that preceded Amtrak's near bankruptcy in 2001–02. During the tenure of the Amtrak Reform Council, Amtrak board members, its president, and other officials assured Congress, the council, and the American people that it was on the "glide-path" to self-sufficiency required by the Amtrak Reform and Accountability Act of 1997. This was supposedly "documented" in Amtrak's strategic plan, marketing plan, and periodic reports. Meanwhile, the most powerful Amtrak board members, instead of fighting for long-overdue reforms, were fighting for more pork-barrel train routes that couldn't even pass the laugh test. Trains actually started running from Chicago to Janesville, Wisconsin (where?). A planned NBC News story about the Janesville train route was so embarrassing that Amtrak, normally immune to any sense of shame, discontinued the route before the story was broadcast.

Day after day, hearing after hearing, Amtrak stuck to its story: "We are going to make it," we are "on the glide-path" to financial solvency. Congress's inability or unwillingness to cut through these lies and finally deal with Amtrak is reason, in and of itself, for removing responsibility for intercity rail from the federal government.

As soon as the ink was dry on the Amtrak Reform and Accountability Act, Amtrak set to work on obstructing and undermining it. While professing to follow Congress's mandate to achieve financial self-sufficiency, the railroad continued with business as usual. Amtrak used funding that was meant for capital investments to balance its daily operations budget. It routinely ignored requests for information required by the Amtrak Reform Council, or provided answers that were incomplete or misleading. And all the while, Amtrak and its lobbying partners worked on Capitol Hill to undermine the council, resisting any change despite Congress's clear mandate for major reform.

Hence the importance of this book. *End of the Line* is about more than the disastrous way Amtrak has operated for thirty years. Amtrak's dismal performance is an object lesson in how a government-funded entity can pursue its own private objectives, at odds with its public mission, and in diametric opposition to the constitutional processes that establish the law of the land. Can we prevent similar bureaucratic coup d'états from nullifying the law in other federal government agencies? The answer should be obvious, but given the lobbying power of special interests, it will not be easy. It will be impossible without courageous, selfless leadership in Congress—and that is not something to be easily counted upon. So far, there is ample evidence of Congressional complacency, and little evidence of continuing courage. This should be a cause for concern beyond even those who care about Amtrak: The fact that much of the Washington establishment apparently doesn't care that the coup has taken place could well embolden other bureaucracies to plot similar courses.

Here is an organization with management that has made a career of taking more from the taxpayers while giving them less in return. Here is a story of how powerful current and former public officials were enlisted to sell failure as success, even when they should have known better. And here is the story of how members of Congress worked on behalf of powerful interests to thwart the very law both houses of the people had enacted. This is not just a sad commentary on Amtrak; it is a sad commentary on the modern workings of the American political system and portends well neither for the republic nor democracy. Where were the servants of the people when Amtrak burned an act of Congress in its proverbial fireplace? On the train.

All of which bring us to the bottom line. The principal obstacle to improving passenger rail in the United States is Amtrak. As long as those claiming to support passenger rail service are captured by the interest of Amtrak's employees and vendors, intercity rail service will be as ineffective (or even less effective) than it is today. And a lot of money will be wasted in the process.

The "Blue Ribbon" panel said that Amtrak had to go. The Amtrak Reform Council found that Amtrak had to go. And Joe Vranich, who probably knows as much about intercity rail in the United States as anyone, says Amtrak has to go. More importantly, this book sets out a vision by which intercity passenger rail in the United States can contribute much more, by following the market and management reforms that have been so successful elsewhere in the world.

WENDELL COX

Mr. Cox was a member of the Amtrak Reform Council from 1999 to 2002, and is principal of Wendell Cox Consultancy in metropolitan St. Louis. He also serves as a visiting professor at the Conservatoire National des Arts et Metiers (a national university) in Paris.

Acknowledgments

I am grateful to the American Enterprise Institute for Public Policy Research for support throughout the preparation of this work, in particular to Kim Dennis and Ryan Stowers. I want to thank AEI President Christopher DeMuth for recognizing the importance of this work. And my editors, Samuel Thernstrom, Lisa Ferraro Parmelee, and Anne Beaumont patiently did all of the things good editors do to improve the readability of a book; thank you for your brilliant work.

I need to tip my hat to two other organizations, the Cato Institute and the Reason Foundation. Parts of chapter 3 are based on a paper I wrote in conjunction with Cornelius Chapman and Edward L. Hudgins, *A Plan to Liquidate Amtrak*, sponsored by the Cato Institute and published February 7, 2002. Parts of chapters 4 and 5 are based on a paper I wrote with Edward L. Hudgins, *Help Passenger Rail by Privatizing Amtrak*, also sponsored by the Cato Institute and published November 1, 2001. I gratefully acknowledge the Cato Institute for permission to reprint several passages.

Portions of appendix C, which gives details of rail privatization experiences throughout the world, were extracted and updated from a paper I wrote in conjunction with Robert W. Poole Jr., *Replacing Amtrak: A Blueprint for Sustainable Passenger Rail Service*, sponsored by the Reason Public Policy Institute and published October 1997. I gratefully acknowledge the Reason Foundation for permission to reprint several passages.

Finally, I am indebted to my wife, Marie, for her patience as I locked myself away for exceptional amounts of time to create this work. Everyone should be so fortunate as to have a supportive, loving spouse like Marie.

Introduction

Having second thoughts about one's convictions is a growth experience. I should know, because I had helped create Amtrak, and later advocated its expansion. In my exuberance for train travel, I was one of Amtrak's staunchest supporters. I've since recognized that my advocacy ignored powerful forces in the travel marketplace, and I helped perpetuate a discredited transportation concept. I offer a *mea culpa* to American travelers, commuters, and taxpayers. But this book is about more than trains—it is about a government enterprise that has failed so spectacularly that fundamental principles of business and good government are violated.

When Amtrak was formed, it was expected to enhance America's mobility by taking over the failing passenger train system operated by private railroad companies and revitalizing it. Advocates said Amtrak would become "modern," and that putting all intercity trains under one organization would be cost-effective, thus improving the competitiveness of trains. Amtrak's first chairman, David W. Kendall, declared, "This new system can and will succeed because it unifies for the first time the operation and promotion of the nation's rail passenger service. Now, a single management can devote its energy exclusively to serving this passenger."[1] Amtrak would bring about a new Golden Age of rail service. For good measure, politicians promised that Amtrak would eventually earn a profit.

What we have today is far different. Instead, Amtrak is nearly insolvent—seemingly always just one more government bailout away from bankruptcy—and it racks up high costs disproportionate to its meager traffic. The railroad fails America by running too many trains where they are not needed—a form of rolling "pork barrel." Amtrak is unable to lift itself out of a morass of its own making.

Public subsidies for passengers riding Amtrak long-distance trains are expensive. In the 1970s, former transportation secretary William T. Coleman said it would be cheaper for taxpayers to buy airline tickets and give them to passengers for free than to continue to subsidize their train rides. That view was echoed in 1998 by Wendell Cox, an economist and member of the Amtrak Reform Council, who pointed out that airline fare revenues per passenger-mile were less than Amtrak subsidies per passenger-mile, so it would probably be less expensive for the government to buy every Amtrak rider a discount air ticket.[2] And in 2003, as Amtrak costs continued to mount, the Union Pacific Railroad's chief executive, Dick Davidson, said of long-distance train riders, "You could buy them a plane ticket and save money."[3] Each of these critics was correct.

In many cases, the reader need not take my word for the facts and assertions reported here. Because I expect Amtrak to contest my viewpoints, the work is exhaustively documented and footnoted. In many cases I used Amtrak's own words as they appeared in planning documents, press releases, news interviews, and congressional testimony. Also, the work synthesizes findings in nearly two dozen reports published since 1997 by the U.S. General Accounting Office (GAO),[4] the inspector general of the Department of Transportation, the Amtrak Reform Council, and a special "blue-ribbon" panel assembled by a congressional committee. (The last two have completed their missions and are no longer in business.)

Some confusion exists regarding the Amtrak Reform Council and the Amtrak Reform Board. The Amtrak Reform Council was an oversight body given specific powers to look into Amtrak affairs and make recommendations. The Amtrak Reform Board holds fiduciary responsibilities for the railroad, makes policy decisions, and has hiring and firing authority over Amtrak executives.

As a point of disclosure, I served from February 1998 through July 2000 as a member of the Amtrak Reform Council. The Citizens Against Government Waste encouraged the appointment, which was made by Republican Senator Trent Lott of Mississippi. During my service, I experienced repeated attempts by Amtrak to stall responses to the council's requests for information or to refuse to respond at all. Yet the council was required by statute to request specific information for inclusion in reports to Congress. I concluded that the council was unable to fulfill effectively the oversight role that Congress had intended when creating the agency. My resignation allowed me to speak more freely about Amtrak's deceptive campaign that it was on its way to becoming "profitable" (as Amtrak then defined the term). I also warned against granting additional billions of dollars in subsidies to finance "white elephant" Amtrak high-speed train schemes. I am gratified that I had a role in exposing such utter nonsense, including testifying before the Senate Commerce, Science, and Transportation Committee.[5] My resignation also meant that I had no vote in the final council recommendation that Amtrak be broken apart.

I'm often asked what I think of Amtrak's latest president, David Gunn. On the one hand, I ought to feel indebted to Mr. Gunn for making me look good. In previous years I said Amtrak should never purchase another Acela Express train, and Amtrak sharply criticized me. Gunn took over the helm and revealed he would never buy another Acela Express train. I found fault with Amtrak for starting a money-losing program to carry freight in special cars attached to passenger trains, and Amtrak insisted I was wrong and that the program would become profitable. Gunn killed it for being a money-loser. I said Amtrak owed it to taxpayers to make its books transparent, and Amtrak refused, citing "confidentiality." Gunn has reconfigured the books in a more commonsense way and ordered the posting of financial information on Amtrak's website. Also, giving credit where credit is due, Amtrak has made some recent strides in its marketing campaigns, reservations system improvements, station cleanliness, equipment utilization, and cost controls.

On the other hand, Amtrak's leadership is still heading in the wrong direction. Think of the captain of a ship who is fighting mightily to keep afloat while water leaks in through faulty seams, the equipment breaks down, and the crew is disgruntled. The captain may do a wonderful job fixing leaks and repairing machinery, and may even have the resources from government subsidies to give salary increases to the crew. The captain succeeds in making it to port—but the problem is, it is the wrong port. That is what is happening with Amtrak. Locomotives are being repaired, but the trains are still heading in the wrong direction.

I prefer a nonfiction author to reveal *why* he is writing a book. In my case, I hope to document further how Amtrak is hopelessly flawed and to present possible solutions. Three primary issues emerge in this work:

- The subsidies needed to keep Amtrak operating will continue to reach all-time highs despite the railroad's claims of lowered expenses and improved performance. The facts need to be on the record as to how and why Amtrak is frittering away billions of taxpayer dollars. The subsidy per Amtrak passenger is far higher than anything we find in our aviation or highway systems.

- Amtrak's credibility has plummeted to new lows. This book addresses how growing radicalism within the railroad causes it routinely to threaten to shut down when it has cash-flow problems—even saying it will halt trains on the busy lines where no justification exists for shutting down. Amtrak's promises about future progress are hollow.

- Amtrak has demonstrated a reckless disregard for public safety by ignoring critically needed safety upgrades in its New York tunnels—an issue of added importance in an age of terrorism. It is vital that we remove key facilities like the New York tunnels from Amtrak's bureaucratic grip and transfer them to a regional or local authority that will provide the competent stewardship that train passengers have every right to expect.

The focus of this book is on developments since the passage of the Amtrak Reform and Accountability Act of 1997 (ARAA). In explaining the need for the ARAA, Republican Senator John McCain of Arizona, chairman of the Commerce, Science, and Transportation Committee, said: "Let there be no mistake. Amtrak is on the brink of bankruptcy. Fundamental reforms are needed immediately if there is to be any possibility of addressing Amtrak's financial crisis and turning it into a viable operation. This measure is long overdue, and some fear, as I do, that even with these reforms Amtrak may not make it."[6] Amtrak indeed failed to reform. The intent of this book is to catalogue how that happened; it will demonstrate that Amtrak did not then, nor does now, plan to undertake reforms other than cosmetic ones.

Chapter 1 provides a brief history of Amtrak, which will be helpful for readers who may not be familiar with the many years of mismanagement that led up to enactment of the ARAA in 1997. Chapter 2 outlines the proposed reforms, which actually were quite modest, and how Amtrak thwarted them. It tells how Amtrak managed to receive a massive tax refund—even though it has never paid income taxes—and how the railroad receives hidden subsidy after hidden subsidy. These developments reinforce arguments to liquidate Amtrak and favor replacement operators.

Chapter 3 addresses Amtrak's insatiable demands for more subsidies and includes a chronology of Amtrak's repeated shutdown threats. Developments since the reform attempt prove conclusively that Amtrak's future is hopeless, and preserving Amtrak is irrational. The federal government's effort to maintain the Amtrak status quo is worth censure. Amtrak represents Washington's difficulty in freeing itself of the grasp of special interests who are big spenders, not of their own money, but of taxpayers' money. The result is that Congress appropriates billions of dollars in subsidies without demanding serious changes to a dysfunctional rail system.

Further, congressional requirements that Amtrak spend money on capital improvements to lightly used routes are outrageous. Spending on long-distance routes fails to provide public benefits commensurate with the billions of taxpayer dollars needed to buy new trains and improve fixed infrastructure. Such wasteful spending leaves little for the heavily trafficked routes that indeed require capital improvements and costly security arrangements in an age of terrorism. In short, throughout Amtrak's history, it has devoted too much of its budget to where it is not needed, and not enough to where it is.

I wish every editorial writer in America would read chapters 4 and 5, entitled, respectively, "Myths About the Value of Amtrak" and "Fallacies About the Cost of Amtrak." When the Amtrak Reform Council recommended Amtrak be broken apart, these save-Amtrak arguments were made by some members of Congress and most railroad labor union officials. The chapters counter arguments by the small number of railroad buffs who argue with evangelical zeal to preserve Amtrak's nearly useless and breathtakingly costly long-distance passenger trains; it also counters false promises about future Amtrak-style high-speed trains.

Chapter 6 addresses the chilling threat of terrorism against rail passenger systems. Amtrak receives no criticism from me regarding current-day *threats* of terrorism against passenger trains or stations. The nation must focus on the prospects of terrorist attacks on all types of trains (not just

Amtrak's), railroad stations, bridges, and tunnels. Ominous indeed are comments by Homeland Security Secretary Tom Ridge, who said his agency cannot apply an aviation standard to railroads and that "the security environment for trains will never resemble aviation."[7]

Where Amtrak and I part company, however, is when it comes to the condition of the railroad tunnels in New York City. Literally, lives are at stake should a train accident occur in the tunnels, with their inadequate firefighting equipment and constricted passageways that hamper passenger evacuation. Amtrak has known about the critical need for safety-related improvements for nearly thirty years, yet has done little about it. The urgency of performing these upgrades is greater than ever because of the possible consequences of an act of terrorism aboard a train.

Chapter 7 outlines how, in recent years, Amtrak has managed to alienate its major institutional customers—local commuter agencies and state transportation departments. Boston is a prime example, but it is likely that other public agencies that have contracts with Amtrak will seek alternative operators in the future.

It's time to replace Amtrak with something more workable and relevant. Chapter 8 focuses on what Great Britain, Japan, Canada, and the United States have done to privatize and devolve publicly owned railroads. This chapter and appendix C also outline how fifty-five nations are privatizing, franchising, or devolving their Amtrak-style railroad systems. A little more than a decade ago, every national passenger railroad in the world was owned and operated on the socialist model of a state-run enterprise. Today the only countries in the Western Hemisphere that run an essentially nationalized passenger rail system are the United States, Canada, and Cuba. On this score, Washington has more in common with Havana than it does with Mexico City, Buenos Aires, or countless other capital cities south of the Rio Grande.

Chapter 9 describes capabilities to replicate such lessons here and delves into the monopolistic practices Amtrak uses to thwart private-sector competition. I'm often asked, "Since private railroad companies got out of the money-losing passenger business years ago, how can we return trains to the private sector?" Fair question. The answer is that we need public-private partnerships whereby companies will compete for contracts to run trains, and companies are ready to do that. We need to create a sensible plan where

Amtrak is phased out while responsible private-sector operators take over the Amtrak routes that are worth continuing.

The chapter also examines the experimentation underway in the commercial airline and intercity bus industries. Air service is becoming more affordable to travelers in more places as a result of more efficient aircraft designs, relaxed labor work rules, cost reductions related to airline bankruptcies, and a lessened emphasis on high-cost hub airports. Amtrak—with its fundamental inability to reduce labor costs—will need even higher subsidies to compete against tomorrow's more nimble competition.

The conclusion addresses the difficulty of seeking change in Washington, D.C., which thrives on an entitlement mentality and pork-barrel spending sprees. Many books have been written about Washington's inability to abolish ineffective programs, a "hardening of the arteries," so to speak. One such work, Jonathan Rauch's *Demosclerosis*, vividly illustrates the many ways government has "calcified."[8] Similarly, Brian Tracy has discussed what he termed "psychosclerosis"—"your natural tendency to fall in love with your own ideas, and then to vigorously defend them against anything new."[9] These concepts help explain Amtrak's relationship with Congress, where both institutions fail to respect American taxpayers and travelers, leave vital improvements unfunded, thwart minor reforms, and then falsely promise that Amtrak will somehow become successful. The chapter calls for the elimination of disincentives toward private-sector involvement in rail passenger service.

The appendices present extensive information not found anywhere else in one place—the repeated warnings from government oversight agencies about Amtrak's financial practices and condition; a chronology that delineates the excessive delays in Amtrak's Acela Express development program; and an account of the widespread nature of railway privatization and devolvement, which clarifies how the United States is out of step with countries throughout the world on this issue.

Information in the tables, gleaned from dozens of government studies, documents how Amtrak financial forecasts are way off the mark; illustrates how puny Amtrak's total traffic is when compared with that of airports; outlines the financial losses per passenger on different routes; describes how the majority of Amtrak passengers are concentrated on just a few lines; and, most tragically, summarizes the number of fatalities in terrorist attacks on rail facilities worldwide (671 people between 1998 and 2004).

Amtrak is an enterprise with a negative net worth, unable to run itself in a business-like fashion. This brings up a point about my view of Amtrak as a business. I now serve corporate executives and entrepreneurs as a business performance coach. I help leaders define the next levels of success for their enterprises and help them achieve their goals and objectives. In so doing, I'm struck by how clients demonstrate vision, risk-taking, integrity, conscientiousness, skill, sensitivity, and determination to reach well-designed goals. Amtrak, however, routinely makes appalling decisions. Examples include opening a Wisconsin train line that supposedly would "enhance the area's economy"—a train that often ran empty and lost more than a thousand dollars for *each passenger* it carried.[10] In Indiana, Amtrak started a new train on a slower schedule than had been in effect on the route in 1925, more than three quarters of a century ago. Amtrak's lack of sound decision making at the very time it was ordered to undertake reforms is nothing short of astonishing.

While Amtrak is not worth saving, it is possible to save America's most important trains. A decade ago, Amtrak's chief financial officer Elizabeth Reveal expressed a view that remains salient today:

> I think there's two questions: "What's the future of passenger rail in America?" There is a completely separate question, which is, "What's the future of Amtrak?" You can imagine a brilliant future with passenger rail with Amtrak gone.[11]

The federal government does not run a national airline. It does not operate a national bus company. It does not own the interstate highways (the states do), nor does it own toll roads, commercial airports, or bus terminals. From a public policy standpoint, there is no justification for the federal government to own and operate a national railroad passenger system that is essentially irrelevant to the transportation marketplace. It is time to establish a new paradigm for railroad passenger service in America.

1

A Brief History of Amtrak

Throughout most of the twentieth century, intercity travel by railroad in the United States declined. The deterioration started in 1923, as automobiles started to become widespread, and, with the exception of World War II, it continued unabated through the 1950s. This trend accelerated in 1958, when Boeing 707 jetliners began connecting cities on much faster schedules than propeller-driven aircraft. By 1969, the end of the passenger train was nearly at hand. As Professor George W. Hilton wrote in a study for the American Enterprise Institute for Public Policy Research, "The number of trains, which had reached 20,000 in 1920, was down to 500, and over 100 of these were the subject of discontinuance proceedings."[1]

In 1967 Anthony Haswell founded the National Association of Railroad Passengers, a lobbying organization for the preservation and upgrading of passenger trains. His efforts converged with other forces, resulting in the creation of a new federal program: Amtrak, officially known as the National Railroad Passenger Corporation. The publicly sponsored railroad was established under the Rail Passenger Service Act of 1970.[2] In passing the legislation, Congress anticipated the need for subsidies for only a limited time until Amtrak could become self-supporting.[3] The legislation was signed by President Richard Nixon and became law on October 30, 1970, and Amtrak assumed responsibility for intercity rail passenger service on May 1, 1971.[4]

Nixon administration correspondence mistakenly estimated that some Amtrak routes, such as Chicago–Los Angeles, would be "very profitable," while accurately anticipating that others, such as Philadelphia–Pittsburgh, would incur a "substantial deficit." The Transportation Department concluded, "It is expected that the corporation would experience financial losses for about three years and then become a self-sustaining enterprise."[5]

In fact, Amtrak has always run at a loss and has required substantial subsidies from federal, state, and even local governments (for train stations) to keep it afloat. It is likely that if the advocates of saving railroad passenger service in 1970 could have envisioned what would result from the creation of Amtrak, they would have chosen another path. Anthony Haswell, who today occasionally is referred to as the "father" of Amtrak, has said on several occasions, "I feel personally embarrassed over what I helped to create."[6]

This book will not provide much detail regarding the 1971–96 Amtrak saga, or outline the many revisions in Amtrak's statutory authority or planning procedures during that time. Suffice to say that Amtrak has made many costly mistakes. In the 1970s, for example, it erred in bowing to political pressures to add routes in rural West Virginia and Montana that failed to attract appreciable traffic levels. During the same period, the railroad also miscalculated by using its monopoly powers to dampen development of an independent Auto-Train passenger service. It approved for passenger service the use of a diesel locomotive, designed primarily for freight trains, that had a tendency to derail at the higher speeds that passenger trains travel. And it was reluctant to discontinue poorly performing routes until forced to do so by President Jimmy Carter's administration. Similarly poor decisions in the 1980s caused Amtrak to flounder from one fiscal crisis to another, a pattern that was repeated in the 1990s and continues to the present day. Amtrak seems inherently unable to learn from hard lessons.[7]

Amtrak's problems persist for two fundamental reasons. The first is the premise held by many that giving Amtrak bigger subsidies will ameliorate its problems—a notion that ignores the facts. In the six years since the passage by Congress of the Amtrak Reform and Accountability Act, infusions of $6.5 billion in federal funds have provided Amtrak with more taxpayer largess than in any equivalent period in history. Despite this, the railroad's problems are more intractable than ever.

A second reason was offered by Hilton, who wrote that Amtrak's failure stems directly from the logic whereby the corporation was established. After addressing market demand and measures of consumer responsiveness, he concluded that travelers favor rival modes of transportation that are faster (primarily air) or less expensive (automobile and sometimes the bus) over train travel.[8]

Amtrak's problems persist because the organization spends its capital subsidies on fruitless programs and remains insensitive to the travel marketplace. The inescapable conclusion is that while the United States needs passenger trains in selected heavily populated corridors, it does not need Amtrak's antiquated, far-flung route system, high operating costs, poor management practices that deflect innovation, and capital program with abysmal rates of return. Citing the railroad's determination to pursue business as usual instead of reforming, the *Wall Street Journal* editorialized that Amtrak was "one of the worst-run businesses in the country. . . . The Enron of American transportation."[9]

2

The Failure of
Amtrak Reform Efforts

When Amtrak was created in 1970, it was given rather vague goals to increase ridership, and then-Secretary of Transportation John A. Volpe predicted the new rail corporation "could be profitable within perhaps three years."[1] Proclaimed Arthur D. Lewis, one of Amtrak's eight incorporators, "You're going to see the greatest business turnaround in history."[2]

Amtrak's ridership gains have been hard-won, and the railroad has never achieved profitability. It has never come close—and yet, it insists that all will be different in the future. Year after year, we have heard that Amtrak's fortunes will improve—and year after year, Amtrak skirts bankruptcy, even as it blocks efforts to enact modest reforms. This incoherence and lack of credibility are reflected in Amtrak's tendency to present conflicting statements regarding the same set of facts. For instance, Amtrak's 2004 request for federal subsidies states, "Amtrak enters 2004 in its strongest financial position in years." At the same time, it declares that full funding of $1.798 billion is critical, and it fails to note that the amount is Amtrak's largest-ever subsidy request for one year.[3]

According to an auditor's statement in Amtrak's consolidated financial report for fiscal year 2003, the railroad has a history of sizable operating losses and is highly dependent upon substantial federal government subsidies to sustain operations. Without continuing subsidies, the auditors caution, "Amtrak will not be able to continue to operate in its current form and significant operating changes, restructuring or bankruptcy may occur."[4] Despite a string of announcements about growing ridership, passenger ticket revenues were down in fiscal year 2003 as Amtrak kept lowering fares. And notwithstanding curtailment of several costly programs—such as an

12

ill-designed plan to carry freight (which Amtrak called "express") in special cars attached to passenger trains—the net loss climbed once again, this time to $1.274 billion for the year. Amtrak has consistently failed to take appropriate steps to avoid bankruptcy.

A Blue-Ribbon Call for Major Change

Many warnings about Amtrak's unavoidable need for ever-growing subsidies have gone unheeded, including well-documented admonitions issued prior to the passage in 1997 of the Amtrak Reform and Accountability Act. In June 1997, the Working Group on Inter-City Rail, also known as the "blue-ribbon panel" on Amtrak, came to far-reaching conclusions about the railroad:

- Amtrak is awash in red ink, buffeted by conflicting missions and ballooning debt, and represents an untenable outlook for passenger rail in the United States.

- Amtrak has missed its financial targets and faces a major liquidity crisis and probable bankruptcy.

- Amtrak's funds should be directed toward the routes with the greater market potential, which are primarily the higher density intercity corridors.

- Amtrak's monopoly should end, and passenger rail service should be opened to competition.

- Amtrak does not properly compensate freight railroads for the costs of Amtrak-caused freight train delays, and contracts with them should be renegotiated.

- Amtrak's long-distance trains make more sense as "rolling National Parks."

- Separate and independent ownership of the railroad infrastructure and passenger train operations would serve as a fundamental mechanism to introduce competition in rail service.

- Amtrak requires large subsidies from taxpayers, and those subsidies are not directed to activities of maximum benefit.
  Continued funding of Amtrak has little hope of success and
  would be irrational—a true waste of taxpayers' money that
  potentially exacerbates Amtrak's problems. Genuine renewal of
  national passenger rail service will not be resolved by political
  rhetoric nor by periodic last-minute infusions of cash.[5]

The panel, which was created by the leadership of the House Transportation and Infrastructure Committee, recommended creation of a new holding company named Amrail to own Amtrak's infrastructure and organize the
eventual breakup and privatization of Amtrak. The report cited precedents
where railroads have been separated into different entities, referring to countries as diverse as Australia, the Czech Republic, Japan, Mexico, and
Sweden.[6] As one of the panel members concluded, "Amtrak is a terminal
patient in need of radical surgery."[7] Seven years later, despite serious efforts
to enact even modest reforms, nothing has changed.

The Amtrak Reform and Accountability Act of 1997

The blue-ribbon panel was part of a reform process that had begun earlier.
Congress knew it had to do something about Amtrak, which was facing
imminent bankruptcy, especially as its shaky financial condition was
aggravated by costly restrictions imposed by federal law. Movement to
end the status quo started when the House of Representatives passed a
bipartisan reform measure, the Amtrak Reform and Privatization Act of
1995, by an overwhelming 406-to-4 vote.[8] The legislation would have
eliminated some costs and permitted better business decision making. In
addition to having bipartisan support, the bill was endorsed by rail labor
unions. This reflected its compromise nature. For instance, to ameliorate
Amtrak's costly "labor protection" requirements, the bill called for an
accelerated bargaining process with no restrictions on the eventual labor-
management agreement. Unfortunately, the bill died in the Senate, prin-
cipally because of the opposition of the trial lawyers' lobby to any reform
of the unlimited tort liability in passenger train accidents.

In 1997, a nearly identical bill was introduced, the Amtrak Reform and Accountability Act.[9] This time, however, the labor unions opposed the bill and took many Democrats with them. The reform legislation began passing through the legislative stages on virtually party-line votes. The Clinton White House offered no support for reform proposals, bowing to two favored groups of contributors—organized labor and the trial lawyers.

These events occurred against a background of increasing crisis at Amtrak. The U.S. General Accounting Office projected that Amtrak, which already was borrowing to meet payroll, would exhaust its credit resources by mid-1998. Meanwhile, members of the Brotherhood of Maintenance of Way Employes threatened to strike Amtrak nationwide on October 22, 1997, for higher wages.[10] It was unclear how Amtrak could afford any settlement while on the verge of bankruptcy. The situation was reminiscent of the final days of the Penn Central Railroad, which threatened cessation of operations in 1973 as a result of a labor strike against the already bankrupt carrier. It had taken the federal government—which created Conrail in response to the crisis—thirteen years, $8 billion in taxpayer funds, and five federal laws to put the northeastern freight railroad network back in operation on a private-sector basis.

As the Amtrak Reform and Accountability Act wended its way through Congress, the Clinton administration tried to remove whatever teeth it had to protect the Amtrak status quo. A pivotal moment came when the Taxpayer Relief Act of 1997 was amended by Senate Finance Committee Chairman William Roth, a Republican from Delaware, to include an unearned $2.184 billion "tax refund" to Amtrak. Roth was under pressure from railroad unions in his home state to "do something" to help Amtrak. However, the amendment set off a furious reaction in the House, where Bill Archer of Texas, Republican chair of the Ways and Means Committee, and Bud Shuster, Republican from Pennsylvania and chair of the Transportation and Infrastructure Committee, insisted the tax bill require that reform legislation be enacted as a condition of payment. This provision was the reason Bill Clinton and Congressional Democrats permitted the ARAA to pass. Amtrak needed the $2.184 billion, and couldn't get it until Clinton signed the reform law, which he did on December 2, 1997.

The reforms were intended to require Amtrak to operate more like a legitimate business. The law repealed a ban on the contracting-out of services, eased the ability of states to create interstate compacts to run passenger rail service, and modified certain liability provisions. It abolished a statutory requirement that Amtrak employees receive generous severance benefits should a route be discontinued, instead permitting Amtrak and the labor unions to negotiate new severance agreements.

The law meant that for the first time the federal government would establish a method of measuring Amtrak's progress in tightening its fiscal belt, and it required Amtrak to operate without federal operating grants by the end of fiscal year 2002 (actually, the month was modified from September to December 2002). A provision established the Amtrak Reform Council, a bipartisan oversight commission charged with monitoring Amtrak's financial performance. The council—with only five employees—would share oversight with the much larger staffs of the GAO and the inspector general of the Department of Transportation.

The Amtrak Reform Council's overall responsibilities were to evaluate the railroad's performance and make recommendations for achieving cost containment, productivity improvements, and financial reform; submit to Congress an annual report that assessed Amtrak's progress; and report quarterly to Congress on Amtrak's use of the "tax refund" received under the Taxpayer Relief Act of 1997. A highly visible responsibility was to issue a "finding" should the council determine that Amtrak would fail to meet the ARAA's operating self-sufficiency requirement. Should such a "sunset trigger" be implemented, the council would have ninety days to submit to Congress "an action plan for a restructured and rationalized intercity rail passenger system." In turn, Amtrak would have to submit a different plan to Congress— one that outlined its "complete liquidation."[11] As a safeguard, the Amtrak plan was to be reviewed by the GAO and the DOT's inspector general.

With these provisions of the ARAA, Washington gave the appearance of initiating reforms at Amtrak.

The Clinton Administration's Unqualified Reform Board

Another stipulation of the ARAA was the replacement of Amtrak's board of directors, with whose lack of leadership and resulting bankruptcy threats Congress was dissatisfied. The statute required that a new seven-member "reform board of directors" replace the existing board by March 31, 1998, or soon thereafter. Senator John McCain said that new leadership was imperative, that a "new culture" needed to be adopted by Amtrak employees and management, and that changes should start at the very top. To ensure that the new board would be qualified to perform its important tasks, eligibility criteria were incorporated in the new law.[12] The law stipulated that members be individuals with "technical qualifications, professional standing, and demonstrated expertise in the fields of transportation or corporate or financial management."

The Clinton administration created two problems that snarled the process of seating a reform board. First, it nominated candidates who did not have the qualifications required by the law. Second, it delayed the nominations and forced senators to choose between hurriedly confirming the candidates or throwing Amtrak into a fiscal crisis in 1998. Here is how Anthony Haswell explained it:

> When the White House announced its director picks on May 22, not one name met the Reform Act's criterion specifying private-sector transportation experience. Moreover, two of the nominees . . . are holdovers from the old board that Congress specifically sought to abolish when it passed the reform legislation. Senator John McCain had warned the president in February that members of the old board should not sit on the new one. The administration stonewalled until June 29, eighteen hours before the deadline, when Amtrak stood to lose its 1999 authorization if a new board—consisting of at least three outside directors plus the secretary of transportation—was not seated. Faced with the specter of an Amtrak funding crisis and shutdown, the president signed the appointments of three directors confirmed by the Senate two days earlier.[13]

What was needed on Amtrak's reform board were business-turnaround experts, but Clinton's nominees included two former governors, Michael S. Dukakis of Massachusetts and Linwood Holton of Virginia, the then-sitting governor of Wisconsin, Tommy G. Thompson, and the mayor of Meridian, Mississippi, John Robert Smith. Two of the members began campaigning for

Amtrak to initiate money-losing services to serve their constituents. Mayor Smith routinely advocated creating a new route linking Atlanta with Dallas via Meridian, which would have lost many millions of dollars annually. In December 2000 he reported that Amtrak was hiring and training crews for the new service, and that from the day Amtrak reached agreement with the Kansas City Southern Railway the service could be operational within ninety days.[14] Startup was delayed as Amtrak learned $44.6 million was required to build new train sidings and signals along the route.[15] By 2004, all new route proposals were put on indefinite hold because of Amtrak's financial condition. Meanwhile, Governor Thompson succeeded in his quest to create a Chicago–Janesville, Wisconsin, Amtrak service. After he left the board, it was discontinued because of low ridership and the highest per-passenger deficit in the system. The reform board's record of success on larger institutional issues was similarly disappointing.

As terms expired for Clinton's appointees to the reform board in 2003 and 2004, the Bush administration selected highly qualified executives to fill the vacancies. Nominated were Robert L. Crandall, the former chairman and CEO of AMR Corporation and American Airlines; Louis S. Thompson, retired as a railway advisor for the World Bank, who had been involved in the privatization-franchising of state railways in many countries; Floyd Hall, an executive who has engineered turnarounds at ailing companies, including Kmart, Singer Sewing Machine Company, and Grand Union Company; and Enrique J. Sosa, who oversaw worldwide operations while president of BP Amoco Chemicals and served in executive roles at the Dow Chemical Company.[16] The Senate stalled the confirmations of all of them for many months, despite growing vacancies on the board, and in 2004 the Bush administration was forced to issue recess appointments for Hall and Sosa.[17]

Projecting a "Glidepath" to Profitability

For more than a decade Amtrak has promised financial results it can't deliver, with no apparent consequences. The reform board faced this problem as well—and failed to fix it. In 1992, then–Amtrak chairman W. Graham Claytor Jr. pledged, "Amtrak continues to reduce its need for federal operating support and hopes to eliminate it altogether by the end of the decade."[18]

TABLE 2-1
AMTRAK FORECAST FOR OPERATING SELF-SUFFICIENCY
(millions of dollars)

	FY 1999	FY 2000	FY 2001	FY 2002
Revenues	1,866	2,184	2,396	2,501
Expenses	2,796	3,092	3,215	3,253
Operating Profit/(Loss)	(930)	(908)	(819)	(752)
Capital for Progressive Equipment Overhauls	76	77	78	80
Depreciation/Noncash Expenses[a]	370	470	499	487
Budget Gap	(484)	(361)	(242)	(185)
Excess Mandatory RRTA	166	172	179	185
Test for Self-Sufficiency	(318)	(189)	(63)	0

SOURCE: National Railroad Passenger Corporation (Amtrak), *Strategic Business Plan FY 1999–2002* (Washington, D.C.: Amtrak, 1998), summary handout sheet, 1.

NOTE: Amtrak's test for self-sufficiency does not include paying taxes under the Railroad Retirement Tax Act (RRTA); such taxes are the railroad equivalent of the employer contribution of Social Security payroll taxes.

[a] Noncash expenses also include certain employee benefit related expenses.

In fact, financial losses worsened. Next, between 1995 and 1997 Amtrak advocates repeatedly urged a substantial increase in subsidies to Amtrak to finance improvements sufficient to bring about operating profits—a "glide-path" whereby each year Amtrak's losses would decline and in a few years Amtrak would be operationally self-sufficient. In October 1998, Amtrak developed a strategic business plan which, it claimed, would

> meet the dual objectives of creating a more vibrant, modern national rail system and becoming operationally self-sufficient by the end of fiscal year 2002. [See table 2-1.] Amtrak's ultimate vision is to provide a market-based national system whose economic viability is due to both passenger revenue and the contribution of successful commercial ventures.[19]

Soon thereafter, George D. Warrington was named president of Amtrak. He echoed the plan, predicted a bright future, and promised that

Amtrak would "be the envy of all transportation providers."[20] The following year, Amtrak said it had

> made significant progress towards meeting the ambitious objectives stated in that plan. . . . [T]he corporation is on track to meet the goal of operational self-sufficiency by fiscal year 2003, and to continue growing beyond fiscal 2003 while remaining operationally self-sufficient.[21]

The railroad also announced that service would be initiated on eleven new route segments, but did not explain how adding more money-losing services would bring it closer to self-sufficiency.

Governor Thompson, serving as chairman of the reform board, was bullish. In October 1999, he criticized *Business Week* for implying that future subsidy needs would be nearly double the amount Amtrak claimed, and declared that "Amtrak is on track to eliminate the need for federal operating support."[22] Soon thereafter, he told the Senate that Amtrak would "operate free of operational subsidies in the fiscal year 2003. I am convinced of that. . . . This board has established for Amtrak a clear-cut mission—deliver performance, not promises."[23]

In 2000, Governor Thompson said, "We are keeping our commitment to Congress and the American people to run Amtrak like a business and we continue to achieve solid financial improvement." The boosterism apparently impressed Moody's Investor Services, which raised Amtrak's credit rating to A3, based partly on "Moody's expectation that operational self-sufficiency will be achieved."[24] When the Amtrak Reform Council issued its first report, which contradicted Amtrak predictions on self-sufficiency, Governor Thompson said, "They're wrong. We have developed a very good game plan. . . . We are arguing very vociferously we are going to make it."[25]

Showing consistency, in late 2000 Governor Thompson again promised financial health, saying, "Amtrak is well on its way toward achieving operational self-sufficiency by fiscal year 2003," as he defended against a charge that a high-speed rail bill was a bailout. "We don't need a bailout," he declared.[26] His testimony that day apparently proved too much for Phyllis Scheinberg, the GAO's associate director for transportation programs, who said at that Senate hearing, "Amtrak is largely no better off than it was a year ago."[27] Undaunted, eight months later George Warrington again expressed confidence that Amtrak would reach self-sufficiency.[28] In the five years since then, Amtrak has never come closer than $521 million to self-sufficiency, and that only after heavy borrowing.

It is fair to observe that most organizations have difficulty projecting future performance. Publicly held corporations have to be particularly diligent because of Securities and Exchange Commission regulations. But Amtrak is a breed unto itself—it has a long history of issuing ridership, cost, and financial projections that are way off the mark.

Consider ridership. On numerous occasions the GAO has questioned the traffic forecasts upon which Amtrak bases its revenue projections as being too optimistic. A 1976 report made note of Amtrak's projection that the "number of passengers will increase from 17.3 million in fiscal year 1975 to 32.9 million in fiscal year 1980—a 90 percent increase—and revenue passenger miles will increase from 3.8 billion in 1975 to 8.6 billion in 1980—a 126 percent increase."[29] The actual 1982 passenger count was 21.2 million, 35.6 percent off the estimate, and revenue-passenger-miles totaled 4.6 billion, off by 46.5 percent. To this day, Amtrak does not come close to carrying the levels of traffic projected in 1976. Unsubstantiated projections have remained a hallmark at Amtrak for several decades; its unrealistic "glidepath" estimates to self-sufficiency are but the latest example.

Squandering Amtrak's Unearned IRS "Tax Refund"

Central to events during 1997 was the passage of the Taxpayer Relief Act (TRA), which required that the Internal Revenue Service provide Amtrak with a $2.184 billion income tax refund, even though Amtrak has never paid federal income taxes. The action was shocking to those who advocate spending restraints and was denounced by the National Taxpayers Union, which stated, "We know of no other entity or taxpayer being treated in such a favored manner."[30] As Senate Commerce Committee Chairman John McCain said,

Given that Amtrak is exempt from most federal tax burdens, this scheme represents the greatest train robbery since the James Brothers retired. How we can give a corporate tax refund to a quasi-government corporation that has *never* paid federal corporate income taxes defies imagination. It's too bad the American taxpayers aren't so favorably treated. I think every taxpayer would like the chance to receive a tax refund they aren't legally owed. . . . One has to question just how far Congress is willing to go in its quest to find funny-money for Amtrak.[31]

At the time, Amtrak argued for the funding by asserting it would "make it *less expensive* to operate the national passenger rail system"[32] (emphasis added) and promised to "invest the funds in a manner that would bring the railroad to operational self-sufficiency."[33] And indeed, in providing the money, Congress directed that it be spent on "the acquisition of equipment, rolling stock, and other capital improvements" and payment of interest and principal on obligations incurred for such purposes.[34] It also required the Amtrak Reform Council to report whether the railroad's "tax refund" expenditures were used on high-return investments that would improve the bottom line.

So the council asked Amtrak what its projected rates of return were for each project it had financed. This type of analysis was a common practice on freight railroads, where officials would decide which capital improvements (track and signal work, new facilities or closing of old ones, bridge replacements, curve straightening, congestion elimination, and so forth) should receive priority based on rates of return. But common-sense good business practices for freight railroads were utterly foreign for Amtrak.

The first Amtrak report on TRA-financed projects boasted of the "wise investment" that Amtrak was making of its resources, and that funds were being committed for "high rate-of-return" projects selected after "rigorous evaluation."[35] In fact, a closer look at the report revealed that Amtrak was still following long-discredited spending patterns by failing to target high market-growth opportunities for investment and by spreading $360 million across a broad geographic area. Half of the spending went to the least profitable routes, where it produced no noticeable return on investment.[36]

Amtrak's "geographic balance" approach to capital investment was alarming because Amtrak's ridership and market potential was far from geographically balanced. More than half of Amtrak's passengers were concentrated in the Northeast and California. The dispersed manner in which Amtrak committed TRA funds was another effort to prop up its weak, politically inspired route system at the cost of a market-based system. Amtrak was again marginalizing itself in a marketplace where it held a microscopic three-tenths of 1 percent of the travel market.[37]

When questioned, Amtrak officials could not show how TRA expenditures would reduce losses on poorly performing routes, restrain overall cost growth, or improve cash flow. All indications were that Amtrak was not serious about reforming its wasteful ways. By 2000, the Amtrak Reform Council found significant problems in TRA expenditures, stating, "Amtrak has not used a significant portion of the funds for the kinds of high-priority, high-return investments that will help its bottom line."[38] A year later, the council reported that about 26 percent of TRA commitments were for expenditures that most companies would consider ordinary operating expenses or required capital expenses.[39] Once again, Amtrak failed to direct its capital funding to achieving maximum benefit.

Skepticism regarding Amtrak's financial management was confirmed in mid-2001 (only nine months after Governor Thompson had adamantly declared, "We don't need a bailout"), when Amtrak took the unbelievable step of mortgaging Pennsylvania Station in New York in order to secure a $300 million loan needed to keep the trains running.[40] Senator McCain said, "I am informed this transaction was out of desperation because Amtrak would become insolvent within the next month without an immediate infusion of cash."[41] A letter that he wrote jointly with Senator Phil Gramm revealed additional details:

> Apparently, Amtrak's financial condition is so severe that without an emergency infusion of cash provided by this deal, it would face immediate bankruptcy. The situation is especially troubling considering that Amtrak continues to boast it is on a "glidepath" to operational self-sufficiency. Clearly, Amtrak has been dishonest to Congress and the American public regarding its true financial condition. . . . [P]rior to this latest financial maneuver, Amtrak

lacked the funds to even cover operating costs needed to carry them from June to October 1st when the new fiscal year begins. It is quite disturbing to find out Amtrak is now financing over a 17-year period three months of operating costs—an "asset" which depreciates to zero on October 1st.[42]

Placing the $300 million mortgage on Penn Station was an act of desperation comparable to a family taking out a home equity loan on their house to purchase groceries and other living expenses without changing their lifestyle or knowing how the loan will be repaid. In the real world, such tactics almost always result in bankruptcy. So far, however, Amtrak's endlessly tolerant Uncle Sam has always been willing to open the federal purse for another bailout.

The Amtrak Reform Council Pulls the "Sunset Trigger"

Amtrak's deteriorating finances were such that by July 2001, just after the Penn Station mortgage story emerged, GAO representative JayEtta Z. Hecker warned Congress, "It is very unlikely that Amtrak can operate a national intercity passenger rail system as currently structured without substantial federal operating support. The outlook for it achieving operational self-sufficiency is dim."[43] By September, George Warrington apparently had given up on the idea of self-sufficiency and was quoted as declaring that the requirement was "inappropriate, impractical and irrational in the context of recent events and public service expectations."[44]

The GAO's view was correct. On November 9, 2001, the Amtrak Reform Council determined that Amtrak would not be operationally self-sufficient by December 2002, as the ARAA required.[45] This finding of the council was the trigger for the Amtrak "sunset" provisions of the ARAA. The council was then required to develop a plan to restructure Amtrak, and Amtrak was required to develop a plan for its "complete liquidation." The council said its decision was based on Amtrak being "in a weaker financial condition today than in 1997," with a 2001 loss that was its "highest ever."[46]

The council also found that Amtrak's assets—its trains, tracks, and stations—were in worse physical condition than when the ARAA was passed, and that the railroad had consistently engaged in counterproductive transactions that had weakened its financial condition. The council cited obviously "imprudent" financial practices, such as the $300 million mortgage on New York's Penn Station, as well as additional debt and asset liens that would limit options and sources of cash flow in future years. This extraordinary borrowing had tripled Amtrak's debt since 1995, just six years, to $3 billion, increasing its costs for debt service to about $200 million annually.[47]

In public presentations to council members, the Amtrak Reform Council's senior financial analyst, Michael Mates, raised concerns that the new Acela Express service was not generating the additional passenger traffic and revenues that Amtrak had forecast (see chapter 4). The railroad had used this prediction to justify its investment of approximately $1.4 billion in Acela Express equipment, shops, and infrastructure upgrades. The projected 2 million–person increase in ridership was expected on the New York–Boston segment, where three-hour trip times would make the Acela Express competitive with air shuttles (taking into account travel time to and from airports). Amtrak had estimated that the additional passengers would generate another $300 million in ticket revenues and, after paying direct train operating costs, contribute $180 million to overhead and for capital costs. However, Amtrak had deployed many of the Acela Express train sets on the New York–Washington segment, where they offered minimal time-savings over the Metroliner trains that were already providing three-hour trip times. Mates noted that south of New York, the Acela Express provided less capacity and, most likely, less revenues, since Metroliner trains had seven cars while Acela Express trains had six.

The council concluded that Amtrak could not conceive and implement improvements needed in intercity rail passenger service in the United States, and that it was a critically flawed company.[48] The council noted many difficulties, among them that

- Amtrak was in a weaker position than it was prior to passage of the ARAA.

- Costs were growing faster than revenues.

- Management made little use of the reforms enacted under the ARAA. For example, although Amtrak was given authority to cut unprofitable routes, it had not done so.

- Amtrak had no standard in place to measure the productivity of its workforce, which was essential since labor constituted more than 50 percent of operating costs.[49]

To create a more effective passenger rail program, the council's plan recommended that a new business model be implemented. The existing corporation, the National Rail Passenger Corporation, would be restructured into three entities. First, Amtrak would become a federal oversight agency responsible for administering the nation's passenger rail program, with services eventually provided under contracts that included performance requirements.[50] Next, a government-owned and -operated corporation would control the Boston–Washington rail infrastructure.[51] Finally, a train-operating company would provide service during an interim period, after which the oversight agency would permit private companies to place competitive bids to operate some Amtrak routes.[52] Overall, the council's plan would introduce competition through franchising in arenas currently monopolized by Amtrak.

The council believed that, as is the case throughout our free-market economy, competition would drive down costs and improve service quality and customer satisfaction. Competition would help minimize losses, but in all likelihood would not eliminate the need for operating subsidies. Some Amtrak services—specifically its long-distance trains—would need to be offered on a negative-bid basis—that is, the bidder requiring the least subsidy would be awarded the franchise.[53]

A Plan to Liquidate Amtrak

With its finding that Amtrak would fail to meet the ARAA's operating self-sufficiency requirement, the Amtrak Reform Council had pulled the "sunset trigger" and produced its plan for restructuring. In turn, the statute stipulated that within ninety days of the finding, the railroad must "develop and submit to the Congress an action plan for the complete liquidation of Amtrak, after having the plan reviewed by the GAO and the inspector general of the Department of Transportation for accuracy and reasonableness."[54]

The cost to the public treasury of liquidating Amtrak remained unclear. The GAO reported difficulty in estimating costs because they would depend upon uncertainties, including Amtrak's debt and financial obligations at the time of liquidation, the market value of its assets, and proceeds from the sale of its assets. Moreover, the GAO disagreed with an Amtrak estimate that liquidation would cost between $10 billion and $14 billion, saying most of the costs identified by Amtrak were not liquidation costs. "For example," the GAO said,

> after a liquidation, the costs Amtrak currently pays to operate, maintain, and rehabilitate infrastructure (such as tracks and stations) could be borne by other parties as a result of decisions to provide passenger or other rail service, especially on the Northeast Corridor. In this regard, existing commuter rail agencies and others that operate on Amtrak tracks might assume some of these costs.[55]

Amtrak, however, insisted on including all of these costs in its calculations, even though the GAO had already examined the "full faith and credit" questions associated with liquidating a government-assisted enterprise and concluded that the United States government would not be liable for Amtrak's labor protection obligations and certain other debts.[56] The agency also discovered that

> If Amtrak had been liquidated on December 31, 2001, secured creditors and unsecured creditors—including the federal government and Amtrak employees—and stockholders would have had about $44 billion in potential claims against and ownership interests in Amtrak's estate. The federal government would have been by far the largest claimant, accounting for about 80 percent of the value of all creditor claims and ownership interests.[57]

Liquidation represents a proceeding in which diverse and competing claims can be resolved. Moreover, if Amtrak were to be liquidated, most of its assets probably would end up in private hands through the process, having been sold by the trustee to the highest bidder after notice, a hearing, and any required auction process. Many of its operations—for example, the Northeast Corridor routes—would probably continue under new owners. Money-losing routes would no doubt be discontinued, with some assets transferred by new owners to more promising routes. The extent to which U.S. intercity rail passenger service would be restructured in a liquidation is impossible to predict, although forecasts would be easier if a franchise system were established that induced private companies to bid on Amtrak assets needed for future operations.

Few policymakers and taxpayers understand that liquidation could be a calm, logical process, and that legal and historical precedent would guide an Amtrak liquidation inasmuch as railroads have undergone the process for more than a century. In the 1890s, when railroads were the *primary* mode of passenger transportation in America, insolvency was widespread.[58] More than 27,000 miles of rail were taken over by courts, and another 40,503 miles of track were sold at foreclosure sales of railroad assets between 1894 and 1898.[59] No grave national crisis resulted; in fact, the creative destruction of failed railroads produced a fresh start for the lines affected, with new capital, no disruption in service, and enhanced prospects for the future.

Amtrak presents a profile similar to that of a typical nineteenth-century troubled railroad. It operates unprofitable lines for which there is insufficient demand. Its financiers—taxpayers, not robber barons—hold long-term obligations, such as Amtrak's non-interest-bearing $3.8 billion note to the U.S. Treasury that matures in the year 2975, a note that would undoubtedly yield less than its face value if sold currently.[60] Given Amtrak's dire circumstances, it is logical to employ liquidation procedures, namely Chapter 11 of the bankruptcy code,[61] to do as the capitalists of the nineteenth century did—recognize the problem, cut financial losses, and liquidate in a proceeding in which diverse and competing claims can be resolved.

Amtrak Blocks Liquidation Plans

Long before the Amtrak Reform Council pulled the "sunset trigger," Amtrak had worked to make it difficult for the council to grapple with the railroad's fiscal condition. From the outset Amtrak hindered the council's ability to perform, starting in July 1998, when Representative Robert Andrews, Democrat from New Jersey, included language in the transportation appropriations bill barring the council from using any funds for expert "outside consultants."[62] The ban took hold at the very time Amtrak increased the tempo of issuing misleading statements to the press and Congress.

The GAO also was frustrated by Amtrak obstructionism. In one dispute that became public, Amtrak refused to reveal how it had developed projections of a $105 million bottom-line improvement. "We asked and asked. They never gave us any support for their numbers," said Jim Ratzenberger, the GAO's assistant director for transportation issues.[63]

Amtrak's response to the council's having set sunset provisions in motion was a typical bureaucratic defense mechanism—blame someone else. Amtrak said that America should "recognize that we have a policy problem, not an Amtrak performance problem," and that Congress should provide still more funding.[64] Not one Amtrak board member, executive, or press spokesperson apologized for consistently misleading the public about being on a "glidepath" to operational self-sufficiency. According to council member Wendell Cox,

> Amtrak conducted itself as if it were operating under the Amtrak Business as Usual and Unaccountability Act. The company specifically ignored congressional reforms that would have improved cost efficiency, such as contracting-out services and using more efficient private companies to provide some train service.[65]

He declared Amtrak incapable of financial discipline, saying the railroad had "long operated as if its role is to incinerate the taxes paid by the American people."[66]

Amtrak defenders contended that the September 11 terrorist attacks nearly five months earlier had heightened demand for train service, and self-sufficiency was no longer a meritorious objective. But in fact, although reservations may well have risen for a very brief period when airlines were grounded and Reagan National Airport in Washington, D.C., was closed, overall train traffic during that period actually declined (see chapter 4). In congressional testimony, Amtrak Reform Council Chairman Gilbert E. Carmichael warned, "Amtrak does not have any effective oversight of its business plans, its funding requests or its financial and operational performance. Nor are its many business operations flexible, innovative or responsive to customer needs."[67] Amtrak's financial credibility was so far eroded that the corporation's ability to obtain additional financing completely collapsed. By March 2002, Amtrak was in a dispute with an outside auditing firm over whether it could be identified as a "going concern."[68]

Despite the ongoing financial crises, Congress took the astonishing step of blocking issuance of the liquidation plan the ARAA had required Amtrak to develop. Senators Joseph Biden of Delaware and Ernest "Fritz" Hollings of South Carolina, both Democrats, attached an amendment to the defense appropriations bill that prohibited Amtrak from spending funds to prepare such a plan.[69] The amendment, which both obfuscated Amtrak's spending practices and helped to exacerbate them, represented the worst possible adherence to the status quo.

Blocking the preparation and issuance of the liquidation plan was a contrivance to help Amtrak, but its unintended effect was to inspire critics to equate Amtrak with the spectacularly failed Enron Corporation. Wendell Cox of the Amtrak Reform Council wrote, "If there is an Enron of the public sector, it is Amtrak."[70] Kevin Horrigan, a *St. Louis Post-Dispatch* columnist, discouraged the idea of Amtrak playing a role in its liquidation, writing, "This is like leaving [Enron Chairman] Ken Lay in charge of reorganizing Enron."[71] Stephen Moore, president of the Club for Growth, looked at Amtrak subsidies and asked, "When does this madness end?" adding, "Amtrak makes Enron seem like a well-run firm by comparison."[72] Ken Bird, an Amtrak supporter-turned-critic, who regrets having organized groups in New York and Illinois to support expansion of Amtrak, said "Amtrak is a rolling Enron that should be allowed to go bankrupt."[73]

The Amtrak-Enron comparison was well-deserved. After all, hadn't Congress used its lawmaking powers to do what Enron's auditors did with paper shredders? Both hid from public view the details and scope of a financial disaster in the making. In blocking the release of the liquidation report, Congress perpetuated for months the idea that Amtrak was some-how salvageable. By June, only four months after the council found Amtrak's financial condition unsustainable and six months after the Biden/Hollings amendment, the railroad once again threatened to shut down operations nationally, including independently financed commuter rail services, because of a "surprise" cash shortfall. Had Biden and Hollings not interfered, the threat of an impending Amtrak bankruptcy would have been exposed earlier. A shutdown was averted by a $100 million emergency loan from the U.S. Department of Transportation.

A Heritage of Suppressing Information

Amtrak and its supporters have a tradition of suppressing information adverse to the railroad. During the 2002 financial crisis, Senator John McCain said to a committee about to hear testimony from Amtrak:

> I trust one of the subcommittee's goals in holding today's hear-ing is to receive an accurate assessment of Amtrak's current financial situation and not to simply sit through another day of testimony from Amtrak as it spins the "facts," provides only half-truths, and makes more promises that will go unmet . . . I note that [Amtrak President George] Warrington's written testimony fails to mention a single word about the [Penn Station] mortgage transaction or its actual financial situation today. . . . Amtrak's testimony before the Congress this year . . . did not give *any* indication about Amtrak's looming financial crisis. Isn't Amtrak under an obligation to provide the Congress with accurate and timely information? Do we need to start swearing in Amtrak witnesses before our hearings begin in order to help ensure we receive honest testimony? One comment about the Penn Station mortgage which you may find of interest. When my office requested a copy of the trans-action last week, Amtrak responded that it was a "private" mat-ter. How can such a deal be a "private" transaction when, as I learned this week, it includes a provision which conveniently

allows for the federal government (in other words, the American taxpayers) to repay that mortgage on Amtrak's behalf? I'm convinced we simply cannot rely on the statements from Amtrak officials if we want to know the facts when it comes to Amtrak.[74]

The Amtrak Reform Council also suffered from Amtrak's resistance to basic inquiries, a problem that I, as a member, had experienced firsthand.[75] The council's first chair, Christine Todd Whitman, asked me to examine how Amtrak was spending its tax refund and draft a report that, if approved, would fulfill the ARAA's requirement to inform Congress of Amtrak expenditures. Amtrak officials were unwilling over a seven-month period in 1998 to provide adequate information to demonstrate how current capital expenditures would move Amtrak toward balancing its operating budget. The reports it eventually filed were vague and non-responsive.

One example of Amtrak's refusal to provide adequate information involved a program to carry freight in special cars that the railroad had initiated to boost revenues. Press releases about the program disclosed only revenues, not operating or startup costs. The return on investment was an issue because Amtrak claimed that moving freight could help make the system profitable. Requests for more information went nowhere. In a meeting on September 24, 1998, I asked Amtrak board members Tommy Thompson and Michael Dukakis to ensure that the railroad would provide the council with proper financial data about the program. Governor Thompson agreed to do so. Months later, Amtrak provided sketchy figures that did not remotely approach the quality of a report that would have been expected for an internal review in a private company. The experience illustrated the Amtrak Reform Board's lack of seriousness about its fiduciary responsibilities. Amtrak's indifferent treatment of the council's sitting members also extended to the council staff. In one particularly telling instance, Amtrak changed the allocation methodology used to prepare its Route Profitability System (RPS) reports in a way that deceptively minimized the financial losses of its worst trains—the long-distance trains. Digging into the details and discovering Amtrak's manipulation of data became a saga.

Congress required Amtrak to include these RPS reports in its annual report to Congress. But the council staff noticed that the 2001 RPS reports were not in conformance with previous years' reports. Amtrak had assigned unrelated non-passenger revenues (also called "non-core" revenues) earned on one part of its system to other parts. For example, by assigning non-core income from real estate along the Boston–Washington line to trains that operate nowhere near the line, Amtrak made that line seem like it was earning money that it was not.

Council staff questioned the new methodology and the "improved" financial performance of many routes, but Amtrak staff provided no explanation for the change. After repeated requests to senior Amtrak executives, and after the council staff enlisted the help of the Senate Commerce Committee, Amtrak eventually provided a fiscal year 2001 report in the format used in earlier years. And, to no one's surprise, council staff discovered that most trains were showing greater losses from fiscal year 2000 to fiscal year 2001. Clearly, the trend was inconsistent with Amtrak's official position at that time that Amtrak was on the glide-path to operational self-sufficiency, and Amtrak's accounting gimmicks had been designed to cover up this disappointing performance.

Why would Amtrak pull Enron-like accounting maneuvers that obfuscated poor performance? Because changing the methodology had significant political benefits. First, by allocating non-core revenues to trains with the greatest operating losses, the worst-performing trains did not look as unprofitable. Second, the practice arguably misled Congress into thinking that all revenues attributed to a train would disappear if the train were discontinued; in fact, these non-core revenues would remain (e.g., on the Boston–Washington line) if these money-losing trains were terminated. Finally, because non-core revenues and profits increased from fiscal year 2000 to fiscal year 2001, the new methodology resulted in RPS reports that showed financial performance improvements on trains that in fact were experiencing mounting losses.[76]

The GAO suffered a similar experience with Amtrak statements, noting they could not be reconciled with audited statements.[77]

The council's staff considered this battle a success because it had shed greater light on where Amtrak was losing the most money. Unfortunately, the episode was but one of many. Amtrak's intransigence on matters large and small was calculated to impair the ability of the five-person staff to carry out the council's mission.[78]

The news media noticed Amtrak's efforts to obscure its increasing deficit and emphasize ridership gains. "From its press releases, you'd think that Amtrak is finally headed on the fast track toward prosperity," wrote Mark Murray in the *National Journal*. "Unfortunately, with its glowing statements and press releases, Amtrak seems to be telling only part of the story." When questioned, an Amtrak spokesman said the company's press releases hadn't highlighted Amtrak's growing costs because expenses were often "trickier" to describe, especially when dealing with capital depreciation.[79]

Believing that Amtrak was not being fully forthcoming about financial issues, Anthony Haswell, acting as a citizen advocate for more of a market-based train system, asked the railroad to disclose financial information on its individual train routes and services, along with the analysis it used to justify adding money-losing routes to the system. Upon Amtrak's refusal, Haswell sued in July 2001 under the Freedom of Information Act in an attempt to provide transparency to Amtrak's accounting system and allow the public to determine how much money individual Amtrak routes were losing each year.[80] The suit was resolved when some information was provided and other information was not, but that is not the point; the point is that Amtrak's uncooperative attitudes have been extended to anyone who exercises his legal obligations or rights to question the organization's judgment.

In no period since its formation has Amtrak misled so many people in so many ways as it has since passage of the ARAA in 1997. The railroad disputed the findings of independent agencies that warned about bankruptcy; the new "reform board" members blundered in not discontinuing the worst-performing trains and, in defiance of sound business practices, adding more money-losing trains; management repeatedly issued misleading ridership, cost, and financial projections; the organization received an unearned "tax refund" and spent a good portion of it unwisely; and officials stonewalled Congress, the Amtrak Reform Council, and interested citizens who wanted to know more about the precarious state of its finances. The result of this multifaceted, underhanded campaign was that it succeeded in defeating implementation of true reforms.

The Amtrak Reform Council no longer exists, but its warnings about Amtrak continue to ring true. Experience is showing that the council was the responsible party trying to create a truly modern train service that is relevant to the market. As we will see in the next chapter, Amtrak has become mired in one fiscal crisis after another despite the disproportionately generous subsidies it continues to receive for the small number of people it serves. Few Amtrak observers were surprised as the railroad's management in recent years threatened to shut down again and again, a tactic to force additional funds from Congress and the taxpayers.

3

Amtrak's Present Condition

The more traffic Amtrak carries, the more money it loses. The railroad's net loss in fiscal year 2003 increased to $1.274 billion from $1.132 billion the year before, despite having carried more passengers.[1] Amtrak's highest passenger-count ever was matched by its highest loss ever. The only saving grace is that Amtrak is also largely irrelevant to the needs of America's travelers. If Amtrak were phased out, America's travelers and commuters would still have ample means of reaching their destinations by riding trains run by private-sector contractors or by taking alternate modes of transport. This fact only further emphasizes the folly of continuing to support Amtrak's ever-growing demands for financial support.

Since the first Amtrak trains began rolling, federal taxpayers have put nearly $27 billion into the railroad, and states have contributed several billion more. (See table 3-1.) These are staggering figures—even more so, however, because the billions of dollars in subsidies have done nothing to make Amtrak self-sufficient or at least provide a greater return to taxpayers; instead, Amtrak continues to rely on the continued generosity of the federal purse. The Congressional Budget Office has found that "in recent years Amtrak has lurched from one fiscal crisis to the next," and that billion-dollar-plus subsidies have been "insufficient for Amtrak to sustain its current service safely and reliably over the long run."[2] In addition to planned subsidies, Washington has had to provide emergency bailouts and supplemental appropriations to reduce the risk of an Amtrak bankruptcy. There is no sign that this will ever change—absent radical restructuring of Amtrak.

Amtrak's Role in Passenger Transport

Amtrak plays a minor role in contributing to America's mobility. An examination of the fifty busiest airports in the continental United States makes it clear how irrelevant Amtrak is to America's travelers. Each of the top sixteen airports serves more travelers every day than does Amtrak's entire national system. Atlanta, with 76.3 million travelers passing through its airport in 2003, served more than three times the number of people who ride Amtrak nationwide. (See table 3-2.) In Texas, the total number of Amtrak travelers in 2000 was less than one quarter of 1 percent of the number of air travelers. (See table 3-3.) Amtrak also suffers by comparison to other forms of public transportation. More than 32 million trips are taken each weekday in the United States on all forms of transit—primarily buses, but also subway and light rail systems. This is more than 450 times the number of trips taken aboard Amtrak intercity trains.[3]

The most generous estimation of Amtrak's market share found that Amtrak provides 1 percent of all intercity passenger-miles traveled on commercial carriers in 2000. (See table 3-4.) The Congressional Budget Office noted:

> The railroad's 5.5 billion passenger-miles that year pale in comparison with the 516.1 billion traveled on airlines (92.2 percent) and the 37.9 billion traveled on buses (6.8 percent). Travel by private automobile reigned supreme, accounting for more than 2.5 trillion passenger-miles in 2000.[4]

Estimates based on passenger trips rather than passenger-miles show an even smaller Amtrak role. In 1997 the Congressional Research Service estimated that Amtrak's traffic of 20 million passenger trips per year constituted about 0.3 percent of such trips in the United States, while automobile travel represented 80.8 percent, commercial airlines, 16.8 percent, and intercity bus, 1.1 percent. Even private aircraft, with 0.6 percent, generated twice as many passenger trips as Amtrak.[5]

TABLE 3-1

HISTORY OF AMTRAK PASSENGER USAGE AND FEDERAL SUBSIDIES

(millions of dollars, except for passenger column)

Fiscal Year	Operating Funds	RRTA	General Capital	Bos-Wash Capital	One Sum	IRS "Tax Refund"	Totals	Annual Passengers Carried (millions)
1971/72	40.0						40.0	16.6a
1973	170.1						170.0	16.9
1974	146.6		2.5				149.1	18.7
1975	276.5						276.5	17.4
1976	357.0		114.2				471.2	18.2
TQb	105.0		25.0	50.0			180.0	
1977	482.6		93.1	225.0			800.7	19.2
1978	561.0c		130.0	425.0			1,116.0	18.9
1979	625.0c		130.0	479.0			1,234.0	21.4
1980	670.4		191.0	362.0			1,223.4	21.2
1981	709.2		187.1	350.0			1,246.3	20.6
1982	522.4	36.0	176.6	170.0			905.0	19.0
1983	561.5	44.0	94.5	115.0			815.0	19.0
1984	562.1	56.0	98.3	100.0			816.4	19.9
1985	551.7	76.0	52.3	27.6			707.6	20.8
1986	500.7	88.0	2.0	12.0			602.7	20.3
1987	468.5	112.0	26.5	11.5			618.5	20.4
1988	413.6	121.0	46.2	27.5			608.3	21.5
1989	410.6	144.0	29.4	19.6			603.6	22.2
1990	388.1	133.0	83.6	24.4			629.1	22.0
1991	343.1	144.8	132.0	179.0			798.9	22.0
1992	331.0	150.2	175.0	205.0			861.2	21.3
1993	351.0	146.0	190.0	204.1			891.1	22.1
1994	351.7	150.5	195.0	225.0			922.2	21.8
1995	392.0	150.0	230.0	200.0			972.0	20.7
1996	285.0	120.0	230.0	115.0			750.0	19.7
1997	222.5	142.0	303.0	175.0			842.5	20.2
1998	245.0	142.0	250.0			1,091.8	1,728.8	21.1
1999					571.0	1,091.8	1,662.8	21.5
2000					521.0		521.0	22.5
2001					521.0		521.0	23.5
2002					1,038.2		1,038.2	23.4
2003					1,043.0		1,043.0	24.0
Loans			1,119.6d		100.0e		1,219.6	
Totals	11,043.8	1,955.5	4,306.9	3,701.7	3,794.2	2,183.6	26,985.7	

continued on next page

(continued)

SOURCES: *Background on Amtrak* (Washington, D.C.; Amtrak, September 1978), 11; *2001 Assessment of Amtrak's Financial Performance and Requirements*, CR-2002-075 (Washington, D.C.: Office of Inspector General, U.S. Department of Transportation, January 24, 2002), executive summary charts and tables, figure 5; Kenneth M. Mead, inspector general, U.S. Department of Transportation, testimony before the Senate, Appropriations Committee, Subcommittee on Transportation and Related Agencies, *Amtrak's Financial Condition*, 107th Cong., 2nd sess., June 20, 2002, 3; Mead, testimony before the Senate Committee on Commerce, Science, and Transportation, *Hearing: Amtrak*, 108th Cong., 1st sess., April 29, 2003, 9; U.S. General Accounting Office, *Amtrak Will Continue to Have Difficulty Controlling Its Costs and Meeting Capital Needs*, GAO/RCED-00-138 (Washington, D.C.: U.S. Government Printing Office, May 2000), 19; U.S. General Accounting Office, *Increasing Amtrak's Accountability for Its Taxpayer Relief Act Funds*, T-RCED-00-116 (Washington, D.C.: U.S. Government Printing Office, March 15, 2000), 1; U.S. General Accounting Office, *Amtrak's Financial Crisis Threatens Continued Viability*, T-RCED-97-147 (Washington, D.C.: U.S. Government Printing Office, April 23, 1997), 12; U.S. General Accounting Office, *Amtrak: Financial Condition Has Deteriorated and Future Costs Make Recovery Difficult*, T-RCED-94-155 (Washington, D.C.: U.S. Government Printing Office, March 17, 1994), 18; National Railroad Passenger Corporation, *Annual Report 1983* (Washington, D.C.: Amtrak, 1984), notes to financial statements, 25n4; Congressional Research Service, *Amtrak and Federal Financial Assistance: Background and Selected Public Policy Issues* (Washington, D.C.: Library of Congress, September 9, 1998), 7–10.

NOTES: The above figures are direct disbursements and exclude hidden subsidies granted to other agencies that nonetheless benefit Amtrak. Examples include grants and/or loans from the Federal Transit Administration, Housing and Urban Development, Federal Railroad Administration, or funds/loans received under the Congestion Mitigation and Air Quality Improvement program and the Transportation Infrastructure Finance and Innovation Act of 1998. Figures exclude direct state operating subsidies to Amtrak, which totaled $136 million in FY 2003, $128.5 million in FY 2002, $123.1 million in 2001, and $111.5 million in 2000. Also excluded are indirect state and local capital subsidies to rail infrastructure and equipment that aid Amtrak. Finally, to supplement public funding, the Transportation Department's inspector general reports Amtrak tapped private financial markets to borrow an additional $2.2 billion from 1998 through 2003.

[a] Ridership is for fiscal year 1972 only, as 1971 was only May 1 through June 30, a partial fiscal year.

[b] Transition quarter. Start of federal fiscal year changed from July 1 to October 1. Ridership not available.

[c] Includes appropriations of $25 million in 1978 and 1979 for partial repayments of government-guaranteed loans.

[d] In the 1970s, Congress gave Amtrak guarantee authority to borrow $880 million in a government-guaranteed loan program. Amtrak stated in 1983 that it would not ever be likely to repay the debt, and $880 million in debt plus $239.6 million in interest owed to the U.S. Treasury's Federal Financing Bank was repaid through an appropriation to DOT of $1,119,635,000.

[e] This loan prevented an Amtrak system shutdown because of a cash shortage. On July 3, 2002, Amtrak executed a $100 million loan under the FRA's Railroad Rehabilitation and Improvement Financing Program for qualified capital expenditures. The loan bears interest at 1.81% per annum, and is secured by various Amtrak-owned right-of-way properties and facilities. The loan was scheduled to be repaid on November 15, 2002, or the date Amtrak had access to funds from its fiscal year 2003 appropriation in an amount that exceeds $100 million, whichever came later. Public Law 108-199 defers repayment of the loan plus accrued interest until after fiscal year 2004. This loan requires Amtrak's compliance with certain conditions which include: improving financial controls and accounting transparency, submission of monthly performance reports, and providing a list of expense reduction options to Congress and the DOT.

TABLE 3-2

COMPARISON OF AIRPORT USE WITH AMTRAK NATIONAL SYSTEM

City and Airport	Total Passenger Traffic Calendar 2003	Average Daily Passenger Count	Multiple of Average Daily Amtrak System-wide Traffic
Hartsfield-Jackson Atlanta International Airport	76,325,955	209,112	3.18
Chicago O'Hare International	63,772,680	174,720	2.66
Dallas/Ft. Worth International	49,241,481	134,908	2.05
Los Angeles International	48,791,020	133,674	2.03
Phoenix Sky Harbor	36,007,688	98,651	1.50
Denver International	35,445,714	97,112	1.48
Las Vegas McCarran International	34,032,343	93,239	1.42
Minneapolis-St. Paul International	31,615,224	86,617	1.32
Houston Intercontinental	30,999,012	84,929	1.29
Detroit Metropolitan Wayne County	30,803,900	84,394	1.28
New York Kennedy International	27,415,375	75,111	1.14
Newark Liberty International	27,331,950	74,882	1.14
San Francisco International	26,462,795	72,501	1.10
Orlando International	26,260,525	71,947	1.09
Seattle-Tacoma International	25,623,016	70,200	1.07
Miami International	24,762,770	67,843	1.03
Amtrak National System Traffic[a]	*24,000,000*	*65,753*	
Philadelphia International	22,906,508	62,758	0.95
New York LaGuardia	22,357,293	61,253	0.93
Charlotte Douglas International	22,217,332	60,869	0.93
Boston Logan International	21,341,001	58,468	0.89
Cincinnati/N. Kentucky International	20,734,990	56,808	0.86
St. Louis Lambert International	19,887,651	54,487	0.83
Baltimore-Washington International	19,165,547	52,508	0.80
Salt Lake International	17,827,878	48,844	0.74
Chicago Midway	17,365,966	47,578	0.72
Fort Lauderdale International	16,938,776	46,408	0.71
Tampa International	15,255,864	41,797	0.64

continued on next page

TABLE 3-2 *(continued)*
COMPARISON OF AIRPORT USE WITH AMTRAK NATIONAL SYSTEM

City and Airport	Total Passenger Traffic Calendar 2003	Average Daily Passenger Count	Multiple of Average Daily Amtrak System-wide Traffic
Washington Dulles International	15,123,353	41,434	0.63
San Diego International Lindbergh Field	15,065,828	41,276	0.63
Pittsburgh International	14,094,651	38,615	0.59
Washington Reagan National	13,502,284	36,993	0.56
Metropolitan Oakland International	13,252,454	36,308	0.55
Portland International (Oregon)	12,035,406	32,974	0.50
Orange County (CA) John Wayne International	10,989,144	30,107	0.46
Memphis International	10,742,040	29,430	0.45
San Jose International	10,115,787	27,714	0.42
Cleveland Hopkins International	9,956,063	27,277	0.41
Kansas City International	9,708,904	26,600	0.40
New Orleans Louis Armstrong International	9,272,181	25,403	0.39
Sacramento Metropolitan	8,756,340	23,990	0.36
Nashville Metropolitan	7,867,262	21,554	0.33
Raleigh Durham	7,809,720	21,396	0.33
Houston William P. Hobby	7,413,978	20,312	0.31
Indianapolis International	7,313,900	20,038	0.30
Austin Robert Mueller Municipal	6,318,950	17,312	0.26
Milwaukee General Mitchell Field	6,285,856	17,222	0.26
San Antonio International	6,261,620	17,155	0.26
Hartford Bradley International	6,168,522	16,900	0.26
Ontario (CA) International Airport	6,085,320	16,672	0.25

SOURCE: U.S. Department of Transportation, Bureau of Transportation Statistics, http://www.transtats.bts.gov/, following this series of links: "Aviation," "Air Carrier Statistics (T-100 Market)," "T-100 Market," "Analysis" links for "Origin Airport" and "Destination Airport," and "Top N" analysis summary for each; once collected, the origin and destination figures were added to arrive at the total passenger traffic for each airport.

a Every airport above this line has traffic greater than Amtrak's national system traffic by the multiple shown.

TABLE 3-3
AIRLINE AND AMTRAK RIDERSHIP BY STATE

	Enplanements (CY 2000)	Amtrak Ridership (FY 2000)	Variance	Airline Per-Day Boardings (CY 2000)	Amtrak Per-Day Boardings (FY 2000)
Alabama	2,776,979	25,670	2,751,309	7,608	70
Alaska	4,829,951	0	4,829,951	13,233	0
Arizona	20,642,747	42,511	20,600,236	56,555	116
Arkansas	1,790,435	10,895	1,779,540	4,905	30
California	87,490,852	3,524,366	83,966,486	239,701	9,656
Colorado	20,491,110	123,437	20,367,673	56,140	338
Connecticut	3,704,343	450,147	3,254,196	10,149	1,233
Delaware	3,650	360,129	-356,479	10	987
Florida	59,471,956	472,737	58,999,219	162,937	1,295
Georgia	40,598,775	73,182	40,525,593	111,230	200
Hawaii	18,000,690	0	18,000,690	49,317	0
Idaho	1,888,457	2,258	1,886,199	5,174	6
Illinois	42,010,517	1,474,478	40,536,039	115,097	4,040
Indiana	4,919,443	62,475	4,856,968	13,478	171
Iowa	1,587,916	27,500	1,560,416	4,350	75
Kansas	659,431	16,181	643,250	1,807	44
Kentucky	13,754,511	4,334	13,750,177	37,684	12
Louisiana	6,201,560	98,942	6,102,618	16,991	271
Maine	1,006,890	0	1,006,890	2,759	0
Maryland	9,779,728	853,622	8,926,106	26,794	2,339
Massachusetts	14,363,339	657,650	13,705,689	39,352	1,802
Michigan	20,068,350	263,566	19,804,784	54,982	722
Minnesota	17,386,301	75,788	17,310,513	47,634	208
Mississippi	1,278,180	44,729	1,233,451	3,502	123
Missouri	21,640,199	235,329	21,404,870	59,288	645
Montana	1,269,715	67,508	1,202,207	3,479	185
Nebraska	2,178,072	19,263	2,158,809	5,967	53
Nevada	20,524,654	38,844	20,485,810	56,232	106
New Hampshire	1,622,599	925	1,621,674	4,445	3
New Jersey	17,729,937	1,805,241	15,924,696	48,575	4,946
New Mexico	3,291,295	47,090	3,244,205	9,017	129
New York	36,983,184	4,966,719	32,016,465	101,324	13,607
North Carolina	18,975,322	262,525	18,712,797	51,987	719
North Dakota	557,579	41,264	516,315	1,528	113
Ohio	11,619,977	82,580	11,537,397	31,836	226

continued on next page

TABLE 3-3 (continued)

AIRLINE AND AMTRAK RIDERSHIP BY STATE

	Enplanements (CY 2000)	Amtrak Ridership (FY 2000)	Variance	Airline Per-Day Boardings (CY 2000)	Amtrak Per-Day Boardings (FY 2000)
Oklahoma	3,546,904	36,634	3,510,270	9,718	100
Oregon	7,619,265	297,929	7,321,336	20,875	816
Pennsylvania	24,013,673	2,407,781	21,605,892	65,791	6,597
Rhode Island	2,704,988	196,075	2,508,913	7,411	537
South Carolina	3,154,536	90,039	3,064,497	8,643	247
South Dakota	611,624	0	611,624	1,676	0
Tennessee	11,565,566	25,329	11,540,237	31,686	69
Texas	65,012,104	123,847	64,888,257	178,115	339
Utah	9,608,387	15,369	9,593,018	26,324	42
Vermont	450,393	52,221	398,172	1,234	143
Virginia	20,883,138	2,115,520	18,767,618	57,214	5,796
Washington	16,077,008	518,331	15,558,677	44,047	1,420
West Virginia	410,139	17,160	392,979	1,124	47
Wisconsin	4,692,873	260,077	4,432,796	12,857	713
Wyoming	367,286	0	367,286	1,006	0
Totals	**701,816,528**	**22,388,197**	**679,428,311**	**1,922,785**	**61,338**

SOURCE: U.S. Senate Banking, Housing, and Urban Affairs Committee, "Airplane and Amtrak Ridership by State," table provided to Amtrak Reform Council, Congressional Budget Office, and U.S. General Accounting Office, unpublished and undated (circulated in early 2002).

TABLE 3-4

INTERCITY TRAVEL BY RAIL, AIR, AND BUS, SELECTED YEARS, 1960–2000

(billions of passenger-miles)

	1960	1970	1980	1990	2000	Percentage of 2000 Total
Air Carriers	31.1	108.4	204.4	345.9	516.1	92.2
Railroads	17.1	6.2	4.5	6.1	5.5	1.0[a]
Buses	19.3	25.3	27.4	23.0	37.9	6.8
Total	**67.5**	**139.9**	**236.3**	**375.0**	**559.5**	**100.0**

SOURCE: *The Past and Future of U.S. Passenger Rail Service* (Washington, D.C.: Congressional Budget Office, September 2003), 7.

[a] This is the most generous allocation of intercity travel by rail that can be found in any current-day study.

It is on behalf of this minuscule role that Washington has experienced one crisis after another regarding Amtrak and has striven mightily to keep the railroad afloat.

Amtrak's Finances since the Failure of Reform

Amtrak continues to be a prime candidate for bankruptcy—a fact that would surprise anyone who may have believed Amtrak's glowing reports about revenue increases.[6] The strongest warnings of Amtrak's dire financial condition came in 1997, when the GAO examined issues related to an Amtrak liquidation to help position the government for such an eventuality.[7] But the evidence of Amtrak's dire financial condition has only continued to mount since then.

Federal oversight agencies issued approximately thirty reports between 1997 and 2004 that quantified Amtrak's financial condition, reviewed its nonproductive policies, and warned about its substandard performance.[8] The reports focused on the operation of trains whose expenses far outstripped revenues, the substandard upgrading of the Boston–Washington line, the failure to invest capital in the most promising services or where safety needs were greatest, and the execution of flawed job-protection agreements with labor organizations.

Adding to the wealth of information were many Congressional hearings, where experts categorized Amtrak's disappointing performance and urged innovative solutions. One witness, for example (William J. Rennicke, vice president of Mercer Management Consulting Inc.), noted that Amtrak's operating efficiency had continued to decline despite the ARAA's having granted it flexibility to improve performance by altering or discontinuing high-cost, low-yield routes. Passenger-miles per employee dropped from nearly 250 in 1992 to about 214 in 1999, and train-load factors (the percentage of seats occupied) dropped from 51 percent in 1992 to 45 percent in 1999.[9]

The warnings about Amtrak have been numerous (see appendix A) and so eloquent that Washington's response begs the question of why the reforms mandated thus far have been so minor. Anthony Haswell has observed, "In view of Congress's impatience with Amtrak's chronic deficits and underwhelming market performance, the reforms it demanded were relatively few and unobjectionable."[10]

Amtrak's Fossilized Route Structure

In nature, when something is fossilized, it is preserved long beyond the era in which it sprouted, grew, and died. Amtrak routes—particularly the long-distance ones—are fossils because they, too, continue to exist far beyond the time in which they sprouted, grew, and gasped their last healthy breaths.

Unlike Amtrak, America's aviation and bus networks routinely adapt to shifting market patterns by abandoning little-used services and adding services elsewhere. Even the highway network has, to a limited degree, discarded roads whose time has passed. The evidence can be found in the disappearance of parts of famed U.S. 66 and of city streets in American "rust belt" communities like Pittsburgh, Pennsylvania, which vanished along with the factories they once served.

A primary contributing factor to Amtrak's fossilization is an unparalleled job-protection agreement. Virtually no Americans, regardless of industry or occupation, including bus line and most airline employees, have a labor-protection plan. Amtrak has one with rules that make it costly to end service over poorly used lines or, in certain circumstances, move an employee more than thirty miles from an existing employment location. Discontinuing service completely on a route activates an employee-severance package that is one of the costliest labor provisions found anywhere. For many years Amtrak employees were entitled to one year's salary and benefits for each year worked, up to six years. The protections were a disincentive to the adaptation of Amtrak's system to marketplace demands long after Amtrak's enabling legislation required the provision to be negotiated.[11] The prospective payments were such a liability that merely the threat of their kicking-in was used from the 1970s through 1997 to argue against the discontinuation of costly long-distance trains.

The protection clause made downsizing or restructuring Amtrak difficult and deterred talk of privatization and devolvement of trains to regional or state authorities. Congress, in drafting the ARAA, wanted to limit severance to six months—which would still be the most generous arrangement in the United States. In a compromise, the ARAA removed all statutory employee-protection provisions covering Amtrak employees and instead required Amtrak and the unions either to negotiate new provisions through collective bargaining or to submit the issue to binding arbitration. Amtrak and the unions chose binding arbitration. In a November 1999 decision, a three-member arbitration board retained the "triggers" for implementing protective benefits for employees—closure of a route or a reduction in frequency below three round-trips per week, or closure of a maintenance facility or transfer of work to another facility more than thirty miles away. Not much changed.

The preexisting terms were eased somewhat. Employees were required to have at least two years of service to be awarded protection; the maximum duration of benefits was reduced from six years to five; employees were required to have more years of service, on a sliding scale, to reach maximum benefits; and no employee protection would be required for the first two years of any new service commenced after the arbitration. Even so, as the Amtrak Reform Council concluded, "Despite the improvements achieved by Amtrak through this arbitration, Amtrak's new labor protection obligations to employees, particularly those with many years of service, remain significantly higher than those of non-railroad corporations in the United States economy."[12] (See table 3-5.) Hence, Amtrak's route network remained significantly more inflexible than any airline's or bus company's system.

Shutdown Threats

For many years, one of Amtrak's chief means of strong-arming Congress into meeting its need for subsidies has been to threaten to shut down various passenger routes. By 2003, Amtrak took the practice to new heights by repeatedly threatening to shut down its entire national system. That broader scheme includes halting operations on the few properties that Amtrak owns, which include most of the Boston–Washington line and Chicago Union Station. This would hurt innocent parties, such as non-Amtrak commuter trains that carry millions of passengers being unable to enter their most important terminals (e.g., New York, Philadelphia, Chicago). Also, Amtrak

TABLE 3-5

AMTRAK AND AVERAGE U.S. EMPLOYEE SEVERANCE PAY

Length of Employment	Amtrak Employees		Average U.S. Employee	
	Wages	Medical/Dental	Wages	Medical/Dental
Under 2 Years	None	None	None	None
2 to 3 Years	0.5 Year	0.5 Year	None	None
3+ to 5 Years	1.0 Year	1.0 Year	None	None
5+ to 10 Years	1.5 Years	1.5 Years	None	None
10+ to 15 Years	2.0 Years	2.0 Years	None	None
15+ to 20 Years	3.0 Years	3.0 Years	None	None
20+ to 25 Years	4.0 Years	4.0 Years	None	None
Over 25 Years	5.0 Years	5.0 Years	None	None

SOURCE: Wendell Cox, Amtrak Reform Council, concurring statement published in *An Action Plan for the Restructuring and Rationalization of the National Intercity Rail Passenger System* (Washington, D.C.: U.S. Government Printing Office, February 7, 2002), 71.

would hobble freight train operations in some of the nation's most industrialized areas. This practice is certain to continue until Congress takes steps to ensure that facilities remain open so that commuter and freight trains are able to keep running during an Amtrak shutdown.

Regardless of whether Democrats or Republicans controlled the White House or Congress, Amtrak has always been able to bully the federal government into meeting its need for subsidies—with one major exception, which occurred in 1979. Consider this brief timeline:

- *Carter administration, 1977:* Amtrak President Paul H. Reistrup ordered service cuts on four long-distance routes and some reductions of Metroliner service because of a $50 million budget shortfall.[13]

- *Carter administration, 1979:* In a unique example of cost-cutting prompted by a financial crisis, several thousand miles of nonproductive routes were discontinued, including a Chicago–Seattle train, the North Coast Hiawatha; the New York–Kansas City National Limited; and the Chicago–Miami Floridian.

- *Reagan administration, 1981:* A proposed $613 million budget, about two-thirds of Amtrak's request, caused Amtrak President Alan S. Boyd to warn that all Amtrak trains would be discontinued in thirty-six states, but would continue on the Northeast Corridor.[14] In 1985, another Amtrak president, W. Graham Claytor Jr., said an appropriation of $480 million was insufficient, and the railroad must have $684 million or all operations would cease.[15]

- *Clinton administration, 1994:* Amtrak said it would eliminate some trains and furlough 5,500 workers because a $962 million subsidy for the year left a $173 million shortfall. Thomas Downs became the first Amtrak president to cast doubt on the wisdom of operating a national system of long-distance trains, and under him some service discontinuances were permanent, such as the ending of a slow, lightly used Dallas–Houston train. This was the first time that Amtrak's cash crisis led to serious talk of a bankruptcy.[16] Said Downs: "We are chapter eleven-able by our creditors. We can be put in bankruptcy with relative ease."[17]

- *Bush administration, 2002:* Amtrak President David Gunn threatened to shut down all service in July unless a $200 million emergency loan was approved within three weeks.[18] Soon after, Standard & Poor's cut Amtrak's credit rating to BBB-minus, one step above junk status, and Amtrak's auditors refused to certify the railroad as a "going concern."[19] Both actions made obtaining additional bank loans impossible. Additional draws on the federal treasury represented the only recourse.

The last threat apparently tried the patience of the White House; Ronald Utt at the Heritage Foundation reports that in return for additional financial support the administration wanted "the resignation of Amtrak's unqualified board of directors, ambitious cost-cutting goals, and the adoption of competitive contracting agreements common in European and Asian passenger-rail systems."[20] Amtrak wouldn't budge.

Gunn's actions were widely seen as inflammatory after so many Amtrak promises of brighter days to come. As the *Wall Street Journal* editorialized,

> Imagine if [Enron's chairman] Ken Lay had the gall to demand a federal bailout at a Congressional hearing on Enron's accounting shenanigans. Well, that's just about what Amtrak President David Gunn did on Capitol Hill. . . . [W]e have [no sympathy] for his attempt to initiate a game of chicken with Congress or for his apparent determination to pursue business as usual at one of the worst-run businesses in the country. Amtrak's request comes after Amtrak's auditors discovered it lost $100 million more in fiscal 2001 than previously believed.[21]

There was no need to knuckle under to Amtrak's blackmail—"Fund us, or we'll shut the whole system down, including the handful of trains that are actually popular"—and yet, that is just what Congress and the White House have done. In fact, history shows that railroads entering bankruptcy can continue essential operations. In 1970, the Nixon administration refused to guarantee a $50 million loan to the Penn Central Railroad. The company filed for Chapter 11 bankruptcy, but the trains continued to operate, thanks to the provisions of railroad bankruptcy laws and actions taken by the railroad's bankruptcy trustees.

It was politically and administratively easier for the Bush administration and Congress to avert the 2002 shutdown by approving a last-minute, $100 million loan and another package of up to $170 million in assistance.[22] Yet Amtrak persisted in making threats to halt rail service unless its federal subsidies were increased yet again. Amtrak's record of additional shutdown threats in 2003 and 2004 is nothing short of astonishing:

- *January 14, 2003:* Gunn warned Congress that if his $1.2 billion funding request were reduced, Amtrak would "have no other choice but an orderly shutdown of all service this spring or sooner."[23] One week later he added, "I really can't believe anyone wants to go through what we went through last summer for a couple hundred million bucks. We almost bought the farm."[24]

- *July 11, 2003:* A congressional committee proposed Amtrak funding of $580 million, less than in the two previous years, but more than in 2000 and 1999. Amtrak said the "unrealistic" figure would lead to the immediate shutdown of all Amtrak operations, including the Boston–Washington corridor, all commuter service operating over Amtrak lines, and all state-supported regional service, including the extensive California system. Said Gunn: "You would shut down. It would be a chaotic shutdown."[25]

- *September 1, 2003:* Disagreeing with a House Appropriations Committee consideration of $900 million for fiscal year 2004, Gunn warned, "Failure to fully fund this request, I fear, will quickly bring on the next crisis."[26]

- *September 17, 2003:* Unions representing Amtrak workers threatened to walk off their jobs and shut down the railroad for one day on October 3 to pressure Congress to increase Amtrak subsidies. Besides stopping intercity passenger service, the walkout would have affected commuter trains in major cities.[27] Court action delayed the strike through July 2004, when a court effectively ruled against Amtrak's unions.[28]

- *September 30, 2003:* David Gunn said a $900 million subsidy proposed in the House and a $1.35 billion proposed in the Senate (the most Amtrak thus far had been likely to receive in a single appropriation) were insufficient to prevent a fiscal year 2004 Amtrak shutdown.[29] Disagreeing, DOT Inspector General Kenneth M. Mead said Amtrak could "maintain reliability" and "meet its obligations" by combining the $1.35 billion amount with its $200 million in carryover funds from 2003.[30]

- *February 10, 2004:* For fiscal 2005, Amtrak asked for nearly $1.8 billion in federal subsidies. The Bush administration proposed giving the railroad $900 million if no reforms were carried out, or $1.4 billion if reforms occurred. Gunn warned, "The president's number is a shutdown number."[31] Amtrak did not agree to reforms to make it more deserving of the higher appropriation.

- *July 21, 2004:* The *Philadelphia Inquirer* reported a prediction by Gunn that the $900 million figure would force an Amtrak shutdown by February 2005.[32]

One enterprising journalist unearthed that Gunn's Amtrak threats were nothing new—since the early 1980s he had habitually warned he would shut down transit systems while serving as head of rail operations in New York, Philadelphia, and Toronto.[33]

As suggested earlier, it would be one thing if these shutdown threats were limited to Amtrak trains. But the interconnectivity of the rail system, and Amtrak's inclination to hold commuter rail traffic hostage if any Amtrak track, stations, or personnel are used, means that an Amtrak stoppage could halt non-Amtrak commuter trains in America's largest cities, including New York, Philadelphia, Chicago, and Los Angeles.[34] These trains are far busier than Amtrak's, and because the threats abuse innocent commuters, the relationships between Amtrak and commuter-rail authorities have deteriorated. (See chapter 6.)

Disproportionate Subsidies

Another striking sign of Amtrak's poor fiscal health is its extraordinary and excessive subsidy-to-revenue ratio. A 1998 GAO study found that "Amtrak spends almost $2 for every dollar of revenue it earns in providing intercity passenger service. . . . Three Amtrak routes spent more than $3 for every dollar of revenue, and 14 routes lost more than $100 per passenger in fiscal year 1997."[35]

Astonishingly, Amtrak supporters ignore these facts and argue that Amtrak actually receives too little federal support. In 2001, for example, Amtrak's share of the federal transportation budget was "only" $521 million, less than 1 percent of all transportation spending. However, if an even-handed standard is applied, Amtrak receives significantly more than its fair share. As transport expert Robert Poole of the Reason Foundation has explained,

> In 2001, highways received $33.5 billion in federal funds. But every dime of that came from federal gasoline taxes paid by

drivers who use the highways. This is not a subsidy; it's simply a user tax, paid by highway users to build and maintain the highways they drive on. Likewise, aviation received $12.6 billion in federal funding in 2001. Most of that came from user taxes paid by passengers and private pilots, and was used to pay for air traffic control and airport improvements. The several billion of general-fund monies for aviation went to pay for safety regulation by the FAA; that is how we pay for all the federal safety regulatory agencies. It is only Amtrak that receives actual federal subsidies—monies taken from general taxpayers for the direct benefit of users of the rail mode. People who fly or drive receive no such federal subsidy.[36]

Ronald Utt and Wendell Cox, who have said that Amtrak consistently misleads the public regarding subsidies, have turned the argument around to show what would happen if subsidies were provided to highway and aviation travelers at the same ratio Amtrak passengers receive them:

It would take $1 trillion annually to provide the same level of subsidy per mile to auto users as Amtrak receives. That is more than one-half of the federal budget. It would take $110 billion to subsidize air users at the same rate as Amtrak passengers. Compare this to the less than $50 billion that the nation spends every year, mind you out of user fees, on the nation's highways and air system. The nation deserves a higher standard of discourse.[37]

User fees also have a unique value: An individual not driving an auto or flying does not pay into the highway or airport funds. An individual not riding Amtrak still pays to subsidize Amtrak through income taxes or numerous other taxes collected by federal and state governments.

Disproportionately generous subsidies to Amtrak are nothing new. In 1982, the Congressional Budget Office examined transportation subsidies and put a value on aid to Amtrak:

The comparison showed that on a passenger-mile basis, Amtrak passengers were subsidized at a level more than one hundred times the next closest alternative means of passenger travel. Each Amtrak passenger was subsidized at the rate of 23.6 cents per passenger-mile, while commercial airline passengers received two-tenths of one cent and private auto passengers about one-tenth of one cent.[38]

Aviation and highway user fees are directed to systems that enjoy a staggering level of use. While America cannot survive without its aviation and highway systems, Amtrak's disappearance would be insignificant outside of the Boston–Washington corridor and a precious few other high-density lines serving highly populated areas.

Hidden Amtrak Subsidies

As egregious as these subsidies are, they fail to represent many additional ways in which taxpayers support Amtrak because they do not reflect the other subsidies the railroad receives from a multitude of government agencies and private freight railroads. A comprehensive accounting of Amtrak's true cost to taxpayers has never been made by Congress or any agency, which is regrettable because Amtrak's financial reporting system does not fairly represent the public support the railroad receives. Republican Senator Wayne Allard from Colorado has said,

> I have grown increasingly skeptical about what is going on with Amtrak. It seems they found a way to pick up government subsidies all over the place. . . . We found that we even have the Federal Transit Administration subsidizing Amtrak.[39]

The criticism is justified. Amtrak has restrained cost growth in its accounts because many of its expenditures are kept on ledgers at other agencies, such as the following:

Income Tax Return. In 1999 the GAO testified that Amtrak recorded a portion of its taxpayer-financed "income-tax refund" as "revenues."[40] (See chapter 2.)

Loan Default. In the 1970s, Congress provided Amtrak with guaranteed loan authority to borrow nearly $1 billion. The administration and Amtrak concluded in 1983 that Amtrak would likely never repay the debt, and arranged for the U.S. Treasury's Federal Financing Bank to be repaid through a special appropriation.[41] On October 5, 1983, the Federal Railroad Administration paid off Amtrak's $880 million loan, as well as $239 million in accrued interest, and a new loan for the $1.12 billion in funds was executed between Amtrak and the federal government. That note matures on November 1, 2082, and will be renewed for successive ninety-nine-year terms.[42] Because the Federal Railroad Administration paid the $1.1 billion obligation, it does not show up in Amtrak financial summaries. Nevertheless, Americans born today will pay taxes on this debt at least through the year 2082—even if Amtrak is shut down and all expenses related to passenger trains somehow magically disappear today.

Federal Transit Administration. The Federal Transit Administration (FTA) carries on its books grants for significant upgrades to Amtrak's Boston–Washington line that are shared with commuter agencies. The GAO found that in a five-year period, Amtrak's capital subsidies funded about 42 percent of the capital expenditures on the corridor, while grants from the FTA and state and local sources funded 58 percent. (See table 3-6.)[43] The FTA has funded improvements at many common-use facilities, such as New York's Penn Station and Chicago's Union Station, as well as work at stations where Amtrak is the only rail-service provider, such as the ones in Elizabethtown, Pennsylvania, Rome, New York, and Milwaukee, Wisconsin.[44] Pennsylvania announced a plan in mid-2004 to commit $72.5 million to pay half the cost of upgrading the Amtrak-owned Philadelphia–Harrisburg line; FTA funds may cover up to $56 million of the state's obligation.[45]

Federal Railroad Administration. Amtrak benefits from grants for technology development, train station improvements, historic building restorations, and railroad–highway grade crossing improvements carried on non-Amtrak accounts. The newest additions to FRA's shouldering of Amtrak costs are some security inspections in train stations.[46]

TABLE 3-6
SOURCES OF CAPITAL SUBSIDIES ON NORTHEAST CORRIDOR LINE

1988–93 Averages	Amtrak	State and Local	Federal Transit Administration	Total Non-Amtrak
Expenditures ($ millions)	105.1	93.1	54.5	147.6
Percentage of Total	41.6	36.8	21.6	58.4

SOURCE: U.S. General Accounting Office, *Northeast Rail Corridor: Information on Users, Funding Sources, and Expenditures,* RCED-96-144 (Washington, D.C.: U.S. Government Printing Office, June 27, 1996), 12.

NOTE: Amtrak total is derived from adding an average of $76.2 million of Northeast Corridor Improvement Program funds and $28.9 in general capital subsidies on the corridor annually. Capital expenditures were for major upgrades and the maintenance of track, stations, signal systems, and high-speed-rail improvements. The degree to which Amtrak and the commuter railroads receive mutual benefits from these expenditures varies.

Housing and Urban Development. The loan-guarantee provision of the Community Development Block Grant Program, HUD section 108, has benefited Amtrak in at least one instance: It helped to finance the relocation of a reservation call center from Fort Washington, Pennsylvania, to Philadelphia.[47]

Congestion Mitigation and Air Quality (CMAQ) Improvement. CMAQ, a Federal Highway Administration program, has partially funded facilities used by Amtrak. Examples include renovation of the Worcester, Massachusetts, Union Station, a planned Los Angeles–Las Vegas train, and construction of a new station in Sturtevant, Wisconsin.[48] Amtrak is hoping to establish a precedent for future CMAQ funding of plans "located outside of non-attainment and maintenance areas which have heretofore been generally ineligible."[49]

Transportation Infrastructure Finance and Innovation Act of 1998. In November 2000, $140 million was made available in the form of TIFIA loans to support the Penn Station Redevelopment Corporation, chartered in 1995 by the New York State Urban Development Corporation. The corporation is overseeing the conversion of Manhattan's John A. Farley post office, which was built in the same neo-classical style as the long-gone monumental Pennsylvania Station, into a station for Amtrak to use instead of the current subterranean Penn Station.[50] An estimated $315 million will be spent, with the U.S. Postal Service paying some of the costs as part of a redevelopment effort; commuter trains will continue to use the existing station.[51]

Federally Imposed Local Tax Exemptions. In a case of lowering Amtrak's tax bill at someone else's expense, the ARAA exempted the railroad from local property taxes levied in Beech Grove, Indiana, the location of a major Amtrak maintenance facility. The elimination of tax revenue placed a greater burden on local taxpayers.[52] The ARAA also exempted "Amtrak's passengers and other customers from most state and local taxes, fees, and charges."[53]

State Funds. Amtrak has benefited from a multitude of state programs. The northeastern and mid-Atlantic states, from Maine to Virginia, invested more than $4 billion between 1992 and 2001 in infrastructure and operations that directly or indirectly support Amtrak, and they expect to spend an additional $3 billion from 2002 to 2006. The states also fund improvements that mutually benefit intercity and commuter service, such as station improvements, track capacity enhancements, bridge repairs, and signal system upgrades. The analysis that provides these figures includes payments to Amtrak for intercity trains as well as payments by commuter railroads for use of Amtrak-owned tracks and facilities.[54] The calculations include expenditures that directly support intercity service, such as a $1 million grant from New York State to Wayne County to build a new Amtrak station in the town of Lyons.[55] California has expended more than $1 billion to purchase locomotives and coaches for Amtrak, build stations, and improve tracks and signaling systems.[56]

Local Funds. Some counties finance major infrastructure improvements that benefit Amtrak. For example, counties between Los Angeles and San Diego created a joint powers board to purchase and upgrade most of the line used by Amtrak. A number of communities use municipal or transit agency funds to build new train stations or upgrade old ones. A recent example is a new train station constructed across the river from Albany, New York, in Rensselaer, for $53.1 million; while most of the cost was contributed by federal and state budgets, $1.5 million came from the Capital District Transportation Authority.[57] Amtrak costs local taxpayers in other ways, too. In La Crosse, Wisconsin, prior to 2003, Amtrak paid $1 a year in rent to use the city-owned train station. The city persuaded Amtrak to agree to $16,000 annually, but as Amtrak faces the lease expiration in 2005 it notified the city that its national policy is not to pay rent.[58] In New Hampshire, Amtrak expects the citizens of Exeter to begin paying the $40,000 annual cost for insurance on the train station; the town already maintains the station, pays the utilities, mows the lawn, and plows the snow.[59]

International Assistance. Apparently, the extensive direct and indirect subsidies outlined above are insufficient to meet Amtrak's needs. David Gunn believes Canada should contribute up to $20 million for track improvements to benefit Amtrak's Seattle–Vancouver, British Columbia, train, a route that lies predominantly in the United States.[60]

If that happens, it would not be the first time Canada helped Amtrak, and the highly unusual circumstances of that previous occurrence deserve special mention. The *Ottawa Citizen* reported that Canada provided loans to help purchase the Acela Express and other equipment, details of which the newspaper said were hidden from public view:

> The federal Export Development Corp. secretly loaned $1-billion to the deficit-plagued U.S. railroad agency Amtrak while the Chretien government sharply cut passenger rail funding in Canada. The money allowed the U.S. government-owned Amtrak to side-step a congressional cap on capital grants, and may have given Montreal-based Bombardier Inc. an undisclosed edge over rival bids to build Amtrak's . . . Acela Express high-speed train. . . . By secretly backing Bombardier's bid, the Canadian government virtually guaranteed Bombardier would triumph over rival bids from Germany-based Siemens, and Sweden-based Asea Brown Boveri.[61]

The loans became controversial because Canadians couldn't find information about them in government reports. As Americans began asking what liabilities Amtrak had incurred, Amtrak and Canadian officials denied any wrongdoing. Amtrak emphasized to *Congress Daily* that the loans were "fully disclosed" in a *New York Times* article.[62] But further investigation found only this paragraph in the article to which Amtrak pointed:

> Just as General Motors finances car purchases, Bombardier and GEC Alsthom will provide financing for much of the deal, evidently believing that the trains will generate more than sufficient revenues to pay for themselves. Bombardier and GEC Alsthom plan to borrow the money from banks at preferential rates, because the loans will be guaranteed by the Export-Import Bank, according to Bombardier.[63]

As Anthony Haswell noted, this explanation is quite insufficient:

> A reasonable interpretation is that the builder would borrow money from banks to enable them to pay for construction costs until the trains were delivered to Amtrak. It does not state or imply that money would be loaned to Amtrak by a Canadian government agency in what amount and under what terms. Upon re-reading 1996–1999 Amtrak annual reports, it seems clear that a loan(s) was made to Amtrak from the Canadian Export Development Corporation, as reported in the *Ottawa Citizen*, rather than interim financing assistance for Bombardier without assumption of liability by Amtrak. . . . The underlying issue here is that Amtrak is free to roam the world, without congressional or other government oversight, borrowing money for whatever it wants upon whispering in the ears of lenders, "not to worry—good old Uncle Sap will never let you down."[64]

Newer financial statements reveal that Amtrak has apparently been refinancing some portion of the Canadian loans.[65]

Attempts to Tap Highway and Air Travelers' User Fees

Subsidies from every level of government, along with an unearned income tax "refund," are not enough for Amtrak. The railroad attempts to reach into other taxpayer-funded accounts, including the highway trust fund.

The campaign began in the early 1990s, when Amtrak's Graham Claytor argued in the *Washington Post* in favor of an unprecedented move to transfer one penny per gallon of the gasoline tax from the highway fund to Amtrak.[66] The proposal did not sit well with all newspaper readers, one of whom responded, "I have a suspicion that commuting conditions would be little changed even if the entire defense budget were given to Amtrak."[67] Thomas M. Downs followed Claytor in the Amtrak chairman's seat, and he campaigned to divert a half-cent of the gasoline tax to the railroad.[68] Today, David Gunn pushes for dedicating an unspecified portion of the highway fund to Amtrak, much in the way gasoline taxes are diverted to transit programs.[69]

Amtrak believes airline travelers should subsidize it, too, although the railroad is vague about the assistance it wants. Ronald Utt has noted that users of commercial airlines are subject to a total of eleven separate federal user fees and taxes that fund airport construction and operation, air traffic control, and the safety and security of airlines.[70] As Utt wrote:

> In trying to justify more federal support, Amtrak whines about the new Denver airport that cost $4.6 billion to build, but fails to note that Denver was the only major new airport built in the United States since the late 1960s. Is one major airport in 30 years too much to ask for an industry whose ridership soared nearly 300 percent over the same period? Amtrak also fails to note that Denver airport serves 14 million more passengers each year than Amtrak serves in its entirety.[71]

The Air Transport Association, in noting that the industry in 2004 is squeezed by skyrocketing fuel costs and extra security demands, pointed out, "Airlines remain among the most heavily federally taxed industries in America. Customers pay more federal taxes to fly today than consumers pay to buy alcohol, tobacco or gasoline."[72]

There is no evidence that providing Amtrak with additional capital funding out of the highway or aviation trust funds will result in wise expenditure of those funds. In fact, experience demonstrates that additional financial resources will only provide Amtrak with the means to keep its dysfunctional system intact.

Additional Costs to the Economy

The revival of the freight railroad industry has been nothing less than astonishing. The condition of freight tracks on main lines is the best in U.S. history, and capacity is being expanded to meet growing customer requirements. The companies are moving a record number of ton-miles and doing so with only a fraction of the employees, locomotives, cars, and track required in prior decades.[73] The railroads are laying new tracks on busy routes, buying more efficient locomotives and specialized freight cars to compete better with truckers, and using new technologies to increase workers' productivity.[74]

Every major railroad and most regional railroads are registering traffic growth.[75] In 2004, Union Pacific even found itself having to turn away business when the railroad was slow to hire new train crews fast enough to replace a growing number of retirees at the very time freight shipments shot upward. Freight deliveries were delayed throughout the nation.[76] By mid-2004, railroad delays limited deliveries of raw materials to such an extent that several chemical and cement-making factories curtailed production and retailers reported interruptions in receiving consumer goods. The *Wall Street Journal* reported that the Union Pacific's service breakdowns

> come at a pivotal time for the recovering U.S. economy. In total, railroads carry more than 40 percent of U.S. freight volume, and Union Pacific controls nearly a third of that business. It carries about $300 billion a year of raw materials and finished goods.[77]

Despite such robust traffic growth, freight railroads continue to experience rate pressures from trucking and waterway competitors. The situation is not improved when Amtrak operates its passenger trains over tracks of a freight railroad. Amtrak trains interfere with smooth railroad operations, contribute to delays, and cost freight operators money.

Since Amtrak owns only about 5 percent of the route system it displays in its national system map—namely, most of the Boston–Washington rail line, including links to Harrisburg, Pennsylvania, and Springfield, Massachusetts, and small portions in New York State and Michigan—service over about 95 percent of Amtrak's routes is by virtue of access rights over freight railroads.

Amtrak operates over such lines under terms and conditions the railroads consider unfair. For example, Amtrak has compulsory access to railroads' rights-of-way under federal statute, which also requires Amtrak be given priority over freight train movements. Amtrak's payments for the use of private rights-of-way are limited to "incremental" or "out-of-pocket" costs. The freight railroads believe that this formula forces them to subsidize Amtrak service directly and indirectly.

The direct subsidy is rendered by the freight railroad's inability to charge Amtrak what passenger train movements cost it. One company has been candid about the issue. Richard K. Davidson, chairman of the Union Pacific Corporation, has said that Amtrak underpays the railroad $60–70 million annually for using his railroad's tracks. According to Davidson, a federal policy that permits Amtrak to pay lower rates than commercial customers "is purely a political decision."[78]

The Congressional Budget Office explains why the "out-of-pocket" cost formula, as well as operational priority for Amtrak trains, is less easily endured than in the past:

> That arrangement was put in place in an era when the freight railroads generally had excess capacity and adding a few passenger trains to a route imposed relatively small costs. However, after the regulatory reforms of the Staggers Rail Act of 1980 made it easier to cut uneconomic service, the freight railroads streamlined their route structures and capital investment to a size that more closely matched the demand for service. With business growing in recent years, some freight railroads have experienced congestion on their tracks, and passenger trains have contributed to the costs of delay.[79]

The facts bear out this view. The Congressional Research Service found that the number of track miles owned in the United States declined from 319,000 miles in 1970 to 171,000 miles in 1998.[80] Meanwhile, DOT Inspector General Kenneth M. Mead found that freight rail traffic has increased 64 percent since 1980, with continued growth expected.[81]

Indirect costs occur because the priority of Amtrak trains over freight trains impairs the efficient movement of the latter over capacity-constrained lines. More often than not, when an Amtrak train and a freight train are heading toward each other on a single track, the freight train moves onto a passing siding and waits—often an hour or more.[82]

Amtrak is willing to make incentive payments to railroads for on-time performance—that is, the freight railroads would be rewarded for not causing delays to Amtrak trains—but the effectiveness of these payments is in question. The Department of Transportation's inspector general found that one major railroad in 2002 found it more economical to pay $100,000 in fines for delays to Amtrak, while forgoing $14 million worth of incentive payments—a clear sign of how much money Amtrak-caused delays cost them.[83] Congestion on the rails will only get worse, as several transportation organizations predict freight tonnage moved by rail could virtually double by 2020.

The situation is aggravated when Amtrak runs late—and Amtrak is responsible for many late trains, for reasons ranging from holding a train for connections to mechanical breakdowns. When Amtrak is behind schedule on major rail lines, train dispatchers reach for ulcer medications. Today's railroads value train "slots" in much the same way airlines value takeoff and landing slots at busy airports. A late-running Amtrak train can interfere with a dozen or more freight trains consisting of cars for hundreds of demanding, time-sensitive shippers. When Amtrak delays freight trains, it does not pay the price for shippers' dissatisfaction, nor does it pay financial penalties imposed when just-in-time deliveries are late. Every time a freight railroad company pays for Amtrak-caused delays, the railroad's management, stockholders, and employees are bearing an unjust price. In discussing growing freight train delays, the Union Pacific Railroad estimated that each decrease of average speeds by one mile an hour system-wide "required 250 extra locomotives, 5,000 extra freight cars and 180 extra employees to absorb the decrease in efficiency."[84]

Passenger train enthusiasts demonstrate little sympathy for what they view as inequitable treatment by America's railroad industry. They sometimes argue that the freight lines agreed to charge lower rates to Amtrak as a condition of receiving permission from the federal government to exit the money-losing intercity passenger train business. But that was in 1971. The railroads have paid the price for that transaction over and over again, as has the American economy.

No definitive study has been done of the cost to shippers and consumers of Amtrak-caused delays on freight lines. It is reasonable to argue, however, that cutting lightly used Amtrak trains on the busiest freight lines is in the national interest. Observed one journalist:

> Cutting the Sunset Limited [which travels between Los Angeles and Orlando, Florida] might actually result in fewer trucks on the roads because it would be easier to ship freight by rail if Amtrak weren't given priority on the Union Pacific's tracks. What environmental or economic sense does it make to give 170 passengers on the Sunset Limited priority over a freight train that's keeping 500 trucks off the road?[85]

Another approach worth looking at is the system by which commuter agencies arrange compensation to freight lines, which stands in sharp contrast to the temperamental relationship between Amtrak and the freight railroads. This negotiation is conducted at arms' length on a case-by-case basis, with no federal statute compelling mandatory access. Payment levels are established by mutual agreement. Herzog Transit Services Inc., for instance, operates passenger trains over a Union Pacific–owned line in California. Its senior vice president, Alan Landes, noted:

> This access agreement was negotiated by the commuter authority and the number is not public. Herzog would wager that the access fee is higher than comparable Amtrak incremental access fees by more than one hundred percent.[86]

Some private tour train companies also pay negotiated rates. Freight railroads believe what is good for commuter trains and private operators should be good for Amtrak, too, and they have a point.

Amtrak has long been in a financially precarious condition; its fiscal shenanigans bear constant watching. The railroad has been irresponsible in making repeated shutdown threats, especially when carrying out those threats would harm innocent commuters. Taxpayers' direct and indirect subsidies to Amtrak are greatly disproportionate to the public's minimal use of the train system; and Amtrak is so seriously flawed that its fiscal picture will only worsen. A grim picture, indeed, but one that will change only when serious reforms are implemented.

4

Myths about the Value of Amtrak

Four groups predominate in the quest to preserve the Amtrak status quo: Amtrak management, Amtrak employees, some state transportation officials, and railroad buffs. A common theme is that service will improve and more people will ride the trains, and therefore Amtrak's problems will diminish. A fantasy is that tomorrow's high-speed trains will be so appealing that they will link communities of all sizes and succeed in reducing airport congestion. Intermingled with such illusions are dire warnings that communities will be isolated if long-distance trains are discontinued. Unfortunately, many members of Congress believe that reforming Amtrak's operations would imperil their reelection prospects. These myths and others are worth close scrutiny.

Myth No. 1: Amtrak's Political Invulnerability

Amtrak president David Gunn once told a Canadian reporter that American politicians "don't have the intestinal fortitude to stand up and get rid of passenger rail service."[1] He had a point. Members of Congress fear offending any interest group, no matter how small. But Amtrak benefits from illusory political power. Cutting money-losing train routes is not likely to cost any politician much at the ballot box—and could well be rewarded by the voters.

It is true that cutting Amtrak funding or killing a poorly performing route has the *appearance* of being politically dangerous. After all, constituents often want to preserve local service. Amtrak officials claim it will cost more to discontinue money-losing trains than keep them running, because of exorbitant labor-protection costs (while at the same time refusing to negotiate an end to such extravagant labor protections). Union officials claim that discontinuing a train will create "hardships" on employees and will inconvenience commuters and travelers. State and local agencies argue that Amtrak service is "essential"—regardless of how few people use it.[2] And railroad buffs bemoan the decline of the romance of the rails and grieve over the prospect of losing their local train station. In other words, subsidies to Amtrak are justified because they are a source of nostalgia and emotional fulfillment.

This support for Amtrak is largely illusory. Across the nation, very few people care about Amtrak one way or another, since it serves so few people. Very few Americans, if given the choice, would choose to pay higher taxes to subsidize some Amtrak passengers $300 or more for each trip they take.

The press helps maintain this illusion by drawing a bleak picture if politicians even *talk* about cutting back Amtrak. For example, in 2002 the *Washington Post* focused on a Republican proposal to give Amtrak $500 million less than it had requested, which might have prompted Amtrak to shut down six money-losing long-distance routes. The paper observed:

> Political insiders expressed surprise that the Republicans would take such an action before the November elections. The six trains pass through the districts of several key Republicans who are in tight races . . . The potential political complications illustrate why it has been so difficult to abandon train routes over the past three decades. Rep. John L. Mica of Florida, a senior Republican, is in a fight for his political life in a state where the passenger train and high-speed rail have become an issue. His district would lose the Sunset Limited. Louisville would lose the Kentucky Cardinal just months after Kentucky politicians talked Amtrak into extending the train across the Ohio River from its former terminal in Jeffersonville, Ind. The congresswoman for Louisville is Republican Anne M. Northup, who is in a tough reelection battle.[3]

No subsequent article pointed out that the officials mentioned above, and others in the article, were reelected. Their return to office should have been no surprise, because the historical record shows that politicians who've gone along with *actually* cutting Amtrak have been reelected.

In fact, there is no evidence that any public official has ever lost a seat as a result of reducing support for Amtrak, although over the years Amtrak has been forced to stop service on various routes in twenty states. Trains that no longer operate include the Floridian between Chicago and Miami and St. Petersburg; the North Coast Hiawatha between Chicago and Seattle; the Lone Star between Chicago and Houston; the Mountaineer between Norfolk and Chicago; the Hilltopper between Richmond, Virginia, and Chicago; and the National Limited on a New York–Pittsburgh–Kansas City route. Amtrak also selectively discontinues stops with no serious consequences; for instance, the Capitol Limited no longer stops in McKeesport, Pennsylvania, on its way from Washington to Chicago. In total, 123 station stops have been stricken from Amtrak's map over the years—in communities as large as Phoenix, Arizona, and as small as Keyser, West Virginia—and no one is worse off as a result. (See table 4-1 for the listing of communities.)

Even if Congress were to take a relatively radical step, such as replacing Amtrak with a private operator or forcing Amtrak to discontinue money-losing long-distance trains, it is very unlikely that voter backlash would affect even a single election result. So few people use Amtrak nationwide that it is simply a ballot-box irrelevancy. In areas like the Northeast where significant numbers of people do use Amtrak, loyalty to the trains is more intense than loyalty to Amtrak. Preserving Amtrak is immaterial to how ballots are cast to all but an infinitesimal minority.

Myth No. 2: September 11 Demonstrated the Need for Amtrak

In the immediate aftermath of the September 11, 2001, terrorist attacks and the subsequent shutdown of commercial air travel, it seemed easy to argue that Amtrak was indispensable. In truth, even in this extraordinary circumstance, Amtrak seems to have played a relatively minor role in meeting America's transportation needs. Amtrak claimed that ridership increased on trains throughout the country,[4] particularly for trips of more than four hundred miles; seats were reportedly disappearing rapidly on cross-country

TABLE 4-1

COMMUNITIES NO LONGER SERVED BY AMTRAK TRAINS

State	Communities	State	Communities
Alabama	Decatur, Dothan, Montgomery	Nevada	Caliente, Las Vegas
Arizona	Phoenix	North Dakota	Bismarck, Dickinson, Jamestown, Mandan, Valley City
California	Pasadena		
Colorado	Greeley	Ohio	Athens, Canton,
Florida	Clearwater, St. Petersburg		Chillicothe, Columbus,
Georgia	Thomasville, Valdosta, Waycross		Crestline, Dayton, Lima
		Oklahoma	Guthrie, Perry, Ponca City
Idaho	Boise, Nampa, Pocatello, Shoshone	Oregon	Baker City, Hinkle-Hermiston, Hood River, La Grande, Ontario, Pendleton, The Dalles
Illinois	Chillicothe, Decatur, East Elmhurst, Freeport, Galena, Peoria, Rockford, Streator, Warren	Pennsylvania	McKeesport
		Tennessee	Nashville
Indiana	Bloomington, Fort Wayne, Garrett, Jeffersonville, Lafayette, Logansport, Marion, Muncie, Nappanee, Peru, Richmond, Terre Haute	Texas	Brenham, Gainesville, Laredo
		Utah	Milford, Ogden
		Virginia	Crewe, Bedford, Christiansburg, Farmville, Narrows, Norfolk, Roanoke, Suffolk
Iowa	Dubuque		
Kansas	Arkansas City, Wichita	Washington	East Auburn, Ellensburg, Yakima
Kentucky	Bowling Green, Louisville		
Minnesota	Cambridge, Breckenridge, Duluth, Morris, Sandstone, Willmar	West Virginia	Bluefield, Clarksburg, Grafton, Keyser, Oakland, Parkersburg, Rowlesburg, Welch, Williamson
Mississippi	Batesville, Canton, Durant, Grenada, Winona	Wisconsin	Janesville, Lake Geneva, Superior
Montana	Billings, Bozeman, Butte, Deer Lodge, Forsyth, Glendive, Livingston, Miles City, Missoula, Paradise	Wyoming	Cheyenne, Evanston, Green River, Laramie, Rawlins, Rock Springs

SOURCE: Amtrak train schedules from 1971 through 2004.

NOTE: These communities are no longer served because Amtrak discontinued trains, changed train routes and bypassed communities, or discontinued stops on routes that continue to operate.

trains.[5] Amtrak talked about "coming to the rescue of 100,000 passengers nationwide" and being a "viable form of transportation."[6]

As more aircraft returned to the skies, reports indicated an easing in the number of sold-out trains. By September 20, Amtrak's West Palm Beach traffic was "thinning out and returning to normal."[7] Next, the *Los Angeles Times* reported,

> The surge of passengers who flocked to Amtrak trains in the days after the terrorist attacks has begun to subside, dimming hopes that the intercity rail service could attract lots of new passengers amid the airline crisis. . . . Amtrak officials provided few specifics concerning ridership totals following the September 11 terrorist attacks. They said, however, that ridership nationwide was up an estimated 17 percent in the first week after the terrorism. On [September 26], Amtrak said the increase since the attacks had fallen to somewhere between 10% and 13%.[8]

The Amtrak Reform Council found otherwise, concluding: "The terrorist attacks on September 11 caused a brief spike in Amtrak's ridership. For the month as a whole, however, Amtrak's ridership was 6.4 percent lower than in September 2000 and was 16.3 percent less than projected in Amtrak's Strategic Business Plan."[9]

Hoping to prove that the events of September 11 had fundamentally improved Amtrak ridership, the Reform Council's senior financial analyst, Michael Mates, analyzed daily Amtrak ridership statistics for September 2001. Unfortunately, his analysis failed to confirm Amtrak's estimated 34 percent increase in ridership. While Amtrak's reservations system may have been flooded with inquiries and additional reservations, the actual increases in ridership and average length of passenger trip were very modest. In fact, passenger boardings were 6 percent below the prior year's levels for September. Many people thought about riding Amtrak, it seems, but few actually did so.

Even on long-distance trains, where a passenger surge would be expected as the result of the temporary grounding of commercial airlines, the increases in numbers of passengers and average trip lengths were not significant. With additional coaches added to trains to meet Amtrak's alleged surge in ridership, Amtrak's actual system-wide load factor remained virtually unchanged; on some trains, it actually declined after September 11. These facts were disappointing to everyone who wanted to believe that Amtrak's ridership was up and that some portion of that increase would remain even after airlines resumed full service.[10]

The discovery was a stark reminder of the depth of Amtrak's troubles. With the national aviation system shut down for a while, Reagan National Airport in Washington closed for a longer period, and travelers generally wary of flying, Amtrak still found itself with empty seats. Amtrak's next move was to fill those seats by imposing the greatest fare reductions in American railroad history. For example:

- Amtrak began offering a preposterous one-way fare of $3.40 from Indianapolis to Chicago. That same trip cost $6.23 on the New York Central Railroad in April 1953—adjusting for inflation, $23.95 in today's dollars.[11]

- From Chicago to Detroit, Amtrak was charging only $17.20, a fare that Amtrak itself set at $16.25 in 1971 when it launched operations. Adjusting for inflation, that fare would have been $79.59 today.[12]

- Long-distance routes came in for their share of low fares, such as Philadelphia–Chicago for $16 (the Greyhound bus fare was $72.90) and Cleveland–Philadelphia for $11.70 (Greyhound was charging $67.00).

- These heavily discounted fares were offered for exceptionally long periods of time, rather than the customary short-term specials offered to boost ridership. On the Texas Eagle (a train that Amtrak calls a "success") empty seats inspired a St. Louis–San Antonio one-way fare of $81.60 that ran from September 25 to December 17, 2001, and again from January 7 to June 14, 2002. In April 2004, the least expensive Greyhound ticket available for round-trip (Monday–Thursday) travel on that route was $273.

Despite unprecedented discounting, Amtrak's 23.4 million riders in fiscal year 2002 was actually fewer than the prior year (23.5 million).

While it is fair to acknowledge that Amtrak may have suffered from an overall travel decline, it is also important to note that the public's fear of flying and record-low fares did not reverse the decline.

Incidentally, Amtrak saw a post–September 11 revenue boost from increased U.S. Postal Service shipments as the federal government temporarily prohibited passenger airplanes from carrying mail. Amtrak's priority at its primary maintenance facility during that period is revealing. Officials at the Beech Grove, Indiana, car overhaul shop asked employees to "double their production" and said "the biggest push" was on repairing mail cars and baggage cars.[13] Performing work on cars to carry passengers was less urgent, September 11 notwithstanding.

Myth No. 3: The Acela Express Will Save Amtrak

The Acela Express, the high-speed train linking Washington, D.C., with New York and Boston, is Amtrak's crown jewel. It's also been, so far, a remarkable fiasco. An attractive train with many amenities, the Acela Express offers faster schedules than the trains it replaced. What remains unclear is how much of a traffic increase the new trains will generate— and at what price. The trains certainly were not cheap. On May 1, 1996, the Bombardier-Alsthom consortium executed contracts with Amtrak worth $1.1 billion to manufacture twenty Acela Express trains, construct maintenance facilities to support the trains, build fifteen "high-speed locomotives" to pull existing Amtrak rolling stock, and provide ongoing management services.[14] But trains were just part of the cost. The GAO has surveyed various accounts and reports that through March 2003, a total of about $3.2 billion (in 2003 dollars) had been spent on the Northeast High-Speed Rail Improvement Project, as follows:

> Amtrak has spent about $2.6 billion and three commuter railroads, two freight railroads, and two state governments have spent about $625 million. Most of Amtrak's spending was for the acquisition of high-speed trains and related maintenance facilities (about $1.1 billion), electrification of the route (about $717 million), and track and infrastructure projects ($652

million). . . . The Connecticut Department of Transportation also plans to spend an additional $250 million to replace catenary between the New York/Connecticut state line and New Haven.[15]

Amtrak first began planning the Acela Express more than ten years ago. The train's saga has been disappointing enough that it deserves its own detailed summary. Appendix B gives a chronological account of problems in train design, delivery delays, component failures, and service suspensions ranging from 1993 through 2004. In May 1993, Amtrak started the Acela Express procurement process, promising that all new trains would be running by 1998.[16] The last train was delivered in June 2003—somewhere between four and five years behind schedule.[17] As one journalist reported,

> Court documents, government studies, audits, congressional testimony and interviews reveal that the high-speed rail project was dogged by problems, testing delays and bloated costs from the start. Amtrak executives consistently exaggerated what Acela would accomplish and masked the extent of the delays and mounting costs.[18]

An especially vivid account of this problem-plagued operation appeared in a lawsuit (since settled) filed against Amtrak in November 2001 by the Montreal-based Bombardier Corporation, the company Amtrak had contracted with to make the Acela. Bombardier sought to recover $200 million in damages, stating that Amtrak had disrupted the company's ability to produce and deliver the trains on time and had caused cost overruns. According to Bombardier's filing,

> As a result of Amtrak's continuing interference, designs have been modified literally thousands of times, large numbers of already completed components have had to be discarded or retrofitted, the equipment has been subjected to thousands of hours of unreasonable and unnecessary testing and management services have been rendered significantly more difficult

and costly to perform. The magnitude of the extra work caused by Amtrak is reflected in the vast contract record—over 19,900 letters, 9,000 engineering change notices, 4,700 retrofit notices and 800 formally recorded meetings.[19]

Amtrak's biggest mistake is that it did not purchase a proven high-speed train model and adapt it to U.S. safety standards.[20] Amtrak certainly had experience with proven train designs. Beginning in 1993, the railroad conducted tests of the X2000, a Swedish-Swiss high-speed train designed to tilt when going around curves. The tilting capability counteracts centrifugal force, which permits trains to take curves faster while maintaining passenger comfort. The tests were highly successful, the train's reliability was exceptionally high, and the interiors received rave reviews from passengers and the press.[21] Amtrak also tested trains from Germany and Spain.

But instead of learning from these experiences, Amtrak went to a new design. It was this decision that brought about the persistent delays in planning and production and the years of diminished revenue-generating capacity.

An action Amtrak took to change the name of the train had a side benefit—it obscured how many years the Acela Express's delivery fell behind schedule. When the order was first placed, the train was called "a new Metroliner"; then it became the American Flyer, and still later, the Acela Express. Hence, a journalist trying to track delays in databases will find it difficult because references to the train kept changing. Regardless of what it was called, there's no question that the train went into operation years behind schedule, and as late as 2004, serious design flaws remain.

Like the Swedish-Swiss X2000, the Acela Express was designed as a tilting train to permit it to travel faster around the many curves between New York and Boston. But after production started, it was learned that the trains were built four inches too wide, making it impossible to put the tilting mechanism to full use. This restricted the Acela's speed and added time to the schedules—a problem that could have been avoided if Amtrak had purchased the X2000. In addition, the Acela Express's top speed between Washington and New York is limited to 135 mph, primarily because going faster would bring down the catenary (the overhead wires that power the trains). As a result, the Acela Express only operates at its top speed of 150 miles per hour on eighteen miles of the entire Boston–Washington route— a stretch at the Rhode Island–Massachusetts border.[22]

Due to these numerous design flaws, the Acela Express trips between Boston and New York generally take three hours and twenty-seven minutes.[23] This does not meet the federal statutory requirement to connect the cities in less than three hours, which would make the trains competitive with air shuttles (when travel time to and from airports is factored in).

Current Amtrak schedules are an embarrassment when compared with the New Haven Railroad's Advance Merchants Limited, which linked New York and Boston in three hours and fifty-seven minutes in 1954.[24] The New Haven Railroad achieved that performance without the benefit of running on a fully electrified railroad (Amtrak's electric locomotives are faster than the diesels used in the 1950s), without tilt-train technology that allows faster speeds, without the advanced signaling systems now in place, and without new tracks virtually the entire distance between Boston and New Haven. In running only about thirty minutes faster than trains a half-century ago—after Amtrak has spent billions on the project—the Acela Express is a testament to Amtrak's inability to bring about advanced high-speed rail service.

Amtrak's disappointing record with the Acela Express also stands in stark contrast with the successes that other countries have had with high-speed rail. Today's Acela Express is slower than Japan's first bullet trains were in the 1960s—trains that are now in museums. Among the world's fifty fastest trains, the Acela Express's highest *average* speed (103 mph, which it only reaches on the brief stretch between Wilmington, Delaware, and Baltimore) ranks a mediocre forty-second.[25]

Moreover, while top speeds weighed heavily in Amtrak's decision to produce the Acela Express, it is the overall travel time that counts in passengers' minds. That is one reason why rail traffic in the Northeast has not yet reached projected levels. Passengers aboard the Acela Express today are riding trains with average speeds that are slower than what Spain offered in the early 1990s, France in the 1980s, and Japan in the 1970s. Also, Japan's bullet trains boasted a 99 percent on-time record, while the Acela Express only managed to raise its on-time performance above 70 percent after it added time to the schedule in 2003, making it easier to arrive "on time."[26]

The Acela Express's problems and unmet expectations are legion:

- While Amtrak has, indeed, achieved ridership gains in the Northeast Corridor, traffic has ebbed and flowed, rather than gaining steadily as Amtrak had predicted it would.

- The GAO has found that Amtrak fell short in upgrading infrastructure and exercised ineffective management of the high-speed project. Amtrak focused on short-term needs while neglecting more important work. While Amtrak electrified the tracks between Boston and New Haven and acquired the Acela Express, it did not properly address other needed infrastructure work, nor did it fully integrate the interests of commuter rail authorities and state governments into the project, even though work involving them was critical to achieving three-hour Boston–New York service.[27]

- By 2004, Amtrak was reducing fares on the Acela Express, abandoning earlier pledges that the train's appeal would be based on value, not price. This was another setback because Amtrak had forecast that two million additional passengers would generate $300 million in revenues annually, a level difficult to achieve with such extensive discounting. The latest discount-pricing actions have taken Amtrak even further away from achieving the profits projected for the Acela Express.

When George Warrington once declared that Amtrak would "be the envy of all transportation providers," he meant that would happen in part because of the anticipated success of the Acela Express. Amtrak's subsequent president, David Gunn, said he would never order another Acela Express—a logical conclusion considering the train's history. Even once-ardent Amtrak advocate Thomas R. Pulsifer, who had defended Amtrak for nearly thirty years, was disillusioned. As the commissioner of an Ohio state agency looking into high-speed rail, he had hoped the Acela Express would succeed. Now, he says, he has deciphered what the word "Acela" means—"I fear it's Amtrak-ese for 'fiasco.'"[28]

Myth No. 4: America Needs a
National High-Speed Rail Network

Is a national high-speed train network necessary to travel in the United States? As discussed earlier, high-speed rail can contribute to mobility in the Boston–Washington corridor and on a few other short-distance routes through heavily populated areas. But there is no need to connect these lines to each other, as the routes will be targeted to regional population clusters no more than three hundred miles apart. Unlike the Interstate Highway System, there is no justification whatsoever for a national high-speed rail network. If Amtrak is allowed to build America's high-speed rail system, the trains will be slow, expensive, and lightly used.

After the Acela Express debacle, Amtrak can no longer credibly claim that its future trains will be as speedy as Japanese bullet trains or French TGVs (*Train à Grande Vitesse*—or train of great speed). Such trains operate at 187 mph on short-distance corridors generally three hundred miles long, where speedy ground travel can compete with air service. They also operate at top speeds on tracks dedicated exclusively to passenger trains because of safety and operating conditions. When high-speed trains share their tracks with freight trains, as they do in the United States, their speeds decline. And whatever the speeds, foreign high-speed trains operate in areas far more thickly populated than is typical for the United States.

Aside from the Acela debacle, there are other reasons for leaving Amtrak out of any plans for new high-speed trains. Amtrak has acquiesced to faulty political schemes, contributing to four enormous deficiencies in current proposals:

- *"High-speed" now also means "slow"*: In other countries, the term "high-speed train" generally refers to trains traveling at 150 miles per hour or more, most often on lines that have no freight traffic. But Amtrak has redefined "high-speed" to mean trains traveling as slow as 90 mph running on tracks congested with freight trains. Amtrak's future trains will rarely be faster than the trains that U.S. rail passengers traveled on in the 1950s or earlier, and Amtrak will be unable to effectively compete with contemporary air travel times.[29]

- *Nonmarketable lengthy routes:* Amtrak has yet to disavow proposals made by politicians and railroad buffs for nonsensical "high-speed train" proposals for excessively long routes such as Washington, D.C.–New Orleans. The 1,152-mile route is so lengthy that not even the fastest European or Japanese high-speed train could compete with air travel. Amtrak permits such talk to continue in hopes that talk of trendy high-speed rail projects will be the impetus for additional federal appropriations.

- *Sparsely populated routes:* Proposals to run Amtrak high-speed trains include routes with few potential customers. For example, Chicago–Omaha is discussed by train boosters, yet Iowa's population of 2.9 million people is nowhere near that of the dense population centers found in Japanese or European cities—the Paris area alone has 10 million people. Another proposal, which is supported by Texas Republican Senator Kay Bailey Hutchison, is to run high-speed trains between Dallas and Texarkana. (Two adjacent communities are named Texarkana, one in Texas, the other in Arkansas, and they have a combined population of less than 125,000.) This represents a tiny travel market.[30]

- *Inability to cure airport congestion:* Amtrak claims that Amtrak-style high-speed trains will ease airport congestion, or "winglock."[31] It stretches credulity to believe that such trains will divert more than a small number of air travelers to travel by rail. Even if every proposed Amtrak high-speed train were running today, it is doubtful that even a single flight would be removed anywhere in the nation's crowded aviation system.[32]

Eleven corridors have been designed either by legislation or by the Department of Transportation for potential conversion into high-speed rail corridors.[33] The GAO has warned, "The ultimate cost of developing these high-speed rail corridors is unknown, but certainly in the many tens of billions of dollars."[34] The National Taxpayers Union has estimated the cost at $100 billion.[35] Most of these projects would be a tremendous misallocation of the nation's resources, equivalent to building long runways in the middle of the Nevada Desert, hundreds of miles distant from cities, and hoping that people will materialize to fill the Boeing 747s.

Some Amtrak advocates believe that high-speed trains will succeed even on routes that have already failed with conventional trains. Calls are made for high-speed trains on segments of long-distance routes wherever political muscle is available. For example, the old Dixie Flagler will probably never again roar down the tracks on its historic route between Chicago, Nashville, Atlanta, and Miami, but railroad buffs have called upon the Federal Railroad Administration to approve a high-speed line on a sparsely populated portion of that route between Nashville, Chattanooga, and Atlanta.[36]

Considering the rural demographics that dominate outside of Atlanta, the small travel market, and the engineering challenges and costs to upgrade freight tracks to permit passenger trains to run at higher speeds, the economics of these proposals are remarkably dismal. Yet train proponents insist that highway traffic congestion has become so bad that alternatives are needed. While that may be true, the idea that Amtrak is the answer is absurd: Most traffic problems occur in urban and suburban areas where people are commuting to work. We could spend billions of dollars on high-speed rail lines like Nashville–Atlanta without solving the highway congestion problems.[37]

Amtrak-style high-speed trains will be colossal failures.[38] As the *Economist* editorialized about one congressional effort to boost high-speed rail, "[G]iving Amtrak control over something like $12 billion in capital spending is insane."[39] Moreover, federal or state appropriations for such programs will help obscure Amtrak's financial plight, still another reason to terminate any planning that involves the railroad. The *Chicago Tribune* observed, "The dream of high-speed rail cannot be an excuse to perpetuate the Amtrak model of heavily subsidized nationwide rail. It's a model for wasted money."[40] For high-speed rail to succeed in America, we must establish a means of inducing private investment and private-sector participation, which would in turn inject some fiscal and market discipline in a process now out of control.

Myth No. 5: America Needs European Trains

Some Americans admire railroads in Europe and think the United States should have trains like the ones there. But this simply ignores exceptionally different environments. *Congressional Digest* summarized Europe's train-friendly circumstances well:

> Conditions in those countries are, in many ways, more favorable to passenger rail transportation than in the United States. Their population densities are higher (which makes train travel more efficient), their fuel prices, including taxes, are higher (which makes driving more expensive relative to other travel options), and their land area is relatively smaller (which makes travel time by train more competitive with air travel).[41]

Even with these favorable conditions, Amtrak-style long-distance trains are in decline in just about every country in the world, even in train-dependent countries like Germany, where rail's share of the passenger market fell from 36 percent in 1950 to 6 percent in 1990, and the Netherlands, whose traffic continues to decline based on passenger-kilometers; the latest totals there dropped from 14.3 billion in 2002 to 13.8 billion in 2003.[42] The industrialized countries registering rail traffic increases are doing so with commuter trains in the large urban areas or with high-speed trains that truly compete with air travel, and their gains are sizable enough to mask the decline on Amtrak-style routes. When nonindustrialized countries like Argentina have privatized their railways, generally the first reform has been to discontinue money-losing long-distance passenger trains.

Myth No. 6: America Needs Long-Distance Trains

A stark fact is how few people use America's long-distance trains. The vast majority of train travel is concentrated on just a few routes. According to DOT Inspector General Kenneth Mead,

Amtrak ridership in 2002 totaled about 23.4 million passengers, and short-distance corridor trains carried 19.8 million (84 percent) of them—47 percent of them in the Northeast Corridor and 37 percent on other corridor trains. The remaining 16 percent of passengers (3.6 million) rode the 17 long-distance trains.[43]

The shift in the ratio to passengers riding short distances will grow as state initiatives continue to stimulate traffic on regional, short-distance trains.

Despite this, several arguments are offered in favor of saving long-distance trains. For instance, it is said they provide "essential" transportation linking small communities to the outside world. In fact, Amtrak serves fewer communities than the aviation system. In 2001, Amtrak had 512 stations, while there were 635 U.S.-certificated airports and several thousand smaller ones.[44]

Another oft-repeated claim is that people in towns along the Empire Builder route, which travels through the northern parts of Montana and North Dakota between Seattle and Chicago, depend on the train to get to the Mayo Clinic in Rochester, Minnesota, or to Shriners' hospitals.[45] We hear that discontinuing the train would be a "hardship"—yet hundreds of communities in those very states are not served by Amtrak. People who live in southern Montana or southern South Dakota, for instance, make do just fine without Amtrak. When they need to reach the "outside world" they drive or take the bus, or travel to another community that has bus or airline service. As Anthony Haswell has explained,

For every community now served by Amtrak, there are literally dozens who do not have train service and have no reasonable prospect of ever getting it. Take Kansas, which has a daily Amtrak train running across its entire length. The state has 161 communities ranging in size from 1,000 to 50,000, yet Amtrak stops in just four of them. Since there are so many smaller communities without Amtrak service, the assertion that it is essential to the relatively few that have it is not credible. . . . Even those places which do have an Amtrak train may not have very useful service, for the train may run only three days a week, arrive and depart during the middle of the night, and often not run on time.[46]

Diehard railroad enthusiasts will still argue that long-distance trains are an integral part of a "national passenger rail system." America does not have such a system. Amtrak fails to serve many popular travel routes simply because of the way trains are routed or gaps in its system. Examples of nonexistent train links include Detroit–Cincinnati, Kansas City–Tulsa, Tucson–Phoenix—the list of unconnected cities is endless.

Given how marginal rail travel is to meeting America's travel needs, there is clearly no justification for keeping long-distance routes as part of a "national passenger rail system" that hasn't existed for decades. C. Kenneth Orski, a transportation management consultant, examined what should constitute such a system:

> Should such a system be a continent-wide coast-to-coast network of interconnected long-distance train routes, as envisioned by many Amtrak supporters? Or should it rather be a system of regional rail services? The answer is self-evident. A coast-to-coast interconnected rail system is neither justified nor needed. Ours is a vast country and there simply is not enough demand for long distance rail travel to make a continent-wide rail network economically feasible. Instead, what is needed is rail service connecting major population centers in heavily traveled corridors. When viewed in this light, it becomes clearer why responsibility for intercity rail services— like for commuter rail services—should properly be vested in regional authorities or state governments.[47]

The prospect of a "balkanization" of Amtrak horrifies train enthusiasts who believe in a national system of interconnected trains. However, in 2002 all of Amtrak's long-distance trains carried only 15.6 percent of total Amtrak ridership, meaning Amtrak was "national" in image much more than in fact. (See table 4-2.) Even Europe does not have a sprawling system like Amtrak. Observed journalist John Tierney,

TABLE 4-2
AMTRAK 2002 RIDERSHIP DISTRIBUTION BY ROUTE

Name of Train	Riders (thousands)	Percent of Total Amtrak Ridership
Long-Distance Trains		
Silver Star	252	1.1
Three Rivers	27	0.5
Cardinal	74	0.3
Silver Meteor	48	1.1
Capitol Limited	46	0.6
Lake Shore Limited	88	1.2
Silver Palm	206	0.9
Pennsylvanian	76	0.3
Auto Train	202	0.9
Empire Builder	368	1.6
California Zephyr	327	1.4
Southwest Chief	256	1.1
City of New Orleans	159	0.7
Texas Eagle	129	0.6
Sunset Limited	97	0.4
Coast Starlight	446	1.9
Total Long Distance	**3,646**	**15.6**
Boston–Washington		
Acela Express/Metroliner	3,214	13.7
Regional	5,760	24.6
Clocker	1,979	8.5
Total Boston–Washington	**10,953**	**46.8**
Other Short Distance		
Ethan Allen	39	0.2
Vermonter	67	0.3
Twilight Shoreliner	215	0.9
Maple Leaf/Empire Service	1,241	5.3
Downeaster	245	1.0
Keystone	949	4.1
Adirondack	91	0.4
Carolinian	215	0.9
Piedmont	44	0.2
State House	226	1.0
Hiawatha	404	1.7
Wolverine	300	1.3
Illini	92	0.4

continued on next page

TABLE 4-2 *(continued)*
AMTRAK 2002 RIDERSHIP DISTRIBUTION BY ROUTE

Name of Train	Riders (thousands)	Percent of Total Amtrak Ridership
Other Short Distance		
Illinois Zephyr	94	0.4
Heartland Flyer	53	0.2
Pacific Surfliner	1,725	7.4
Cascades	580	2.5
Capitols	1,080	4.6
San Joaquins	734	3.1
International	92	0.4
Kentucky Cardinal	21	0.1
Mules	144	0.6
Pere Marquette	60	0.3
Special Trains & Buses	98	0.4
Total Other Short Distance	**8,808**	**37.6**
Grand Total	**23,407**	**100.0**

SOURCE: Kenneth M. Mead, inspector general, U.S. Department of Transportation, testimony before the U.S. Senate Committee on Commerce, Science, and Transportation, hearings, *The Future of Intercity Passenger Rail Service and Amtrak*, 108th Cong., 1st sess., October 2, 2003.

If there were a European version of Amtrak, one centralized monopoly running the continent's trains, it would be pandering to politicians in the Pyrenees and in Ukraine by running a half-empty train from Madrid to Moscow—and subsidizing it with revenues from the Paris-Lyon trains.[48]

Amtrak's origin-to-destination station usage confirms that long-distance passenger trains have passed their prime. In 2000, seventeen long-distance routes carried nearly 4 million passengers, but only about 18 percent of those passengers traveled the full length of a route. Nearly twice as many people (34 percent) rode in the "corridor" portions of long-distance routes. (See table 4-3.)

For example, only 5 percent of the half-million passengers on the Coast Starlight, which travels between Seattle and Los Angeles, traveled end-to-end, while 55 percent traveled on portions that are considered an existing or planned corridor. If the Coast Starlight was replaced with

TABLE 4-3

END-TO-END VS. CORRIDOR PASSENGERS ON LONG-DISTANCE TRAINS

Train	2000 Passengers			End-to-End (%)	Corridor (%)
	End-to-End	Corridor[a]	Total		
Auto Train	233,900	233,900	233,900	100	100
California Zephyr	33,362	72,198	382,002	9	19
Capitol Limited	62,481	16,698	145,196	43	12
Cardinal	3,631	16,087	74,479	5	22
City of New Orleans	39,433	0	200,682	20	0
Coast Starlight	26,174	277,299	505,098	5	55
Crescent	8,561	77,610	265,789	3	29
Empire Builder	40,307	155,159	433,404	9	36
Lake Shore Limited	67,264	99,326	300,989	22	33
Palmetto	28,148	70,524	217,865	13	32
Pennsylvanian	0	33,590	33,590	0	100
Silver Meteor	52,063	69,913	254,229	20	28
Silver Star	34,877	129,397	269,577	13	48
Southwest Chief	47,079	2,683	268,267	18	1
Sunset Limited	13,685	5,972	119,444	11	5
Texas Eagle	2,192	30,675	145,023	2	21
Three Rivers	20,599	55,947	133,206	15	42
Total Long Distance	**713,756**	**1,346,978**	**3,982,740**	**18**	**34**

SOURCE: Kenneth M. Mead, inspector general, U.S. Department of Transportation, testimony before the Senate Commerce, Science, and Transportation Committee, *Hearing: Amtrak*, 108th Cong., 1st sess., October 2, 2003, 14.

[a] Represents the number of passengers who get on and off the train within the confines of a single corridor. Corridors include stations on existing Amtrak corridors and those on planned high-speed rail corridor routes.

shorter trains traveling over the heavily used routes, 95 percent of the passengers would continue to ride the shorter-distance trains on the busiest sections (the Seattle–Portland–Eugene, Sacramento–San Jose, and Santa Barbara–Los Angeles segments). There are other instances where Amtrak trains could be discontinued, with other trains picking up the slack—such as between Harpers Ferry, West Virginia, and

Washington, D.C., where more people ride commuter trains than ride Amtrak.

The cumulative result of efforts by railroad enthusiasts, labor unions, and elected officials—along with some in the railway supplier industry—to preserve Amtrak at all costs is rather sad. The coalition that props up a dysfunctional Amtrak system lacks an adequate political groundswell to put the right trains on the best lines to carry the most people. Federal Railroad Administrator Allan Rutter summed up the situation in recent congressional testimony:

> The present Amtrak route system has changed little over Amtrak's thirty years of existence, seemingly locked in place by history and politics. That is starkly anomalous in America's transportation system. What other transportation company or mode of travel has changed its routes and service so little in the last thirty years? Most transportation providers have changed their systems dramatically over that time span in response to changes in travel patterns driven by economics and demographics.[49]

Myth No. 7: Bigger Would Be Better

In 1998, Amtrak began implementing a strategy to expand service in twenty-one states when it initiated a comprehensive assessment of its system with what it called a market-based network analysis (MBNA). Amtrak described the MBNA as a mechanism to find opportunities to "reduce costs and increase revenue" and "match consumer demand with an efficient operation."[50] Amtrak also said the MBNA would drive expansion and equipment acquisition to accommodate the "best and most profitable passenger rail service."[51] Finally, the effort was designed to "increase our profitability."[52]

In a report to Congress, Amtrak said of the MBNA process that "Amtrak can only grow by servicing markets where research—hard facts and data, not hunches, nostalgia, or historical precedent—indicates a strong chance for success."[53] With that promising beginning, Amtrak then went about ignoring hard facts in favor of wishful thinking about its expansion plans.

The MBNA spawned Amtrak's "Network Growth Strategy," announced in 2000, which called for new or expanded service on four-teen routes.[54] Amtrak claimed that when implemented, it would "add $255 million in revenue by 2003 and expand Amtrak service in twenty-one states." In 2004, the inaccuracy of Amtrak's projections is plain enough: The added trains never generated even minimal consumer demand. Moreover, the trains contributed to higher operating losses.[55] These trains have been so substandard one could reasonably say they violate Amtrak's charter, which mandates that it provide *modern* rail passenger service.[56]

What is "modern?" It certainly does not mean initiating trains that are slower than their predecessors were many decades ago. As part of the Network Growth Strategy, Amtrak launched the Kentucky Cardinal on the Chicago–Jeffersonville, Indiana (which is near Louisville) route to carry passengers and United Parcel Service shipments.[57] The train took twelve hours, forty-five minutes to cover the 307 miles.[58] In 1925, the Pennsylvania Railroad train ran that same route in eight hours, forty min-utes[59]—four hours and five minutes faster than Amtrak's train. Our great-grandparents seventy-six years ago could ride a "milk run," pulled by a steam locomotive and stopping at sixteen towns along the way, and arrive faster than Amtrak, which served only five intermediate stops. Amtrak knew about the seriously deficient track conditions that existed, and the resulting slow speeds, on the line owned by the Louisville & Indiana Railroad Company—but started the new service anyway. Why? Anthony Haswell believes the entire MBNA process "was a deliberate effort to deceive the Congress" and that Amtrak's institutional survival depended upon no train discontinuances but indeed additions to its network.[60]

Of course, in Amtrak's defense, it hasn't seen fit to charge modern fares for tickets on this sadly inadequate train. To encourage traffic, Amtrak cut fares in October 2001 to $3.40 for a one-way Chicago–Indianapolis special fare—about half of the $6.23 train fare in effect in April 1953, which would be $23.95 in today's dollars. In a further effort to boost ridership, the train was extended into Louisville on December 4, 2001. But it did poorly during that busy holiday travel month, carrying an average of twelve passengers each trip.[61] The train, one of the slowest in the world—dubbed by wags a "Conestoga wagon with lights"—was discontinued on July 7, 2003.

The Kentucky Cardinal wasn't the only slow train Amtrak launched as part of its Network Growth Strategy. With Wisconsin Governor Tommy Thompson sitting as chairman of Amtrak's board of directors, Amtrak's "hard numbers" analysis suddenly discovered that a new train to Wisconsin was a certain money maker. The Lake Country Limited was launched in April 2000, with Governor Thompson suggesting the new trains would pay for themselves: "We are not willy-nilly putting new lines in place, because we have to make a profit by 2003."[62] It took two hours and thirty minutes to traverse the 98 miles between Chicago and Janesville, Wisconsin.[63] The 1952 Chicago and North Western train made that run in one hour, fifty-two minutes—thirty-eight minutes faster.[64] Not surprisingly, in its first three months of operation, an average of only ten passengers per day bought round trip tickets for that trip. Amtrak wasn't concerned. "It takes a while to ramp things up," said Amtrak's spokesman, who felt that traffic was "going in the right direction."[65] That ramp-up was not apparent when an *NBC News* "Fleecing of America" segment, aired a little more than a year after the train started, showed only one passenger aboard the entire train.[66] On some days the train ran empty. Knowing of the upcoming NBC report, Amtrak finally bowed to mounting criticism and discontinued the service.[67]

Amtrak's growth strategy also called for new service between Milwaukee and Fond du Lac, Wisconsin, and between Chicago and Des Moines, Iowa. In September 2001, Amtrak dropped plans for the Fond du Lac train because "the mail and express business isn't there to support it."[68] Amtrak also canceled plans for the Des Moines train, as "customers never developed for the mail and express service that would have formed the line's financial foundation."[69] Other eccentric proposals for adding long-distance trains, such as Meridian, Mississippi–Dallas and New York–Chicago via the Canadian province of Ontario, never made it off Amtrak's drawing boards. In 2002, Amtrak's president, David Gunn, finally agreed to forgo any further route expansion as a condition for the emergency $100 million loan he needed to prevent a shutdown of the system.

What "market-based analysis" could have justified adding trains that were slower than those that ran a half-century ago? What "research" predicted that express customers would be found on routes where customers proved nonexistent? It is this behavior that inspired one journalist to observe that Amtrak "is about as reliable in its revenue predictions as Bolshevik five-year planners."[70]

5

Fallacies about the Cost of Amtrak

Amtrak advocates—its management and employees, some state transportation officials, and railroad buffs—share another theme: They have routinely overestimated the revenues that Amtrak would earn, underestimated capital and operating costs, and tortured logic to claim that Amtrak somehow contributes to economic growth. Moreover, they have excused Amtrak's financial failures with an inexhaustible supply of rationalizations. History proves that these groups have no upper limit to spending. When the government granted half a billion dollars to Amtrak annually, advocates demanded higher subsidies. When the billion-dollar mark was reached, advocates wanted still more. Now, Amtrak is asking for nearly $2 billion in direct federal subsidies while ignoring meaningful action to mitigate future subsidy escalation. It is time to scrutinize the fallacies used to justify Amtrak subsidies.

Fallacy No. 1: Amtrak's Revenues
Will Increase Substantially—Someday

Many Amtrak trains lose substantial sums of money. The Amtrak Reform Council examined revenue and costs (excluding depreciation) for fiscal year 2001 and found that fifteen routes lost more than $110 per passenger, and six lost more than $210 per passenger. The largest operating loss was on the Sunset Limited, traveling between Los Angeles and Orlando, Florida, at $347 per passenger. (See table 5-1.) A year after the council's report was issued, the DOT inspector general reported that "the fully allocated losses on some trains (including depreciation and interest) can exceed $500 per passenger."[1]

TABLE 5-1

OPERATING PROFIT-LOSS BY ROUTE, 2001

	Ridership (thousands)	Revenue Excluding State Payments ($ millions)	State Payments ($ millions)	Total Revenue ($ millions)	Total Costs Excluding Depreciation ($ millions)	Profit/Loss on Full Costs ($ millions)	Loss per Rider (full costs)	Operating Ratio[a]
Corridor Trains								
Keystone & Clocker Service	3,021	42.4	2.8	45.2	65.6	(20.4)	$ (6.75)	1.45
Metroliner/Acela Express	2,652	271.2	0.0	271.2	220.0	51.3	$ 19.33	0.81
Ethan Allen Express	42	2.0	0.2	2.2	4.5	(2.2)	$ (52.91)	1.99
Vermonter	69	4.3	1.5	5.8	6.4	(0.6)	$ (9.09)	1.11
NE Direct/Acela Regional	6,262	328.6	0.0	328.6	400.1	(71.5)	$ (11.42)	1.22
NY–Buffalo Empire Service	1,304	52.5	0.0	52.5	89.0	(36.5)	$ (27.97)	1.69
Chicago–St. Louis	254	7.8	3.8	11.5	27.7	(16.1)	$ (63.63)	2.40
Chicago–Milwaukee Hiawathas	424	7.6	5.1	12.6	26.0	(13.3)	$ (31.47)	2.06
Chicago–Detroit– Pontiac Wolverine	295	9.7	0.0	9.7	30.9	(21.2)	$ (71.95)	3.20
Chicago–Champaign Illini	105	3.5	2.4	6.0	9.1	(3.1)	$ (29.75)	1.52
Chicago–Quincy Illinois Zephyr	100	2.7	2.8	5.5	8.2	(2.7)	$ (27.09)	1.49
Okla City–Ft. Worth Heartland Flyer	58	1.2	4.6	5.8	5.2	0.6	$ 9.93	0.90
Pacific Surfliner	1,716	31.0	21.5	52.5	78.6	(26.1)	$ (15.21)	1.50
Cascades	565	15.5	16.3	31.8	38.1	(6.3)	$ (11.21)	1.20
Capitols	1,073	11.7	18.4	30.2	34.6	(4.4)	$ (4.11)	1.15
San Joaquins	712	19.8	23.2	43.0	52.0	(9.0)	$ (12.62)	1.21
Adirondack	100	4.4	2.7	7.1	7.8	(0.7)	$ (7.29)	1.10
International	105	3.4	3.7	7.1	10.0	(2.9)	$ (27.47)	1.41
Kansas City–St. Louis	177	4.5	6.1	10.5	12.6	(2.1)	$ (11.75)	1.20
Pere Marquette	59	1.9	2.2	4.1	6.6	(2.5)	$ (42.61)	1.61
Piedmont	51	0.7	3.2	4.0	5.0	(1.0)	$ (20.35)	1.26
Totals, Corridor Trains	**19,146**	**826.4**	**120.4**	**946.9**	**1,137.9**	**(191.1)**	**$ (9.98)**	**1.20**

continued on next page

TABLE 5-1 (continued)

OPERATING PROFIT-LOSS BY ROUTE, 2001

	Ridership (thousands)	Revenue Excluding State Payments ($ millions)	State Payments ($ millions)	Total Revenue ($ millions)	Total Costs Excluding Depreciation ($ millions)	Profit/Loss on Full Costs ($ millions)	Loss per Rider (full costs)	Operating Ratio[a]
Long-Distance Trains								
Silver Star	266	30.7	0.0	30.7	60.8	(30.0)	$ (112.86)	1.98
Three Rivers	134	26.5	0.0	26.5	59.3	(32.8)	$ (244.69)	2.24
Cardinal	68	4.4	0.0	4.4	17.1	(12.6)	$ (186.91)	3.85
Silver Meteor	252	28.5	0.0	28.5	49.8	(21.2)	$ (84.12)	1.74
Empire Builder	398	53.3	0.0	53.3	98.7	(45.4)	$ (114.14)	1.85
Capitol Limited	154	21.4	0.0	21.4	45.6	(24.2)	$ (157.33)	2.13
California Zephyr	361	51.7	0.0	51.7	103.7	(52.0)	$ (143.93)	2.01
Southwest Chief	265	65.9	0.0	65.9	128.7	(62.8)	$ (236.76)	1.95
City of New Orleans	187	15.3	0.0	15.3	39.1	(23.7)	$ (126.81)	2.55
Texas Eagle	149	22.4	0.0	22.4	60.7	(38.4)	$ (258.25)	2.72
Sunset Limited	110	17.7	0.0	17.7	56.1	(38.3)	$ (347.45)	3.16
Coast Starlight	494	41.2	0.0	41.2	87.1	(45.9)	$ (92.98)	2.11
Lake Shore Limited	293	30.6	0.0	30.6	72.4	(41.9)	$ (142.65)	2.37
Silver Palm	219	28.3	0.0	28.3	57.0	(28.7)	$ (131.31)	2.01
Crescent	265	30.8	0.0	30.8	65.8	(35.0)	$ (132.37)	2.14
Kentucky Cardinal[b]	29	1.4	0.0	1.4	7.6	(6.2)	$ (211.65)	5.39
Pennsylvanian	90	9.2	0.0	9.2	35.4	(26.3)	$ (292.34)	3.87
Auto Train	214	54.6	0.0	54.6	66.4	(11.8)	$ (54.96)	1.22
Carolinian	242	13.5	2.7	16.2	20.2	(4.0)	$ (16.37)	1.24
Totals, Long-Distance Trains	4,190	547.5	2.7	550.2	1,131.4	(581.2)	$ (138.71)	2.06
Grand Total, All Trains	23,335.7	1,374.0	123.1	1,407.1	2,269.3	772.2	$ (33.09)	1.52

SOURCE: Amtrak Reform Council, *An Action Plan for the Restructuring and Rationalization of the National Intercity Rail Passenger System: Report to Congress* (Washington, D.C.: U.S. Government Printing Office, February 7, 2002), 96.

NOTE: Excludes special trains and $4.3 million in unallocated labor expense. Parentheses indicate financial losses.

a Operating ratio is defined as expenses divided by revenues (revenues include subsidies from states).

b Kentucky Cardinal classified as a long-distance train because it was an overnight train with sleeping accommodations; train has been discontinued.

Every few years or so Amtrak launches another revenue-enhancement or cost-control initiative, but to no avail: the deficits continue to increase. Improvements to the financial performance of long-distance trains require employing the same formula as would be used with any other product or service: Revenues must increase faster than costs. The prognosis for reducing the operating losses of Amtrak long-distance trains is very poor.

Amtrak has had both successes and failures in its efforts to enhance its revenue. Amtrak promised that revenues would improve as marketing became more sophisticated and improvements were made to the system. Indeed, revenue has increased because of progress made in several critical areas, such as advertising, reservations and passenger information systems, stations and parking, the establishment of convenient connections with other trains, and the installation of new equipment. For instance:

Advertising. After a history of fits and starts and bad advertising, Amtrak's television, radio, and newspaper messages have become fairly compelling. Amtrak has learned how to design Acela Express advertising to appeal to passengers wanting speedy trips, and long-distance advertising to target leisure travelers who respond to emotional messages. Amtrak has also moved into pay-per-click Internet advertising.

Reservations and Passenger Information Systems. Compared with Amtrak's early years when prospective passengers were frustrated by busy signals when calling for reservations, Amtrak today has a high call-response rate. Its telephone speech-recognition system provides train status, schedule, and reservation information with such accuracy that it has won an award from the Travel Industry Association of America.[2]

Stations and Parking. The dreariest stations, such as the ones in Boston and Worcester, Massachusetts, Rochester, New York, and Pittsburgh, Pennsylvania, have been replaced with more attractive facilities. The grandeur of Washington Union Station has been restored, and terminals have been cleaned and upgraded in Baltimore, Philadelphia, Chicago, Los Angeles, and many small towns. Convenient parking at train stations—

once a near-impossibility in some cities—is available, often thanks to municipalities that finance new parking structures.

More Convenient Connections. Those who admire European-style interconnectivity between trains have argued that Amtrak will benefit from having more links to commuter trains and rail transit systems. Since Amtrak began operating, new lines have been created that feed into its stations at twenty-one locations. Some are as large as New York's Penn Station (with new commuter train routes from New Jersey) and as small as Richmond, California (connecting with the Bay Area Rapid Transit system's trains). The market impact of the new connections is difficult to evaluate, but tens of millions of transit-oriented travelers have easier access to Amtrak today than when the railroad was formed.[3]

New Equipment. Amtrak needed to replace the malfunction-prone trains it inherited when it began operations. Since then, billions of dollars have been spent in several equipment-purchasing cycles for new locomotives, Amfleet coaches, Viewliner cars, double-decker Superliner passenger cars, and Acela Express trains.

On the negative side, Amtrak has had disappointing experiences with three initiatives designed to boost revenues, namely in improving service to create more satisfied customers, improving on-time performance, and launching a program to carry freight.

Service Guarantees. Amtrak launched a "wide-ranging customer service initiative" in 1999, when it began offering a guarantee of "world-class" service. When passengers expressed disappointment with some aspect of their experience with Amtrak, service vouchers of varying values were issued. Simultaneously, Amtrak launched a "competency-based" hiring program designed to select people with the proper experience and also the right traits for customer-service positions. Every month, if the number of customers requesting travel vouchers were below a set threshold, all employees would receive a bonus.[4] The program was similar to one at Continental Airlines, which sent such checks to employees many times as service improved; Amtrak's program lasted several years, and not once did complaints fall below the threshold, nor did Amtrak employees ever receive payments for good service. The program was discontinued, with Amtrak having failed to improve customer service aboard trains.

To this day, on-board service is noteworthy for the complaints it generates. Stories abound about passengers receiving poor treatment, particularly in dining cars on long-distance trains, where Amtrak crews are often inattentive or rude. A stark contrast exists between a disappointing Amtrak dining experience and the cheerful treatment given on dining cars operated by private companies such as the Rocky Mountaineer in Canada or the American Orient Express in the United States.[5] "If you look at customer care or customer quality, we're not any further along in 2004 than we were when Amtrak started in 1971," said Ken Bird, a former long-time Amtrak supporter. He now favors an Amtrak breakup and franchising of train services to private companies.[6]

Improving On-Time Performance. Amtrak acknowledges that late trains represent the single largest area of passenger complaint, and improving on-time performance is a priority. Poor performance is endemic to Amtrak's long-distance trains. From 1998 through 2001, Amtrak issued a series of statements citing improved on-time performance.[7] Unfortunately, Amtrak's method of calculation, both then and now, fails to reflect actual performance because Amtrak injects extra time into its schedules before checkpoints where timeliness is calculated. The April 2004 schedule for the Sunset Limited illustrates the point. The eastbound train leaves Los Angeles and arrives in Pomona, thirty-two miles away, in forty-one minutes. No on-time calculation is made at Pomona. Returning from Pomona to Los Angeles, where performance is calculated, the timetable allows one hour and thirty-seven minutes. The time allowed for the "checkpoint" train is more than twice as long as for the "noncheckpoint" train. Hence, in one community after another along the Sunset Limited's 2,764-mile route from Orlando, Florida, passengers are inconvenienced waiting for late trains that may be officially recorded as "on time."

This is the case for every long-distance train—people in Iowa may wait for a late San Francisco Zephyr; travelers in North Dakota may be angry over a tardy Empire Builder; others in Texas will swear "Never again!" while waiting for the Texas Eagle to show up—yet Amtrak's procedure permits it to avoid officially registering many of the trains as "late" in reports to Congress and the Department of Transportation.[8]

In marked contrast to Amtrak's dismal record, the average delay in 2004 on the 160,000 bullet trains run that the Central Japan Railway operates fell to just 12 seconds—an improvement over the average delays of 18–24 seconds in 1997 through 2001.[9]

Carrying Freight and High-Value Express. In a "commercialization" effort in 1997, Amtrak began to carry freight and express in boxcars or highway trailers attached to passenger trains. Program advocates said it would help Amtrak become "profitable," "reach its financial goals," and "improve the financial performance of passenger trains and help preserve and expand our network."[10] Amtrak strained credulity by claiming the program would not take business from private railroads, as it intended to move "specialty commodities—computer chips, for example."[11] When the media revealed that the railroad was carrying boxcar loads of beer, cranberry juice, soups, steel, and other commodities, Amtrak countered that such moves were "occasional and experimental."[12] Eventually, Amtrak conceded it was moving full freight shipments.

Amtrak also asserted that carrying freight would not interfere with passenger convenience. Yet, a comparison of schedules showed Amtrak adding time to schedules to accommodate freight. In Chicago, St. Louis, Kansas City, Dallas, and Fort Worth, riders sat aboard motionless trains in rail yards while locomotives shunted boxcars on and off the trains.[13] By making passenger train schedules slower, the program violated Amtrak's legal mandate to provide "modern" rail passenger service.

Any optimism there might have been regarding the potential financial benefits of carrying freight and express on Amtrak trains was unwarranted. A year after the program started, traffic was below projections, and about half of the freight-express fleet was sitting idle.[14] Amtrak said it would not discuss profitability until that year's scorecard was in.[15] It is worth noting how Amtrak portrayed as a success the debacle that was eventually revealed:

> Amtrak's mail and express business is a thriving $122 million business, having just enjoyed a 25 percent growth in revenue

over the prior fiscal year. In recognition of the fact that it is no longer a start-up operation, a new strategic business unit has been created that will focus on mail and express operations. Led by an experienced freight executive, the new business unit will develop the strategies necessary to grow the operations to a $400 million business over the next few years.[16]

Belying this rosy picture were program revenues that were significantly below projections, as pointed out by independent government agencies.[17] Amtrak's management made aggressive moves in response, buying or leasing 1,141 freight cars and RoadRailer trailer vans, a number that exceeded Amtrak's entire 743-car fleet of "leisure" passenger cars, baggage cars, and auto carriers used for long-distance trains.[18]

In September 2002, Amtrak acknowledged the program's red ink and announced it would discontinue the freight-express program, although it would continue to carry mail.[19] Amtrak has yet to provide a credible figure as to the program's losses, so the cost to the taxpayers is unknown. Moreover, the induced financial austerity created opportunity costs throughout the system. It is fair to ask: What passenger facilities were not upgraded? What safety improvements were not made? What tracks were not improved? What work with high rates of return was not done to finance a money-losing initiative? Amtrak entered the venture promising it would be profitable and reduce the need for subsidies. The reverse occurred.

Even anticipated financial gains from carrying mail were illusory. Amtrak announced its intention to stop carrying mail by October 2004 because of a "small profit margin."[20] The move was historic, considering that railroads have carried mail on passenger trains since the 1830s. Amtrak's exit from its $60 million contract with the U.S. Postal Service symbolizes an inability to earn a profit from a traditional product line.

Fallacy No. 2: Amtrak Will Control Its Costs—Someday

Getting Amtrak into the black will require progress on two fronts: raising revenues and reducing costs. As we've seen, the prospects for raising revenues are not entirely encouraging. Amtrak has also launched a number of cost-control initiatives over the years, with similarly mixed results. On the positive side, Amtrak has invested in capital improvements that have reduced operating costs and station costs.

For instance, starting in the 1970s, new passenger cars were heated with electricity instead of using a costly, antiquated steam-heating system that was a throwback to the days of steam locomotives. In the 1990s Amtrak made another good decision by establishing a run-through program, whereby trains entering Chicago from one route continued onto another instead of sitting idle in rail yards. The improved equipment utilization produced more seats to sell without Amtrak having to purchase still more new equipment.

Station costs have been reduced in many places when local communities assumed refurbishment costs, maintenance costs, or construction costs for new stations. (See chapter 3, "Hidden Amtrak Subsidies.") At one time, Amtrak utilized high-cost stations in Minneapolis, Minnesota, and Jacksonville, Florida, which have since been replaced with smaller, more efficient facilities.

These steps have helped to control costs at Amtrak—but they have clearly been insufficient. Far more notable have been the failed efforts to control costs. Obstacles the railroad has been unable to overcome include high labor costs; competition from airlines, which have done a far better job of controlling their own labor costs; and an inability to raise fares sufficiently to recoup costs while remaining competitive with airlines.

By far the greatest portion of Amtrak's operating cost is labor. A study completed in 2001 found that labor costs, which include salaries, wages, overtime and benefits, accounted for 50 percent of Amtrak's total operating costs.[21] Recently, Amtrak has lowered its labor costs somewhat by extending operating-crew districts. For example, where at one time a locomotive engineer earned eight hours' pay for operating a train through a 150-mile district (which could take only a few hours), Amtrak over the years has reached agreements with labor organizations to lengthen the districts. New rules like this helped for a time in restraining the growth in labor costs.

Unfortunately, such agreements, which target only a portion of the workforce, have been inadequate in controlling expenses effectively. In

2000, Amtrak completed negotiations with fifteen unions that resulted in wage increases of 2.4 percent per year over five years. However, that figure is misleading because employees also received signing bonuses and retroactive wage payments totaling about $144 million. Amtrak has a long way to go to improve productivity and its competitive position. Transportation Department and Amtrak data show that Amtrak's cost per passenger-mile is four times that of intercity buses and three and a half times that of airlines.[22]

Contributing to the difficulty in controlling costs is that Amtrak does not have standard measures of labor productivity in place, as other railroads do.[23] The GAO reported:

> Many officials of the commuter and freight railroads we spoke with stated that, in general, they track labor productivity with a variety of measures including employees per passenger mile and gross ton-miles per employee. It is especially critical that Amtrak determine the efficiency of its labor force. Amtrak has had difficulty controlling the growth of its labor costs, and labor costs are Amtrak's largest operating cost. Finally, Amtrak incurs a fairly high amount of overtime to provide its services, which may suggest some level of inefficiency in its utilization of its labor force.[24]

Amtrak claimed to have negotiated productivity improvements in its agreements in 2000 to offset about 20 percent of the $260 million in negotiated wage increases[25]—but could not provide documentation for that claim to the Amtrak Reform Council. Even if Amtrak's claims were true, offsetting only 20 percent of labor cost increases is clearly inadequate by normal standards. No company can afford to recover only 20 percent of labor cost increases through productivity gains, particularly one losing millions of dollars in operations. When the Amtrak Reform Council challenged Amtrak over its modest goals for productivity improvements, rail labor organizations lobbied Congress to abolish the council (which failed) or slash its funding (which succeeded).[26]

Hampering improvements is the absence from Amtrak's relationship with labor organizations of the give-and-take that occurs in the private sector, particularly when a company is in trouble. In fact, most U.S. corporations seek to offset 100 percent of wage and benefit increases through productivity improvements. In Greyhound's 2004 contract ratification with the Amalgamated Transit Union, workers agreed to a 2 percent wage increase in 2006 and an increase in the company's contribution to the health plan. Greyhound reported, "These increases are almost completely offset by other contract modifications."[27] And in contrast with Amtrak, America's freight railroads made major strides in improving productivity between 1990 and 2002 by doubling from 4.8 million to 9.6 million the ton-miles (one ton moved one mile) moved annually per employee.[28]

Labor Costs for Amtrak and Airlines: A Stark Contrast. Advocates of long-distance trains refuse to recognize that the introduction of jetliner service nearly fifty years ago changed the economics of long-distance travel forever. As far back as 1958, an Interstate Commerce Commission examination of the San Francisco–Los Angeles rail line noted the sharp contrasts between the economics of planes and trains.[29] George Hilton has summarized the report's economic findings:

> The cost disadvantage was not only in the labor-intensiveness of the trains, which required approximately sixteen employees for a one-way trip, but also in the low utilization rate of equipment. The train and a Boeing 727, as of about 1965, each represented an investment of about $3.6 million. The train could produce one one-way trip per day; the plane with a single crew of seven, could produce two round-trips per day. With a second crew, it could double that output. With the introduction of larger aircraft in the late 1960s, the productivity of aircraft increased. A single stretched DC-8 of 250-passenger capacity assigned to a long-distance route, such as Atlanta–Los Angeles, could turn in more passenger-miles per year than the entire Atlantic Coast Line Railroad, the dominant railroad in East Coast–Florida passenger operations.[30]

The cost disadvantage of trains as compared to planes continues to the present. While today's double-decker Superliner trains, with their expanded passenger capacity and somewhat reduced crew size, are somewhat more efficient than older trains, the train still can make only a single one-way trip each day. Airlines, in contrast, have made tremendous improvements in efficiency since the first jetliners went into operation. An airplane like the Boeing 767 can be twenty times more efficient in use of labor than a long-distance train.[31] While the economics of Amtrak's long-distance passenger trains are generally getting worse, airplane travel continues to become more affordable.

The airline industry is engaged in a fierce cost-control campaign, and new labor agreements have lowered ticket prices. Amtrak and its unions can ignore market forces because Congress has continued to fund Amtrak's escalating deficits. The endless federal checkbook means there is little pressure to negotiate efficient labor contracts. Many airlines have been able to reduce labor costs in part because of their exposure to bankruptcies, competition in the industry, and the risks faced by employees that they could permanently lose their jobs if they do not negotiate competitive contracts.

Airlines have faced an unprecedented set of challenges in recent years. A decline in business travel and the September 11 attacks caused a significant loss of operating revenue in the industry. But the airlines are taking action. The GAO found,

> In response to these new challenges, the legacy airlines reported a goal of $19.5 billion in cost-cutting measures to restore their profitability through 2003. As a group, legacy airlines actually reduced their operating costs by $12.7 billion over the last 2 years. For legacy airlines, cost cutting was greatest in labor and commission costs.[32]

Attempts to reduce airline costs are impressive. Meanwhile, Amtrak's business plan, as usual, is to rely on ever-increasing federal subsidies.

Amtrak Has Difficulty Raising Fares to Raise Revenue. Low-cost airlines have been adding to the competitive pressures in the transportation industry. The GAO determined that low fares are widely available. Between 1998 and 2003, low-cost airlines expanded their presence from 1,594 to 2,304 of the top 5,000 domestic markets and now have a presence in markets that serve about 85 percent of passengers.[33]

The *Wall Street Journal* reports that discount airlines together now control fully a quarter of domestic air capacity and plan to continue growing: "J. P. Morgan, in a survey of new jet orders, estimates the discount group will boost its collective domestic fleet by 250 planes to more than 1,000 by 2006."[34]

Competition with other airlines from discount carriers has caused the average one-way domestic airfare of $311 in 2000 to drop to $276 in 2003; adjusting for inflation, this is a real reduction of more than 17 percent.[35]

The public is responding to these lower airfares. Transportation Secretary Norman Mineta, in observing that the number of people flying in the United States could reach pre–September 11, 2001, levels by 2005, said that the new passengers are not the business travelers upon whom many airlines have depended for revenue, but rather more cost-conscious passengers, who shop for fares on the Internet and fuel the expansion of low-fare carriers.[36] These bargain-hunters also represent the market for intercity buses and long-distance trains.

As competition intensifies and airfares continue to drop, Amtrak will find it difficult to raise prices on long-distance trains to recoup growing costs. With some long-distance trains taking three days to complete their runs, and with Amtrak coach passengers paying fares comparable to discount airline fares, it is impossible for the trains to cover their labor costs, to say nothing of fuel costs, trackage fees, maintenance expenses, and equipment replacement costs, and to contribute to overhead expenses such as the reservations system and headquarters payroll.

A word is also required about sleeping cars used on overnight, long-distance trains.[37] An Amtrak Reform Council analysis showed that approximately 85 percent of passengers on Amtrak overnight trains ride in coach. Expensive capital expenditures and maintenance costs are directed to sleeping cars, which serve the smallest minority of train passengers that can be found anywhere in the Western Hemisphere. Such costs are not recovered through Amtrak's sleeping car fares. Taxpayers should not have to subsidize passengers who use a premium service but do not pay to cover its costs. Train operating losses and capital requirements could be lowered on overnight trains if all sleeping accommodations were eliminated. Reconfigured services could have lower operating losses by running on only the busiest portions of long-distance routes without expensive sleeping-car accommodations.

Amtrak's financial prospects are fundamentally constrained because it cannot control costs or tap into a sizable portion of America's travel market-place. It has no niche. It never had a niche. As far back as 1961—ten years before Amtrak's creation—a commission established to study national transportation policy concluded,

> Railroad intercity passenger service meets no important needs that cannot be provided for by other carriers and possesses no uniquely necessary service advantages. It serves no locations which cannot be adequately served by air and highway.[38]

By Amtrak's sixth year of operation, the GAO warned, "We do not believe Amtrak can operate its present route system at a substantially lower cost."[39] In fiscal year 1977, a review of eleven routes showed that operating losses were high despite route improvements, such as adding new equipment and changing schedules to improve on-time perform-ance. The GAO concluded that increased ridership alone would not elim-inate these losses.[40] What has been true decade after decade remains equally true today.[41]

Amtrak has consistently been unable to reduce the operating losses of long-distance trains. To think it will do so in the future is fanciful. If the railroad cannot raise revenues faster than cost increases, and with subsi-dies surpassing record levels for trains that play a minuscule role in our transport system, the inescapable conclusion is that many trains should be discontinued or restructured.

Fallacy No. 3: Cutting Amtrak Fares
Will Increase Ridership

Despite a critical need for higher fares to recover costs, almost every Amtrak train is offering "sale" prices, almost all the time. Amtrak is deter-mined to build ridership at all costs and bolster arguments for increased public subsidies. Some of the discount fares it offers are lower than what the private railroads charged in the 1950s, and are virtually without precedent on American railroads. In addition to the lower fares Amtrak put into place after the September 11 terrorist attacks (discussed earlier), in 2003 Amtrak discounted even more aggressively:

- A new discount program called "Rail 2 Rail" permitted Los Angeles commuters using Metrolink monthly passes to ride any Amtrak Pacific Surfliner train within their zones without charging the traditional fare differential.[42] Such "giving away" of the greater comfort and faster schedules available on intercity trains to low-fare commuters is a costly practice that private U.S. railroads avoided for more than a century.

- Similarly, Amtrak began permitting Connecticut commuters on cheap monthly passes to ride the Acela Express at no extra charge.[43] This peculiar practice meant Amtrak was boosting traffic on its most expensive trains at unrestricted fire-sale prices.

- Amtrak cut ticket prices on its New Haven–Springfield line, sometimes by more than 50 percent, meaning off-peak, one-way fares between Springfield and Hartford, Connecticut, were reduced from $21 to $10 ($11 for peak trains), and monthly pass fares were sharply reduced.[44]

- Amtrak's premier high-speed service needed a traffic boost, so Amtrak cut Boston–New York Acela Express fares from $127 to $99 without requiring an advance purchase.[45]

The result of all this was that Amtrak succeeded in building ridership in fiscal year 2003 to its highest level ever—24 million passengers—but paid a price as passenger revenue declined by $68 million from the previous year and its yield per passenger fell.

As fiscal year 2004 began, Amtrak asserted that it was toning down its seasonal fare promotions and reviewing its web-based discounts "for possible de-emphasis" because of increased demand.[46] Despite its public pronouncement, Amtrak did no such thing:

- In the first month of the new fiscal year Amtrak lowered fares on the Philadelphia–Harrisburg line by more than 50 percent.[47]

- Amtrak offered "Rail Sale" tickets between Miami and Tampa for $7.[48] (Greyhound's fare was $37.)

- In another effort to help the high-speed Acela Express, as well as Metroliners, Amtrak launched a generous buy-two-get-one-free offer on the Boston–Washington line.[49]

- Amtrak permitted commuters in still another city to ride without paying fare differentials by replicating the Los Angeles Rail 2 Rail program in San Diego.[50]

- The Internet "Rail Sale" offerings continued to be deeply discounted, with New York–Chicago and Washington, D.C.–Chicago tickets available for just $39.90, Chicago–Kansas City for $20, and Chicago–St. Louis for $11.80. In each case Amtrak's fare was generally half the lowest bus fare.[51]

- Amtrak lowered fares by changing the definition of what constitutes a "peak-hour" fare, opening an additional four-hour time window for cheaper fares on Friday and Sunday evenings. Prices dropped for Boston–New York from $79 to $64; Washington–New York from $92 to $74; Albany–New York from $50 to $43; and Philadelphia–Harrisburg, Pennsylvania, from $24 to $19.[52]

- In what could be called the most ridiculous fare of the century, Amtrak began selling tickets between Washington, D.C., and Orlando for $17.10.[53]

As Amtrak lowered fares virtually everywhere, ticket prices increased on other U.S. railroad passenger systems to cover growing costs. Consider this activity in 2004 on six commuter railroads:

- *Boston:* The Massachusetts Bay Transportation Authority increased commuter train fares by varying amounts to help cope with a budget crisis.[54]

- *New York–Connecticut:* The Metropolitan Transportation Authority proposed a 5 percent fare increase on the Metro-North Railroad and Long Island Rail Road lines.[55]

- *Philadelphia:* The Southeastern Pennsylvania Transportation Authority contemplated increasing its commuter fares after agreeing to a new labor accord.[56]

- *Virginia:* The Virginia Railway Express, which runs commuter trains into Washington, D.C., from the state's northern suburbs, put into place in April 2004 a fare increase that averaged 6 percent, but for some passengers reached 18 percent; this was the second year in a row for a fare hike.[57]

- *Los Angeles:* The Metrolink commuter rail system implemented a 4 percent increase effective July 1, 2004.[58]

- *San Diego:* The North County Transit District was considering a fare increase because the agency had begun to spend from reserve funds to meet expenses.[59]

Deep discounting will not stabilize Amtrak, because the railroad is the highest-cost passenger transportation provider in the United States. Amtrak's problems stem from excessive costs, not inadequate revenues. If a high-end company like Neiman Marcus were to slash prices to Wal-Mart levels without adjusting its product line or costs, red ink would flow, despite more traffic coming in the doors. The logic applies equally to Amtrak.

Amtrak's deep-discounting strategy undermines the railroad's arguments for continued subsidies. Now more than ever it is easier to ask: If Amtrak is so vital, why must it practically give away seats to lure more riders? Amtrak's super-low fares have destabilized the railroad and will continue to do so in future years. Furthermore, as a matter of public policy, why should taxpayers subsidize Amtrak's predatory pricing actions, particularly when such actions weaken private-sector companies such as intercity bus companies? These entities have the right cost structure and vehicle size to provide economical transportation service on a more frequent basis if market demand exists.

Fallacy No. 4: Amtrak Contributes to Economic Growth

There can be some relationship between the transportation available in a community and that community's prospects for growth. For instance, for many years corporations looking to relocate considered how convenient a city's air service was and often elected to be near a hub airport. While that is still the case to some extent, hubs are no longer preferred over airports with lower fares and less congestion. Nashville, Tennessee, for instance, which is no longer an American Airlines hub, is served by seven major carriers offering greatly discounted fares; companies moving to the area have cited that as a factor in their decisions.[60] In the 1990s the population of the Nashville-Davidson-Murfreesboro metropolitan area grew to 1.3 million, a 25 percent increase; the area has not had Amtrak service since the late 1970s.

Amtrak's short-distance trains are certainly important to the nation's biggest, most train-dependent cities—primarily those located on the Boston–New York–Washington line—and there's little doubt that the trains contribute to the economic health of those cities. The economic value of having Amtrak service on long-distance routes is far less clear, however.

One study was conducted in Montana that suggested Amtrak's economic effect was positive, but the study was conducted to keep federal subsidies for the Empire Builder, so there is good reason to view its conclusions with suspicion. The study claimed that the train generates nearly $14 million in the state annually, and that its disappearance would be a devastating economic blow.[61] This stretches credulity, considering that the Empire Builder makes only eleven stops in small towns at the northern edge of a state that occupies 147,046 square miles. In 2002, only 368,000 people rode the train (1.6 percent of Amtrak's total traffic), and based on an analysis from the prior year, it is highly likely that one-third of those traveled on the Chicago–Milwaukee–Minneapolis segment. In effect, many passengers on the train get nowhere near Montana.[62]

It is sometimes suggested that Amtrak service is necessary to a community's future, as if people or corporations will move in depending upon whether a passenger train stops there. There is no evidence of this effect. Amtrak serves more than five hundred U.S. communities with trains, and a review of population changes in the last decade has shown no economic or population link. Of the twenty-five metropolitan areas with the fastest population growth, twenty-one had no Amtrak station. The communities that boomed without Amtrak included large areas like Las Vegas, Nevada (with population up by 85.5 percent) and the Phoenix-Mesa-Scottsdale, Arizona, complex (up 45.3 percent). They also included smaller communities like Jackson, Wyoming (up 66 percent); Bend, Oregon (up 53.9 percent); Boise-Nampa, Idaho (up 45.4 percent); and Laredo, Texas (up 44.9 percent).

Of the twenty-five metropolitan areas that suffered the most population losses, six had Amtrak service and nineteen did not. Three of the declining communities are served by Amtrak's Empire Builder: Williston (down 6.5 percent) and Grand Forks (down 5.5 percent), both in North Dakota, and Havre, Montana (down 5.6 percent).[63] No correlation developed to link train service with population changes; however, no evidence emerged, either, that having an Amtrak train stop would induce economic prosperity. Whether a community is served by an Amtrak long-distance train seems to be irrelevant to its economic future. It's worth noting that this is a stark contrast to the strong economic relationship that many communities have with their aviation services.

Fallacy No. 5: America Cannot "Throw Away" Amtrak

One roadblock to reform is reluctance to abandon years of public investment in Amtrak, possibly out of concern that doing so would confirm the waste of Amtrak spending. This is a fallacy for several reasons. First, "sunk costs" are generally defined as costs already incurred that cannot be recovered regardless of future events. When faced with endless losses, officials in responsibly run companies dispose of underperforming assets in the most remunerative way possible, identify the losses as sunk costs to shareholders, and move on.

Defining assets and prior operating losses as sunk costs is beneficial. It is the proper accounting vehicle and appropriate management decision to cut losses on losing propositions and free resources for more worthy ventures. This strategy is appropriate for many of Amtrak's assets. The taxpayers deserve to be free of the constant losses associated with Amtrak's bad investments—not penalized to keep assets in money-losing service forever.

In a reconfigured system, many of Amtrak's assets could be put to better use. Amtrak's primary lines would continue in operation, and its locomotives and passenger cars would be sold or leased to operators for use on existing routes or to launch more popular routes. Amtrak's busiest train stations would continue to serve passengers, both commuters and intercity travelers. After Eastern Air Lines went through bankruptcy and liquidation proceedings, the air shuttle gates at the Washington, New York, and Boston airports continued to handle passengers flying between the cities, albeit on different airlines. Most of Amtrak's assets serving high-density corridors in which they provide market-driven rail transportation services would remain in use by successor private-sector companies.

6

Defending against Terrorism:
Can Amtrak Do the Job?

There are a multitude of good reasons to privatize or devolve Amtrak's services to regional or state authorities that have nothing to do with terrorism. But following the September 11 attacks, and particularly the 2004 Madrid train bombings, this issue must be considered seriously as well. Without disparaging Amtrak security or the caliber of its policing efforts, it is worth evaluating what operational arrangement will be best suited to meeting the threat of terrorism.[1] The danger is very real. Two major concerns, in particular, must be considered:

- For nearly three decades Amtrak has failed to correct serious safety problems in its busiest tunnels—New York City's—which it shares with commuter rail authorities, the major users of the tunnels. Amtrak's long inaction on badly needed improvements could make it impossible to safely evacuate passengers in case of attack or accident. Responsibility for addressing this problem must be given to a state, local, or regional authority.

- Airport-style security at every Amtrak station or along all railroad lines is cost-prohibitive. And in implementing such strong security measures, the additional costs and delays would almost certainly cause slower and later trains, losses in ridership, and a worsened financial condition.

New York's Railroad Tunnels

Amtrak has seriously mismanaged critical fire and safety improvements in the tunnels that lead to Penn Station in New York. For years, Amtrak has failed to invest in the safety of these tunnels, the single most important railroad passenger asset in the United States. For New York travelers, if safety is a concern, they are better off flying.

A terrorist act aboard a train while it was inside one of these tunnels would be horrific. The two North River tunnels, which run beneath the Hudson River and connect New York City to New Jersey, and the four East River tunnels (completed in 1910) are indispensable commuter links. With more than 750 commuter and intercity trains carrying a half-million passengers passing through it each weekday, New York City's Penn Station is the busiest in the nation.

In 2002, the Department of Transportation's review of the New York City tunnels determined that a $900 million investment in firefighting equipment and evacuation facilities was needed to bring them up to modern safety standards.[2] DOT Inspector General Kenneth Mead has described in stark terms the kind of tragedy that has already occurred overseas and is at risk of happening here if this work is not done:

> On November 11, 2000 one of the worst Alpine disasters ever claimed the lives of more than 150 people as a funicular train in Kaprun, Austria caught fire less than one-half mile into a 2-mile long tunnel. Many of the victims died from smoke inhalation as they tried to escape the blazing train through billowing smoke being forced up the tunnel by a chimney-like wind effect.[3]

Recent experience in Maryland showed how a tunnel fire can have widespread consequences. In July 2001, a freight car derailed and caught fire in a tunnel owned by CSX Transportation, located under downtown Baltimore. The fire, which took five days to extinguish, involved chemicals, wood, and other train cargo. One street collapsed from a water-main break related to the fire, light rail trains were halted, parts of the city were shut down, and Baltimore Orioles games were postponed. Effects were felt even farther away as all CSX rail traffic in the Northeast was snarled and fiber optic communications and Internet traffic were disrupted.[4] The havoc may have been a harbinger of even worse things that could happen elsewhere; Jack Riley, director of public safety and justice at the RAND Corporation, has cautioned Congress, "Little is known about how long it might take to restart the passenger and freight rail systems in the aftermath of an attack similar to those of September 11."[5]

Fortunately, no passenger trains were involved in the Baltimore tunnel fire, but that surely would not always be the case in such a disaster. In New York's tunnels, inadequate ventilation and antiquated evacuation facilities would present serious obstacles to saving lives in case of a train fire. The ventilation fans in the East River tunnels cannot vent enough heat and smoke, and cannot reverse direction to bring fresh air to passengers and rescue workers. Again, DOT's inspector general has raised a series of concerns about the longstanding fire-safety needs:

> Narrow, winding spiral staircases and crumbling benchwalls [walkways] are inadequate to support the successful evacuation of what could potentially be thousands of passengers in the event of a serious tunnel fire. Ventilation systems that cannot remove sufficient amounts of smoke or heat could further jeopardize the success of such an operation. . . . The Pennsylvania Station fire and life-safety project began in 1976, and Amtrak, Long Island Rail Road and New Jersey Transit will have spent more than $161 million through 2001 on projects intended to improve the safety of operations in the tunnels. . . . Although this spending has resulted in significant improvements to existing structures, funding has not been secured for some of the more critical tunnel projects. . . . In the North River tunnels, there is no standpipe system at all. With limited options for bringing water to a tunnel fire, the temporary solution has been to install stationary dry chemical extinguishers with 50 feet of hose every 100 feet throughout the tunnels. These may be adequate for fighting a small fire, but they would do little to combat the heat and flames of a large fire. Fire Department officials claim that, "the absence of a standpipe system greatly reduces

the department's ability to attack a fire rapidly in its incipient stage. . . . Poorly designed exit stairways and limited connections between tubes hinder the rapid and safe removal of passengers in the event of a tunnel evacuation. . . . In the East River tunnels, the staircases are steep, single-width, spiral staircases that rise as high as 90 feet, or the equivalent of 10 flights of stairs.[6]

To make matters even worse, there are no landings for people climbing to rest while others pass them, and it would be impossible for passengers to exit the tunnels at the same time that firefighters and emergency workers were going toward the source of the disaster.

Amtrak's Skewed Priorities

A basic principle followed in well-managed companies is to invest capital in the most critical components of the business. Incredible as it may seem—and despite full knowledge of the consequences of explosions or fires in tunnels, and the dangerous precedent set by the recent terrorist bombings in Madrid—Amtrak continues to commit funds to projects of little importance on lightly used lines. For example, Amtrak is spending millions of dollars to repair train cars that are mismatched to today's travel market—sleeping cars and long-distance coaches that, when put into use, will serve few people and only add to Amtrak's financial deficit. Meanwhile, capital dollars are still needed for critical improvements to Amtrak's most important route, the Boston–Washington line.

Funding for tunnel work was boosted in the summer of 2002 with a $76.7 million grant to Amtrak to rehabilitate some structures, modernize ventilation and communication systems, and improve emergency access and egress.[7] To be fair, some work has begun including installation of new lighting and emergency phone systems, temporary repairs to crumbling walkways, and improvements to ventilation. Among incomplete projects is the standpipe system, which firefighters require to get water into the tunnels, new ventilation shafts, and new exit stairwells. The overall project will not be complete until 2009.[8]

Amtrak routinely claims impoverishment as a contributing factor in its being in the position of "playing catchup" on New York tunnel work.[9] Quite reasonably, DOT Inspector General Mead does not trust Amtrak officials to reorder their spending priorities and he has asked Congress to force Amtrak to spend appropriated funds on tunnel work; he said, "It is essential that funds be specifically earmarked for fire-safety needs in the [New York] tunnels. Earmarking the funds would ensure that they could not be diverted for any other purpose."[10]

Local Capital Subsidies and Ownership

The Metropolitan Transportation Authority, which is owned by New York State, has committed $125 million for tunnel safety work in its current five-year capital plan, an indication, officials say, of how serious it is about correcting the problems. The *New York Times* reported that the MTA believes it ought to own the two tunnels leading to Penn Station from Queens that are used exclusively by the Long Island Rail Road, but had been rebuffed by Amtrak in previous attempts to gain control of the tunnels. State officials said the urgency of the situation might persuade federal officials to back a state effort.[11]

The state of New York was in favor of such an effort. Its Senate Standing Committee on Transportation echoed Mead's call for earmarking in a report that decried Amtrak for neglecting the tunnels while pursuing projects like the Acela Express, even though it has known about the problem since it assumed ownership of the tunnels under the terms of the Railroad Revitalization and Regulatory Act of 1976. The committee proposed that the two East River tunnels used exclusively by the Long Island Rail Road be turned over to the state.[12]

The New York State report went easy on Amtrak, which failed to launch meaningful work for decades and was responsible for lengthy delays to projects financed by other agencies. For instance, in 1977 the Long Island Rail Road (LIRR) purchased standpipe equipment for installation in the East River tunnels. It was Amtrak's responsibility to install the equipment; but nothing happened for a year. As John J. Fogarty, the Manhattan Borough Commander of the Fire Department, said, "It seems to me ludicrous that we have 90 percent of the equipment rotting in a warehouse and each day we have the possibility of a tragedy that could be averted by just putting the stuff together."[13]

The failure of Amtrak board members and executives to correct known problems in the most critical piece of infrastructure it owns is one of immense proportions. To remedy it, Amtrak Reform Council member Wendell Cox favors the council's plan to separate the Boston–Washington infrastructure from the rest of Amtrak,

> so that the unique requirements of that important facility can be addressed outside the politics that have made it more important to operate trains through Havre, Montana, than to undertake critically needed safety improvements that put hundreds of thousands of daily commuters in peril in the New York area."[14]

Enacting such reforms would require real acts of vision, selflessness, and determination by Congress, the White House, and state and local authorities. It is a lot to hope for—but nothing less will do. To leave this responsibility in Amtrak's hands would be to continue to place our faith in a system that has disappointed in every possible respect for more than thirty years.

Protecting Trains, Stations, and Infrastructure

Every mode of transportation has unique features that make it inherently vulnerable to attack. Security has improved at airports—"closed and controlled locations with few entry points," as the GAO calls them.[15] Train stations, in contrast, rely on the unencumbered movement of people through many unguarded doorways and trains. Jack Riley has explained the concerns:

> Passenger rail facilities present potentially inviting targets for terrorists for a variety of reasons. They are easily penetrated and may have high concentrations of people. The logistics of a

passenger rail attack are comparatively simple. For example, given the typical passenger density in a passenger rail station, substantial casualties can be inflicted with a backpack-sized bomb. This is a substantially lower logistical burden than the one faced by the terrorists who committed the September 11 attacks. In addition, terrorists likely perceive psychological benefits to attacking passenger transportation networks. Rail transportation, like air travel, necessitates the passengers' willingness to put personal safety in the hands of others. An attack is likely to leave passengers reluctant, however temporarily, to travel on the passenger rail system.[16]

Airport-like security measures, particularly passenger screening, metal detectors, X-ray machines, and hand searches, are impractical for use with railroad passengers. Said David Briginshaw, editor of *International Railway Journal*,

> Rightly, calls from some people for airport-style security measures at stations have been rejected. This would cripple rail travel as the number of people passing through commuter and metro stations far exceeds that of an airport. Adopting such measures would also hand a victory to terrorists.[17]

The new terrorist environment presents special challenges for any rail operator with an Amtrak-like system. What is an operator to do with small rural train stations, which may see a passenger board a train only three or four times a week? Who expects such stations to be equipped with security forces and screening devices, and how would that be financed? Even if Amtrak used airport-like security to screen all passengers boarding its trains, how safe would those passengers be in situations where Amtrak trains share terminals, tracks, bridges, and tunnels with less-screened commuter trains on adjacent tracks? What happens if violence erupts on a train—whether Amtrak or commuter line? Do operators need security staff aboard similar to the air marshal program? And what about the threat of biological, chemical, and radioactive attacks in future years? How are train travelers protected against those weapons?

In the aftermath of the September 11 attacks, Secretary of Transportation Norman Mineta admitted that railroad bridges, tunnels, or computerized train control systems might be vulnerable to sabotage.[18] As Jack Riley explained, "Both freight and passenger rail networks traverse dense urban landscapes that may offer multiple attack points and easy escape as well as vast rural stretches that are difficult to patrol and secure."[19] Whatever monitoring and protective measures are put in effect in upcoming years, the cost is sure to be high.

More is being done to reduce vulnerabilities. The Transportation Security Administration (TSA) has said that railroad security issues are different from those of the airlines; in train stations, the primary concern is explosives. The TSA established a three-phase pilot program to screen luggage and carry-on bags for explosives at stations and aboard trains. Said Asa Hutchinson, an undersecretary at the DHS, in announcing the program,

> The pilot program would not resemble an aviation-type solution to transit and rail, but rather provide the department with a venue to test new technologies and screening concepts. The lessons learned from the pilot could allow transit operators to deploy targeted screening in high threat areas or in response to specific intelligence.[20]

In the program, the TSA tested the feasibility of a bomb-sniffing machine to check passengers boarding Amtrak and commuter trains in the joint-use New Carrollton, Maryland, train station.[21] Next, TSA screened checked baggage in Union Station in Washington, D.C., and in the final phase commuters in Connecticut passed through a specialized railcar equipped with on-board screening technology while the train was in motion.[22]

The DHS has committed more than $115 million in grants to improve rail and transit security, and the Transportation Department intends to provide nearly $4 billion in fiscal year 2005 grants to states and localities, some of which may be used for security-related projects.[23] However, funds are not available for every station, and it would be wise to make careful choices about which Amtrak facilities deserve expensive security and safety upgrades. Facilities that primarily serve long-distance trains that carry few people would naturally be low on the priority list.

Among other considerations in such decisions is the fact that adding an extra layer of security-related costs would only worsen Amtrak's financial performance. An unknown factor is whether future security procedures would put Amtrak at a disadvantage in the travel marketplace—even without a terrorist attack. Jack Riley has pointed out that "security measures resulting in increased fares or longer travel times would likely lead to losses in ridership."[24] Far worse, however, would be a successful attack against a passenger train. In places where Amtrak cannot transport passengers both safely and profitably, one must question whether people would be better off using another means of transportation.

All Train Operators
Are Vulnerable to Attack

Three years after September 11, the United States still seems largely oblivious to the range of threats against America's rail systems—Amtrak trains, commuter railroad lines, subway systems, or tourist-oriented museum trains. Public complacency has continued even in the face of attacks on foreign rail lines. Yet railroad and transit security officers have long known the terror that can be unleashed in rail cars, especially since a 1995 sarin gas attack in the crowded Tokyo subway system killed 11 people and injured about 5,500. The RAND Corporation's Jack Riley summarized the history of worldwide attacks on rail to Congress:

> Between 1998 and 2003, there were approximately 181 attacks on trains and related rail targets such as depots, ticket stations and rail bridges worldwide. Attacks on light rail systems and subway systems are included in these estimates. Attacks have occurred in all corners of the globe, including Venezuela, Colombia, India, Pakistan, Spain and the United Kingdom. These attacks resulted in an estimated 431 deaths and several thousand injuries. Bombs were the most frequently used weapon in these attacks, although firearms and arson have also been used.[25] (See table 6-1 for updated information, with the fatality toll in April 2004 at 671.)

TABLE 6-1

TERRORIST RAIL ATTACKS, 1998–2004

Year	Incidents	Deaths	Notable Incident(s)
1998	48	92	Train bomb in Pakistan kills 23
1999	5	2	Two die in Ethiopia; only fatal rail attack of year
2000	13	0	No rail deaths from terrorist acts
2001	41	275	Angolan rebels kill 252 with bomb, gunfire
2002	60	41	Track sabotage kills 20 in India
2003	14	21	Bomb in Mumbai, India, commuter train kills 10
2004	a	240	Bombs on Madrid commuter trains kill 200; bomb on Moscow subway kills 40
Total	**181**	**671**	

SOURCE: Jack Riley, director of public safety and justice, RAND Corporation, testimony before the Senate Committee on Commerce, Science, and Transportation, *Passenger and Freight Rail Security*, March 23, 2004, 2; 2004 information updated by author April 15, 2004.

a Number of incidents unavailable.

After the September 11 attacks, the nation better understood the vulnerability that exists in aviation, but train security had yet to become a top issue for travelers or policymakers. That changed on March 11, 2004, when explosives left in backpacks were placed aboard four crowded commuter trains in Madrid, Spain, and detonated by remote control, causing 200 fatalities and more than 1,800 injuries.

In early 2004, other assaults, real and threatened, were launched against train passengers. In February, an explosion in a Moscow subway train killed forty riders, and two months later Russian officials found bombs buried under railroad tracks northeast of Moscow. Railroad workers discovered explosives under high-speed rail tracks in France and Spain, which caused tracks to be searched system-wide in a costly and time-consuming process. In France, 10,000 railway employees walked the tracks to look for bombs while trains were patrolled by the police and armed forces.[26] After finding a bomb rigged under the tracks of Spain's Madrid–Seville line, police "combed all high-speed tracks 'kilometre by kilometre' while 45 helicopters [kept] watch from above and police dogs [sniffed] for explosives below."[27]

Sabotage to Amtrak: Real and Threatened

Amtrak has been spared a major catastrophe, but it has not been spared train sabotage, the most famous instance of which was the October 1995 derailment of the Sunset Limited in the desert west of Phoenix, Arizona. The wreck resulted in one fatality and seventy-eight injuries. The act was attributed to one or more saboteurs because of notes left at the scene by the "Sons of Gestapo," which said the wreck was an act of retaliation for federal sieges at Ruby Ridge, Idaho, in 1992 and the Davidian Branch Compound near Waco, Texas, in 1993. Maricopa County Sheriff Joseph Arpaio said:

> The track has been tampered with. We have other evidence to indicate it is not an accident. . . . We have terrorists and terrorism across our nation, and now it's hit our county. We had a problem in New York. We had a problem in Oklahoma City. Now we have problems here.[28]

Evidence pointed to someone with knowledge about railroads, perhaps a disgruntled former employee. Officials noted that the derailment could almost be a copycat crime of the sabotage of the City of San Francisco train in 1939 in Nevada, which killed twenty-four people.[29] No arrests were made in either case.

The only other known case of sabotage against Amtrak came in August 1992, when the Colonial from New York heading toward Newport News, Virginia, derailed at a switch that had been aligned to send the train careening onto a side track.[30] The National Transportation Safety Board reported finding bolt cutters that were used to cut the lock on the switch. Later, two men who had a keen interest in railroads were convicted of the crime.

Public officials and travelers appeared to share the view that these rare acts were random, as opposed to organized terrorist activity.

Security officials have discovered terrorist plots against U.S. rail systems. The first signs came when the FBI warned of possible attacks after pictures of American trains were found in al Qaeda's possession. Next came the arrest in Pakistan of the architect of September 11, Khalid

Sheikh Mohammad, who revealed that a U.S. citizen, Iyman Faris, was ordered to investigate ways of derailing trains. Said Faris's lawyer, David Smith,

> Khalid Sheikh Mohammad was particularly interested in the possibility of causing a derailment on a curve on an elevated line, like on a mountainside. And why? Not because that would kill more people, but because he thought it was spectacular. The plot involved a spectacular "Hollywood-like" effect and would fit in with the World Trade Center attack.[31]

Given this, it is little wonder that the Homeland Security Department and the Federal Bureau of Investigation issued a warning that terrorists could target railroad, subway, and bus systems during the summer of 2004 in major U.S. cities.[32] The question remains, however: Are we willing to do what is needed to best prepare for increasing threats to rail service?

In May 2004, government officials investigated at least seven instances of suspected surveillance along rail lines. Reported ABC News: "While authorities say they do not want to unnecessarily scare commuters, they say the findings fit the pattern of terrorists casing the rail lines for a possible attack."[33] According to the *Washington Times,* the National Geospatial-Intelligence Agency stated in a classified report that there has been a fairly steady stream of threat reporting directed toward the Northeast Corridor rail line.[34] The *Los Angeles Times* was more specific, reporting that "some of the linked intelligence points to a major attack on a choke point in the rail system somewhere along the Northeast corridor, from New York to Washington, and perhaps Boston to the north."[35]

The New York tunnels are the biggest choke point on America's rail passenger system. A check of the Internet in July 2004 showed how easy it was to download from a railfan site a diagram of the tracks and switches and location of the control center for Penn Station. The posting made such information easily available to anyone, including terrorists.

Between May and July, 2004, Amtrak stopped and searched six trains, and placed stations from Washington, D.C. to Boston on heightened alert because of anonymous bomb threats.[36] Bomb-sniffing dogs found no evidence of explosives. Amtrak said, "Unfortunately, bomb threats of this nature are fairly common."[37]

Amtrak's Counterproductive Political Actions

More than safety work is urgently needed in Amtrak tunnels. Basic maintenance necessary to ensure reliable operations has also been neglected. The blackout that hit the Northeast in August 2003 knocked out one of two remaining 12,000-volt cables that feed power from Sunnyside Yard in Queens to New York's Penn Station. Why were those sixty-eight-year-old cables not replaced in the period since Amtrak took ownership in 1976? Why was critical work routinely pushed aside in favor of inconsequential projects?[38] Why has not one Amtrak president made critical maintenance projects like this his top priority?

In fact, David Gunn did the opposite in 2003, arguing to preserve long-distance trains while traveling aboard the Chicago–Seattle Empire Builder. In Milwaukee, he told a journalist that "Amtrak's not broken. What's broken is the inconsistent policy."[39] He vowed to a Minot, North Dakota, reporter that he would fight to preserve Amtrak, to "draw a line in the sand, and defend the national system."[40] In Havre, Montana, Gunn condemned legislation designed to reform Amtrak.[41] In describing his twelve-day, coast-to-coast trip, which included a visit with Montana's governor, the *Great Falls Tribune* said Gunn ridiculed reform proposals, saying, "Other plans are just vague ideas, not real plans."[42] By the time Gunn arrived in Oregon, he was talking about the need for Canada to provide subsidies for the Seattle–Vancouver line.[43]

While Gunn took pains to proselytize in Montana, a low-traffic state for Amtrak, he did not take a twelve-day tour along the Northeast Corridor, where about half of Amtrak's customers are concentrated. He did not put a similar effort into recruiting support to put the New York tunnels in proper order. Gunn is just the latest in a long line of Amtrak officials (some of whom, like Tommy Thompson and Meridian, Mississippi, Mayor John Robert Smith, have been discussed earlier) who have directed Amtrak funding toward parochial political interests rather than objective needs. All of these politically motivated projects failed, and, in conjunction with wasteful expenditures elsewhere, they detracted from Amtrak's ability to meet its responsibility to move millions of people safely aboard the packed trains running on the Northeast Corridor that serve America's biggest city and other major East Coast cities.

The threat of terrorism only heightens the urgency of proposals to remove the responsibility for tunnels and rail lines in the Northeast from Amtrak's atrocious stewardship. Amtrak should be forced to transfer ownership of the New York tunnels and other infrastructure to a state or regional commuter agency. The Amtrak Reform Council proposed creating a special federal mechanism to facilitate such a transfer. Despite David Gunn's assertion, the proposals are not just "vague ideas." They are very real, very sensible, and very urgently needed.

Inequities in Paying for Transportation Security

Enormous amounts of funds are being spent to enhance rail security. Freight railroads have contributed to the creation of a Railway Alert Network to improve communications and alert the industry to potential threats. Amtrak police have worked many hours of overtime because of elevated alerts from the Department of Homeland Security (DHS). Transit authorities have sent police teams to military facilities to learn response tactics from chemical weapons experts. Additional procedures, according to Federal Railroad Administrator Allan Rutter, have included:

> Increased police surveillance; more frequent use of bomb-sniffing dogs to detect explosives; more frequent security sweeps of trains and terminals; and efforts to prevent unauthorized access to train platforms, rail yards, and passenger car maintenance and cleaning facilities. The commuter railroads also provide more frequent notices and job briefings to their employees, instructing them about how to be more vigilant in identifying suspicious persons and packages.[44]

It is relevant to note that the security costs incurred by other modes of transportation are shared by their users. Airline passengers, for instance, pay user fees through their ticket purchases, dedicated to aviation security. The fees, along with airline payments, mean commercial aviation puts about $2 billion annually into its own security, an amount the federal government wants to increase.[45] Thus far, payments for additional terrorism-related security costs for rail passenger systems—regardless of whether they are Amtrak intercity trains, local commuter trains, or urban transit systems—have come from the federal government's general fund.

So, once again, there is a disparity in the United States between what airlines and their passengers are expected to pay and what Amtrak and its passengers are expected to pay (nothing, at least thus far). Is this fair? If security in the post–September 11 world is a national responsibility, then should not airline and train passengers both be free of special security fees? Or, if the transport modes are expected to share the burden, should not Amtrak passengers have to pay additional charges on their tickets just as airline passengers do?

Aviation is not the only mode expected to pay more. Homeland Security Secretary Tom Ridge has put the shipping industry on notice about the need for help in the 360 ports protected by the Coast Guard, saying,

> The federal government cannot afford to pay for the increased security needed to protect U.S. ports from terrorists. We need to talk to the private sector. We don't have enough public money to do everything that needs to be done.[46]

The Port of Portland, Oregon, has agreed that user fees will probably be necessary because the federal government cannot be expected to bear the full burden.

No rail system—whether run by Amtrak, a commuter authority, or a private-sector operator—should be denied extra security resources deemed necessary. It is only reasonable, however, to inject fairness into the way in which train passengers and taxpayers share the added costs.

7

Escape from Amtrak:
State and Local Governments

Amtrak's mounting record of fiscal shortcomings, shutdown threats, and threatened labor strikes have created the broadest and deepest sense of disenchantment seen among local commuter rail officials and state transportation departments in the railroad's thirty-plus years. Today more than ever, state and local officials speak harshly about Amtrak and more freely about finding substitute operators—and they've begun to take action. In coming years, Amtrak may lose much of its commuter rail business. Boston's commuter rail system has dropped Amtrak from the largest single commuter rail contract in the nation. Agencies elsewhere have begun exploring ways to keep their trains running during an Amtrak shutdown while looking to reduce Amtrak's monopolistic stranglehold over passenger operations and facilities. Agencies for which Amtrak provides operating or maintenance services—such as Los Angeles and Northern Virginia—are losing confidence in Amtrak because of high-cost contracts, low quality, inefficient practices, and lack of good-faith negotiating stemming from Amtrak's monopolistic practices where it owns infrastructure. Commuter agencies, knowing that competition nurtures better deals, are poised to stimulate more interest in contracts from the private sector.

Shutdown Threats Harm Commuters

Amtrak has repeatedly threatened to suspend intercity train operations unless Congress grants it more funds—suspensions that would halt America's busiest commuter trains—even though there is no reason why Amtrak could not keep those trains running while shutting down its vast, money-losing national network. The commuter agencies that are threatened with temporary closures because Amtrak cannot keep its fiscal house in order include the heavily used New York, Chicago, and Philadelphia systems. Their trains are not operated by Amtrak, but they share tracks and stations.

Amtrak's has repeatedly manufactured these crises—and so far, has been allowed to. This is akin to giving a minor, bankrupt air carrier control over runway operations and maintenance at a major airport and the power to shut down thousands of flights by other airlines. The railroad's ploy would become still more bizarre were commuter trains to come to a halt in Los Angeles, San Francisco, or Seattle, cities where Amtrak has *profitable* contracts to provide commuter operating or maintenance services.

But regardless of the contractual relationships, there is no reason whatever for Amtrak to stop running such services, as Federal Railroad Administrator Allan Rutter has observed:

> The intertwining of Amtrak and commuter rail operations has resulted in the latter being periodically held hostage over issues relating to the financial condition of Amtrak but otherwise unrelated to commuter service. In recent years we have even witnessed a commuter agency that prepaid for its Amtrak services having been threatened by an Amtrak shutdown because Amtrak had commingled the commuter agency's funds with other funds in Amtrak's accounts. . . . [C]ommuters should not go through the periodic stress and uncertainty brought on by Amtrak's regular flirtation with financial catastrophe.[1]

Commuter authorities are alarmed by Amtrak's threatening tactics because the railroad's fiscal woes have nothing to do with them. The fact is, Amtrak could keep commuter trains running even without funds for its national system of lightly used trains. Traffic patterns expose the fiscal brinkmanship involved. Urban commuter trains carry extensive traffic—411.4 million passengers in 2002, more than seventeen times Amtrak's 23.4 million passengers that year.[2] Crowded commuter trains in congested urban areas should not be halted in Amtrak's perennial fight to preserve its long-distance trains.

Michael Mulhern, head of the Massachusetts Bay Transportation Authority (MBTA), has complained that Amtrak officials "insist on dragging the MBTA's commuter rail situation into a national debate. We believe their intentions are to inflict as much pain as possible."[3] He is correct. With proper planning, commuter operations can continue. Mulhern said, "With a little bit of cooperation from Amtrak, we believe we should be able to keep the local operation up and running while they address the issues with the national railroad. Yet, they refuse to even talk to us about that."[4]

Boston and the Changing Commuter Contract Market

Amtrak held commuter rail operating and maintenance contracts in Boston from 1987 until 2003. With 141,000 weekday passengers being carried over a 350-route-mile system, the Massachusetts Bay Transportation Authority represents the nation's largest single-contract rail operation.[5] It carries more passengers per day than Amtrak's Northeast Corridor does in a week.

Until 2003, Boston was Amtrak's biggest customer. The MBTA had for several years been unhappy with its late trains and high-cost contracts for maintenance services.[6] With a workforce of 1,552, Amtrak used more workers per passenger car and locomotive than seven other comparable North American commuter rail systems.[7]

The MBTA's attempt to outsource to private contractors and obtain greater efficiency and fiscal accountability represented one of the most difficult clashes with rail labor leaders in recent times. In 1999, the MBTA put Amtrak's maintenance contract out for bid in an open and rigorous competitive procurement pursuant to federal guidelines. Four companies submitted bids, three of which came in between $175 million and $195 million for the five-year contract. By comparison, Amtrak's bid was $291 million. The MBTA board voted to award the contract to Bay State Transit

Services, at a savings of $116 million over Amtrak's bid, and signed a contract with the private operator on September 15, 1999.[8] MBTA Chief Operating Officer Mulhern called the Amtrak proposal "regressive both in terms of price and quality. In sum, it was totally inconsistent with modern-day practices."[9]

Labor activists disrupted the process and pressured MBTA to disregard its contract with Bay State Transit Services and extend its contract with Amtrak. Republican Senator Wayne Allard of Colorado described how the unions achieved a goal that was so obviously against the public interest:

> Current Amtrak workers refused to apply for employment which Bay State offered as required by federal law. Amtrak management and the unions representing the workers created a hostile work environment, intimidated Bay State employees, and threatened unfounded lawsuits, all to ensure that Amtrak retained the lucrative MBTA contract. Faced with the potential for what amounted to a strike, which could have stranded Boston commuters, the Federal Transit Administration reluctantly approved a three-year extension of the commuter rail contract for Amtrak. Amtrak, the same bidder that offered the lowest quality service at the highest price.[10]

The labor unions had help from the Clinton administration and some in Congress in their fight to extend the Amtrak contract. Democratic Senator John F. Kerry became a predominant supporter of their cause, which included working to overturn the bid process in a Senate hearing.[11] Next, the Clinton administration hinted it might withhold funds designated for MBTA. Despite Amtrak being dead-last against competitors, the collective pressures worked and MBTA extended Amtrak's contract.[12] The Boston Herald editorialized that

> Bay State taxpayers and commuters have been taken for a ride again and the Clinton Labor Department and members of our own congressional delegation—including John Kerry, who appeared at the hearing to defend the utterly indefensible deal—share in the blame.[13]

"This has probably been the most bizarre turn of events in terms of public policy I've ever seen," said Kevin J. Sullivan, Massachusetts transportation secretary and chairman of MBTA's board.[14] In turn, Bay State Transit Services filed suit against Amtrak and rail labor organizations for engaging in restraint of trade in violation of antitrust laws by pressuring the MBTA "to terminate its agreement with Bay State despite Bay State's vastly superior bid."[15]

During 2001 and 2002, the MBTA continued to be frustrated with Amtrak's poor locomotive and passenger car maintenance, but it took the death of a passenger aboard a train for the MBTA to call it quits with Amtrak. James Allen, a nationally known scientist, experienced a heart attack in July 2002 while aboard an MBTA Framingham–Boston train operated by Amtrak. A doctor and others on board began administering CPR, while the Amtrak conductor ignored pleas for the train to stop at the next station, put Allen in an ambulance, and get him to a hospital, as MBTA policy called for. The train continued, passing two stations located near hospitals. To the astonishment of passengers—and despite their pleas to the Amtrak crew—the train continued to pick up passengers for twenty minutes after Allen collapsed. By the time the train pulled into Boston's Back Bay station, it was too late for paramedics to save him. After that, the MBTA reopened the search for another contractor to replace Amtrak, and officials reportedly vowed to never work with Amtrak again.[16]

A new MBTA bidding process saw three private-sector competitors emerge, and a winner was selected in February 2003.[17] By July, a consortium had taken over the maintenance and operation of MBTA's system from Amtrak in a $1.07 billion contract.[18] *Public Works Financing* explained:

> The new five-year contract, which will save Boston $100 million over the term, was awarded to the Massachusetts Bay Commuter Railroad Co., or MBCR, a consortium comprised of Connex North America, Bombardier and Alternate Concepts Inc. . . . "This deal will have a second and third bounce, in that other municipalities will follow, particularly those wanting to get away from current Amtrak contracts," says Joseph Giglio, a professor of strategy at Northeastern University in Boston, who also advised MBTA. The MBTA already is offering its assistance

to other cities, notes Mulhern: "There is no question that what is taking place in Boston will have enormous significance for the future of commuter rail operations throughout the United States, and potentially on Amtrak, as well."[19]

MBCR resolved the most difficult issues by coming to terms with all fourteen of MBTA's unions, representing 1,400 workers. Included was a $1,000 signing bonus and a 20 percent salary increase over five years.[20] The fact that costs were reduced even though pay increases were granted was another indication that Amtrak had been gouging Boston's transit agency, its paying passengers, and state taxpayers for years.[21] Thomas Till, when he was executive director of the Amtrak Reform Council, observed that if the new contractor "does a good job and demonstrates they can run this thing, then I think it's going to give the whole issue of franchising rail operation and maintenance a new look."[22]

Officials at MBTA believe shutdown threats boosted chances for a new organization to succeed in replacing Amtrak. Michael Mulhern has said,

> All that high-stakes drama that Amtrak pulled off, that turned out to be the best shot in the arm that we could possibly have gotten at precisely the right time. In terms of giving the legislature and executive branch here in Massachusetts a stake in what we were trying to pull off, well, Amtrak did it for me. . . . And just as significant, in the event of another high-stakes drama with the future of Amtrak, we'll be totally insulated from that. We own all our own infrastructure. We operate our own commuter railroad. Yes, we'll have interfaces with some of the Northeast Corridor, but it will be a manageable situation for us this time around, whereas last time around you're talking about a disaster for Massachusetts.[23]

What further helped transit officials was that public support was on their side in disputes with the unions, in part because of the ill will created by a multitude of threatened walkouts. Rail labor organizations had warned they would strike against Amtrak in November 1997 and June 1999 and had conducted public demonstrations at other times.[24] By the time the unions threatened another strike in 2003, MBTA had dumped Amtrak in favor of the private sector, protecting Boston's commuters from the vagaries of Amtrak's labor battles.[25]

In the year since MBCR assumed responsibility for the trains, a mixed report card has emerged. On the negative side, MBTA's General Manager Michael H. Mulhern said MBCR was fined $250,000 in early 2004 for late trains and a shortage of cars that have left passengers standing at peak times. MBCR cites difficulties in making timely repairs to the rail fleet because of late delivery of new wheel sets. On the positive side, in the same period MBCR had an on-time record of between 96 and 97 percent and has logged an average of 1,000 more miles between breakdowns than Amtrak.[26] The on-time performance was good considering that the standard was reduced from six minutes in the Amtrak contract to five minutes, which makes a difference when operating 2,639 trains per week.

MBCR has inherited problems because Amtrak had not maintained MBTA's commuter cars to a high standard. Industry insiders say maintenance may also be suffering because the shops are staffed with former, disgruntled Amtrak employees. Unfortunately, the MBTA contract required MBCR to keep all existing Amtrak staff for one year, which has hampered management's attempts to boost productivity.

Despite these teething pains, it seems clear that the MBTA is more satisfied with MBCR than it was with Amtrak.

Other Cities and Regions

Amtrak's control over local commuter rail has been disastrous—but it may not continue for much longer. Others are following in Boston's footsteps. Some commuter authorities are looking to devolve rail infrastructure from Amtrak ownership to local ownership, while others contracting for service with Amtrak are seeking replacement, private-sector operators. For instance:

Chicago. Metra is fed up with threatened Amtrak shutdowns that have nothing to do with Metra's operations. Amtrak owns the subsidiary that owns Chicago Union Station and has threatened to close the terminal when funds ran short. Local officials want to make provisions for some entity, possibly Metra itself, to keep running Union Station and even assume ownership if necessary. "If Amtrak goes bankrupt, Union Station still needs to function, and, if we have to step in to take up that void, we'll need to do it," said Metra Executive Director Phil Pagano.[27] Metra operates its own trains on some lines and contracts with the Burlington Northern Santa Fe, Union Pacific, and Canadian National railroads for operations on other lines. In a related development, Metra may be granted authority to provide commuter train service between Chicago and Milwaukee through Kenosha, Wisconsin, on a route that closely parallels Amtrak's. Should the extension occur, a policy and operational framework would permit phasing out Amtrak and substituting Metra as the operator.[28]

Los Angeles. The Southern California Commuter Rail Authority, also known as Metrolink, has lessened its dependency on Amtrak in stages. In 1998, Amtrak lost a three-year equipment maintenance contract valued at $40 million to Bombardier Inc.[29] In 2002 Metrolink disqualified Amtrak from bidding on a systems maintenance contract because of insufficient financial capacity.[30] During that year's shutdown threat, Metrolink Chief Executive David Solow had said, "We're looking for a backstop to make sure we aren't affected by what happens with them. . . . We need something solid to fill in if Amtrak is suddenly not there."[31] Metrolink wasn't about to look for "something solid" in Amtrak.

By 2003, Metrolink had arranged to hire RailAmerica Corporation, a Florida-based contractor, to keep trains running if needed.[32] The agency is now indicating it may seek private-sector competitive bids for the operating contract (engineers, conductors, dispatchers) held by Amtrak.

New Jersey. In 2001, the NJ Transit's board of directors voted to take over operation of Amtrak's New York–Philadelphia Clocker service during the next five years to exert better operational control.[33] The vote occurred before George Warrington left as Amtrak's president to become head of NJ Transit; it is too soon to see if Warrington will halt these reform efforts.

New York. Amtrak has no contracts to run trains for Metropolitan Transportation Authority operations like Metro North or the Long Island

Rail Road. But the LIRR is, nevertheless, a major customer, as it uses Amtrak's East River tunnels and Penn Station in Manhattan. The LIRR is the busiest passenger carrier in North America—during the weekday rush hour it carries one thousand people in and out of Penn Station every ninety seconds. The MTA has sought ownership of two of the four tunnels that lead to Penn Station from Queens, which are used intensively by the LIRR.[34] Although Amtrak owns these tunnels, Amtrak trains account for less than 20 percent of their traffic. MTA ownership of the tunnels would help protect New York's commuters from the effects of an Amtrak shutdown, similar to what Boston has accomplished. New York State has also expressed interest in buying other Amtrak facilities (tracks, tunnels, stations, and rail yards) that the LIRR and New Jersey Transit use heavily, but Amtrak is reportedly "not willing to discuss it."[35] Amtrak's efforts to avoid state ownership have not been helped by accidents like the one in April 2004, in which a crowded LIRR train was struck from behind by an empty Amtrak train. One hundred and thirty people suffered minor injuries, and hundreds of commuter trains were delayed during the morning rush hour.[36]

Northern Virginia. The Virginia Railway Express (VRE), which serves commuters in the Washington, D.C., suburbs, has been perturbed about the poor quality of Amtrak's service. VRE may solicit private-sector bids for its $14 million contract if Amtrak's services do not improve. In 2003, the VRE said, "We're getting to the point where they're going to have to tell us how they're going to take care of our services or we'll have to look elsewhere."[37] The *Washington Times* observed, "The deadline is the latest in a year-long reconsideration of the contract. VRE's skepticism started last summer, when Amtrak threatened to shut down its nationwide rail system as it ran out of money."[38]

Amtrak has responded to VRE's threatened independence with further coercion: In 2004, it warned VRE that it would cut off commuter-train access to Union Station or charge astronomically higher fees if it lost the VRE operating contract to a private company. Amtrak claims that it "owns" the tunnel that leads from Southwest Washington to Union Station and can do what it wants.

In truth, the VRE has three options to maintain access to the train station:

- The federal Surface Transportation Board states that STB's jurisdiction may be extended to commuter rail in certain instances, including when the commuter rail agency enters into a contract with Amtrak. This gives the VRE the right to appeal to the STB for an order granting it access to the station at reasonable fees.[39]

- The Department of Transportation holds the mortgage on Washington's train station and the secretary of the department sits on Amtrak's board of directors. The department has leverage to overrule behavior that is contrary to the public interest.

- Amtrak is vulnerable to a lawsuit for engaging in restraint of trade in violation of antitrust laws, similar to the action filed by Bay State Transit Services against Amtrak in Boston.[40]

Amtrak's threats are particularly galling since the federal government gave it these assets in 1976 for free, and Amtrak has benefited from a steady stream of billions of dollars in federal support in the years since then. If the American people don't own these vital transportation assets now, they should take steps to change that promptly.

As we have seen with Boston, Chicago, Los Angeles, New Jersey, New York, and Northern Virginia, infrastructure sharing and contractual relationships with Amtrak are two quite different things, yet a common element remains: Amtrak is a constant liability to smooth commuter train operations.

Amtrak is fighting tooth and nail against efforts to protect America's commuter rail passengers from Amtrak's misfortunes. For instance, in 2003 Congress permitted the Department of Transportation and the Surface Transportation Board to set aside up to $60 million of Amtrak's appropriation to fund commuter rail service should Amtrak cease operations.[41] Moreover, the Department of Transportation approved the $100 million emergency loan to Amtrak under the Railroad Rehabilitation and Improvement Financing Program provided Amtrak agreed to twelve conditions; condition eight was to identify the extent to which commuter operations would be affected in the event of an Amtrak shutdown. Amtrak refused. In December 2003, DOT Inspector General Kenneth Mead said,

We asked Amtrak to provide an analysis of the overhead expenses that would be incurred to operate the Northeast Corridor and commuter rail services if all other services were shut down. . . . Amtrak neither performed the required analyses nor developed the coherent response contemplated by loan condition eight. The information required by this condition is necessary to provide Congress with an accurate calculation of the dollars necessary to keep commuter services operating regardless of Amtrak's financial health. Congress included language in Amtrak's fiscal year 2003 and 2004 appropriations requiring that sufficient funds be reserved to satisfy the contractual obligations of Amtrak for commuter operations. However, without the accurate information that only Amtrak can provide, it is not known whether the reserved funds ($60 million in FY 2004) would be sufficient if they were needed. Amtrak depends on Federal taxpayers for its existence, but in this instance Amtrak management is not meeting its obligation to provide those taxpayers with accurate mandated information. Furthermore, Amtrak's RRIF loan agreement did not include any adverse consequence for noncompliance with loan condition 8. The Government's ability to employ adverse consequences, such as a reduction in appropriations, for noncompliance with Federal requirements is severely impaired because such actions would trigger the very insolvency of Amtrak that the Government is endeavoring to avoid. This sort of situation—a constant battle with Amtrak—underscores the need to give the states greater control of intercity passenger rail services.[42]

In the future, removing commuter rail services from Amtrak's grip will depend on three primary factors:

- Commuters becoming more aware that preserving Amtrak as the contractor to operate their trains will mean poorer service and higher fares.

- Local officials launching a competitive bidding process to lure private-sector operators to replace Amtrak.

- Transferring key facilities such as Washington Union Station, Chicago Union Station, New York's rail tunnels, and the Boston–Washington rail line from Amtrak ownership to state, regional, or local ownership.

State Government Relationships Deteriorate

Amtrak's declining role in commuter rail service may also soon extend to state-supported intercity rail routes. Amtrak operates a number of trains under contracts with states, and displeasure is mounting.[43] Allan Rutter has said that to state governments, "Amtrak has looked like the monopoly utility, dictating prices and conditions of service with little or no apparent connection to the actual costs of that service."[44]

For example, in June 2003, California began studying competitive bidding for its intercity rail services, seeking to cut costs on its $73-million-a-year contract with Amtrak.[45] The California Department of Transportation has said that the study "will also examine how to position California to continue intercity passenger rail service in the event Amtrak is restructured or liquidated."[46]

In Missouri, Amtrak has fought a pitched battle to keep Herzog Transit, a private-sector contractor, from replacing it as operator of the St. Louis–Kansas City passenger trains. In 2003, Herzog offered to run the trains at considerably less cost than Amtrak. Suddenly, Amtrak cut its price for running the trains by $2.5 million. Next, Amtrak denied Herzog access to the St. Louis train station and its reservations system (although airlines are allowed to use the latter).[47] The state elected not to proceed with bids, due to pressure from labor unions, and the service remains under Amtrak auspices for the time being. Herzog Transit said, "We hope that the Missouri Department of Transportation does not enter into any longer length of an agreement with Amtrak than is necessary, so that we may continue to attempt to resolve the issues related to Amtrak."[48]

Not surprisingly, New York has also emerged as a battleground for Amtrak. In 2002, a dispute with Amtrak regarding work required to run higher-speed trains between Albany and New York City became public. After state taxpayers financed up to $100 million in upgrades to Turboliner trains, New York Transportation Commissioner Joseph H. Boardman complained that Amtrak had broken promises, delayed train deliveries, "made unreasonable financial demands and threatened to keep the trains out of service in order to wring more money from the state." He said the trains were "well behind schedule, with frequent changes in specifications."[49] In mid-2003, a state comptroller audit cited Amtrak for failing to provide the transmissions and engines needed to rebuild the trains.[50] By 2004, Amtrak had scaled back on its share of the work, despite years of promises.[51] The issue sparked a lawsuit by the New York Department of Transportation asking for a ruling to force Amtrak to live up to its part of a high-speed rail contract to upgrade tracks, as promised earlier.[52]

As additional commuter agencies and state officials seek alternatives to Amtrak, private-sector companies will become more committed to bidding on contracts. Already, private companies operate parts of commuter train systems in Boston, Chicago, Los Angeles, Miami, San Diego, San Jose, and Dallas–Fort Worth. Some changes in federal law may be needed to permit Amtrak-owned facilities, such as maintenance and servicing yards, to be used by private contractors. But Amtrak's future as a contractor for state and local commuter rail services looks increasingly bleak.

Widespread dissatisfaction with Amtrak culminated in a 2004 federal initiative to establish a "fair bid procedure" for private companies that want to run state-supported intercity passenger trains. A *Federal Register* notice quoted Transportation Secretary Norman Y. Mineta saying that part of rail reform includes introducing "carefully managed competition to provide higher quality rail services at reasonable prices."[53] The notice acknowledged that at the state level "there has not yet been a successful process through which a fair and open competition has resulted in the selection of an operator other than Amtrak." A Federal Railroad Administration demonstration grant of nearly $2.5 million may be issued by early 2005 to help one but not more than two states develop new rules and introduce new competitive processes. Such a change is long overdue.

8

Passenger Railroads:
They Can Work

Amtrak has proven it cannot provide reliable rail service at a reasonable cost. The challenge now is to achieve better results from the public's investments in our trains. How can the future of passenger rail service be separated from the future of Amtrak? The 1997 Amtrak Reform and Accountability Act eliminated Amtrak's statutory monopoly, but Amtrak has been able to stop private operators from taking over its routes by denying them access to facilities it owns or leases. Clearly, a more comprehensive plan for introducing private sector competition prior to dismantling Amtrak is needed. Other countries have successfully discarded their Amtrak-style railroads and improved their ability to serve travelers and tourists at lower costs.

Privatization Options

Privatization involves the transfer of assets or service delivery from the government to the private sector. This may leave very little government involvement in the service, or it may involve public-private partnerships in which the government is still a dominant player.[1] Privatization also includes initiatives that allow the government to *provide* a service without *producing* the service. Privatization has become increasingly popular: more than $1 trillion of government-owned enterprises have been sold off around the world in the last fifteen years, according to Reason Foundation scholar Robert Poole.[2]

Although railroad privatization programs vary widely, they are being implemented around the world in one form or another. In some countries, railroads are sold as complete units. Elsewhere, the government retains ownership of tracks and rights-of-way while services over them are franchised. In other cases, new rail lines are constructed with a mixture of public and private financing. And some national rail lines have been "devolved" to lower levels of government, which in turn arrange for provision of service by private operators. A uniform rail privatization model is unlikely to emerge internationally because each nation has individual market needs, legal precedents, and cultural preferences. Nonetheless, it is clear that many countries have determined that subsidized national railroads are inappropriate in today's fiscal and transportation climate.

Some foreign railroads do earn profits in passenger service, most notably some of Japan's bullet train companies, and privately operated tourist trains in various parts of the world. In several countries, parts of premium services are profitable (for example, the French TGV between Paris and Lyon); these in turn help subsidize operating losses on other high-speed and conventional railroad lines. In Europe, Africa, South America, and the Asia-Pacific regions, many private companies earn profits on the rail franchises, while the subsidies for such franchises are lower than what was required by the Amtrak-like organizations they replaced.

Three primary methods of privatization are direct sale to shareholders, franchising, and "devolution" of authority to local governments contracting with private operators.

The East Japan Railway Company, the West Japan Railway Company, and the Central Japan Railway Company were privatized in 1987; their first listings on stock exchanges occurred in 1993, 1996, and 1997, respectively. This is somewhat similar to how the United States privatized Conrail and Canada privatized the Canadian National Railway (CN). This model would not work for Amtrak, as Amtrak is hopelessly insolvent and lacks the profit potential inherent in these companies.

Franchising (which the Europeans call "concessioning") allows governments to specify service levels and quality standards, while private companies compete for contracts to deliver the specified services. In virtually every instance, this has produced greater revenues as a result of innovative marketing practices and more attractive transportation services, while lowering costs through improved efficiency. British officials report that franchising has also improved knowledge of train operating costs.[3]

Where unprofitable rail service must remain for social reasons, the franchising brings about a public good because trains keep running while subsidy requirements are reduced. Steve Savas of Baruch College has explained the virtues of this approach:

> The most important single attribute of contracting is that when properly done, it creates and institutionalizes competition, which is the underlying factor that encourages better performance. . . . [It also] permits better management, free of most of the distracting influences that are characteristic of overtly political organizations [and] fosters good management because the cost of a service is highly visible in the price of the contract, whereas the cost of government service is usually obscured.[4]

The United States has not pursued franchising, but it has come close with private-sector contracts for commuter train operations in Boston, Miami, Dallas–Fort Worth, and San Jose (as discussed in chapter 7). While this arrangement is not the same as franchising, the participation of the private sector makes it very different from the state-run Amtrak approach.

National governments such as Japan have also "devolved" authority for local rail networks to regional, provincial, or local governments. The United States did, too, by transferring ownership of the Alaska Railroad to the state. This is a good approach for spinning off Amtrak-owned facilities, such as the Boston–Washington line, to regional agencies, and also to enable states to set up their own contracting or franchising arrangements.

Fifty-five Nations Would Do Away with Amtrak

Amtrak advocates would have the public believe that almost everywhere else in the world, nations have endless resources to support national passenger rail systems. In fact, public funding for intercity rail services is drying up overseas. Efforts to preserve Amtrak are contrary to the experiences of fifty-five nations that are privatizing, devolving, and regionalizing their national rail services. (See table 8-1.) Each of those countries, if it were

TABLE 8-1

SUMMARY OF RAIL PRIVATIZATION/DEVOLVEMENT IN FIFTY-FIVE NATIONS

Nation	Franchise to Private Rail Operator(s) Completed or Planned	Public to Private Asset Transfer (fixed or rolling stock)	Private Funds in Rail Capital Projects	Private Funds Raised in Stock Offering	Service Devolved to States, Provinces, Regions	New or Additional Privatization Planning Underway
1 Argentina	✓		✓		✓	✓
2 Australia	✓	✓	✓			✓
3 Austria					✓	✓
4 Bolivia	✓					
5 Brazil	✓					✓
6 Canada	✓	✓	✓	✓		✓
7 Chile	✓					
8 Colombia	✓					
9 Congo	✓					
10 Costa Rica		✓			✓	
11 Czech Republic		✓			✓	
12 Djibouti	✓		✓			✓
13 Ecuador						✓
14 Estonia	✓		✓			✓
15 Ethiopia	✓		✓			✓
16 France	✓		✓			
17 Germany	✓		✓	✓		✓
18 Ghana	✓					✓
19 Great Britain	✓	✓	✓	✓		✓
20 Guatemala	✓					
21 Hong Kong						✓
22 India	✓		✓			
23 Iran		✓	✓			✓
24 Israel			✓			✓
25 Italy	✓					✓
26 Ivory Coast	✓					
27 Jordan			✓			✓
28 Japan		✓	✓	✓	✓	
29 Korea	✓		✓			✓
30 Latvia						✓
31 Lithuania	✓					✓
32 Madagascar	✓					✓
33 Malaysia	✓					
34 Mexico	✓					
35 Mozambique	✓					✓
36 Netherlands			✓			✓
37 New Zealand	✓		✓	✓		✓
38 Norway			✓			

continued on next page

TABLE 8-1 (*continued*)

SUMMARY OF RAIL PRIVATIZATION/DEVOLVEMENT IN FIFTY-FIVE NATIONS

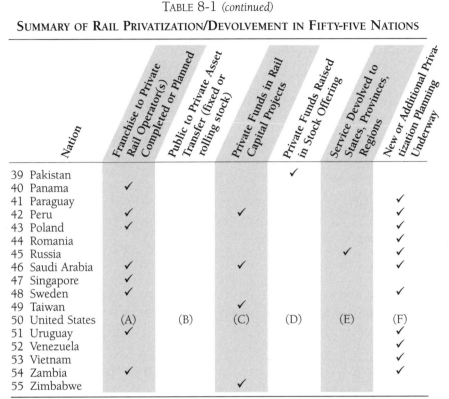

Nation	Franchise to Private Rail Operator(s) Completed or Planned	Public to Private Asset Transfer (fixed or rolling stock)	Private Funds in Rail Capital Projects	Private Funds Raised in Stock Offering	Service Devolved to States, Provinces, Regions	New or Additional Privatization Planning Underway
39 Pakistan			✓			
40 Panama	✓					
41 Paraguay						✓
42 Peru	✓		✓			✓
43 Poland	✓					✓
44 Romania						✓
45 Russia					✓	✓
46 Saudi Arabia	✓		✓			✓
47 Singapore	✓					
48 Sweden	✓					✓
49 Taiwan			✓			
50 United States	(A)	(B)	(C)	(D)	(E)	(F)
51 Uruguay	✓					✓
52 Venezuela						✓
53 Vietnam						✓
54 Zambia	✓					✓
55 Zimbabwe			✓			

SOURCES: Requests for proposals and stories appearing from January 1, 1997, through August 19, 2004, in the *Financial Times, Railway Gazette International, International Railway Journal,* and *Public Works Financing*; testimony of William J. Rennicke, vice president, Mercer Management Consulting, Incorporated, before the House Committee on Transportation and Infrastructure, Subcommittee on Railroads, *Hearing: Restructuring of America's Intercity Passenger Railroad System,* 107th Cong., 2nd sess., April 11, 2002; Amtrak Reform Council, *An Action Plan for the Restructuring and Rationalization of the National Intercity Rail Passenger System: Report to Congress* (Washington, D.C.: U.S. Government Printing Office, February 7, 2002), 97.

NOTE: In the United States, privatization or devolvement has occurred in the following ways:

(A) Some commuter agencies, for example, those in Boston, Chicago, Dallas, and Miami, contract with the private sector to operate or maintain their systems. This is not the same as franchising, but very different from the socialist model of a state-run enterprise as represented by Amtrak.

(B) A public-to-private fixed-asset transfer occurred with the federal government's privatization and sale of the Consolidated Rail Corporation (Conrail).

(C) Private funds are routinely raised in equity markets and invested in freight railroad capital projects.

(D) Private funds were raised as part of the Conrail privatization process.

(E) The federal government devolved railroad service when it transferred ownership and operating responsibilities of the Alaska Railroad to the state; when it transferred ownership of Washington's Dulles and National airports to a local authority; and every time it built an interstate highway.

(F) Various proposals exist to separate Amtrak into different components or to franchise, regionalize, and devolve Amtrak service to regional authorities and states.

home to Amtrak, would phase it out of existence. The Amtrak Reform Council reviewed international privatization efforts and found that:

> Financial pressures have caused governments to implement various programs of reform, restructuring, and privatization of the national railroads of Germany, Sweden, the Netherlands, Italy, and the United Kingdom. The effect of these reforms has been significant. In some cases, higher efficiency and quality have actually permitted a reduction of public support. In other cases, support has increased because the clearer contractual relationships under the new regimes have given governments higher confidence that budgeted funds would be spent effectively and for the purposes intended.[5]

Private and regionalized operation of passenger and freight services worldwide has led to substantial improvement in customer service, increases in traffic, decreases in cost, and a greater return for the government subsidies that continue to be provided. How nations achieve this differs, depending upon a number of factors. Japan and Mexico have chosen to create vertically integrated railway structures where the operator of a service also owns or leases the railroad infrastructure. The European Union is pressing its member nations to institute horizontally separated arrangements whereby private operators utilize tracks and facilities that are owned by the government.

Why are these privatization programs so popular throughout the world? The answer is simple: They save money.

> International examples of privatization of rail and other low-tech assets demonstrate operating cost savings ranging from 3 percent to 50 percent in the first three years of private operation. U.S. examples of outsourcing to private transportation operators show annual operating cost savings in excess of 30 percent. Recent Mercer [Management Consulting] analysis of a European passenger rail system revealed potential cost savings from privatization of infrastructure operations of 9 percent to 11 percent. Because this system is newer and more efficient than

Amtrak, it is likely that Amtrak could achieve even greater savings from a private-sector infrastructure operator.[6]

In its first three years of private operation, the Canadian National Railway, a freight operator, achieved operating savings of 22 percent based on ton-miles.[7] A mainline passenger rail operator, JR West in Japan, achieved an average per-passenger-kilometer operating cost decrease of 37 percent in constant dollars from 1985 (preprivatization) to 1995 (postprivatization); the railroad now operates without subsidies.

Appendix C gives details of rail privatization experiences in other nations, a summary intended to illustrate the scope of such activity worldwide. A few of the more outstanding examples found in Great Britain, Japan, Canada, and the United States are worth exploring here.

Great Britain's Franchising Sparks Record Traffic Boom

British Rail was born in 1948 with the nationalization of four railway companies, but by the early 1990s, it was plagued by poor service and worsening financial losses. Consequently, Prime Minister John Major introduced the Railways Act of 1993, which led to the start of a rail franchising system and the railroad's eventual breakup.

The former British Rail is now sixty separate businesses, twenty-five of which are train-operating companies.[8] Advocates of reforming Amtrak want to replicate the parts of the British experience that worked well (e.g., franchising) and reject the parts that did not (e.g., creating a private-utility monopoly like Railtrack).

Today's train franchisees have succeeded in building traffic on a complex, worn-down system. Ridership was in a virtually continuous downward spiral under British Rail, but today, records are being set for the number of passengers served. In the 2003–4 reporting period, more than 1.1 billion passenger journeys were made on Britain's railway system—the highest level since 1947. Passenger-kilometers traveled, at 40.9 billion, were more than in any year since 1946.[9] (See table 8-2.) This is a spectacular turnaround, especially considering that immediately after World War II, the British rail network was much more extensive, and

TABLE 8-2

BRITISH RAIL RIDERSHIP, 1919–2004

The franchised operators of the privatized British rail system have reversed a downward trend that had been in effect for nearly six decades under state-run British Railways. In 2003/2004, British railway ridership reached the highest level since 1947 based on number of trips, and the highest since 1946 based on passenger kilometers. Since privatization, traffic based on the number of trips has risen 45 percent, and traffic based on passenger-kilometers has increased 36.3 percent.

Year	Passenger Trips (millions)	Trip Growth since 1995/1996 Privatization	Passenger-Kilometers (billions)	KM Growth since 1995/1996 Privatization
1919	2,064		—	
1923	1,772		—	
1928	1,250		—	
1933	1,159		—	
1938	1,237		30.6	
1946	1,266		47.0	
1947	1,140		37.0	
1948	1,024		34.2	
1949	1,021		34.0	
1950	1,010		32.5	
1951	1,030		33.5	
1952	1,017		32.9	
1953	1,015		33.1	
1954	1,020		33.3	
1955	994		32.7	
1956	1,029		34.0	
1957	1,101		36.4	
1958	1,090		35.6	
1959	1,069		35.8	
1960	1,037		34.7	
1961	1,025		33.9	
1962	965		31.7	
1963	938		30.9	
1964	928		32.0	
1965	865		30.1	
1966	835		29.7	
1967	838		29.1	
1968	831		28.7	
1969	805		29.6	
1970	824		30.4	

continued on next page

TABLE 8-2 *(continued)*
BRITISH RAIL RIDERSHIP, 1919–2004

Year	Passenger Trips (millions)	Trip Growth since 1995/1996 Privatization	Passenger-Kilometers (billions)	KM Growth since 1995/1996 Privatization
1971	816		30.1	
1972	754		29.1	
1973	728		29.8	
1974	733		30.9	
1975	730		30.3	
1976	702		28.6	
1977	702		29.3	
1978	724		30.8	
1979	748		32.0	
1980	760		31.7	
1981	719		30.7	
1982	630		27.2	
1983	695		29.5	
1984/1985	701		29.7	
1985/1986	686		30.4	
1986/1987	738		30.8	
1987/1988	798		32.4	
1988/1989	822		34.3	
1989/1990	812		33.3	
1990/1991	809		33.2	
1991/1992	792		32.5	
1992/1993	770		31.7	
1993/1994	740		30.4	
1994/1995	735		28.7	
1995/1996	761		30.0	
Privatization				
1996/1997	801	5.2%	32.1	7.0%
1997/1998	846	11.2%	34.7	15.7%
1998/1999	892	17.2%	36.3	21.0%
1999/2000	931	22.3%	38.5	28.3%
2000/2001	957	25.7%	38.2	27.3%
2001/2002	960	26.1%	39.1	30.3%
2002/2003	976	28.2%	39.7	32.3%
2003/2004	1,104	45.0%	40.9	36.3%

SOURCE: Passenger trips and passenger-kilometers from Strategic Rail Authority, "National Rail Trends," June 2004, table 1.1, "Passenger kilometers by ticket type (billions)," and table 1.2, "Passenger journeys by ticket type (millions)," at http://www.sra.gov.uk/pubs2/performance_statistics/nrt_june04/nrt0604 (accessed August 8, 2004).

commercial airline competition was minimal compared with today. Since privatization, the number of passenger journeys has increased 45 percent, and Britain now has Europe's fastest-growing railway—ahead even of Spain and France, whose state-run railways have started new high-speed train services.[10] One operator, Central Trains, surveyed passengers in mid-2004 and learned that 30 percent of passengers had not used the train in more than twenty years.[11] On weekdays, the British system carries approximately 3 million passengers, about forty times the number Amtrak carries.[12] The *increase alone* in British train traffic since privatization is greater than Amtrak's *total* ridership, a staggering fact.

Britain is in the midst of a massive replacement of its old passenger trains and by 2005 will have one of the youngest fleets in Europe.[13] The Strategic Rail Authority reported that at the time of privatization in 1996, the average age of the national passenger rail fleet of vehicles was more than twenty-two years; by the end of 2004, the average age will be fourteen years.[14]

Today, twelve franchisees are running gleaming new locomotives and passenger cars.[15] One company, South West Trains, is placing in service 785 new Desiro carriages, worth £1 billion, in a phase-in to be completed in 2005—the single largest order for new trains since privatization.[16] Compared with the old "slam-door" fleet they replace, the Desiro trains enhance safety with automatic sliding doors. They also offer what today's customers expect—air conditioning, audio and visual information displays, and greater comfort. Meanwhile, on the Great North Eastern Railway (GNER) trains, passengers with wireless laptop computers have access to Internet and e-mail services from anywhere on the train.[17]

Chris Green, chief executive of Virgin Rail and a former British Rail managing director, has said that much of the fleet replacement simply would not have happened had British Rail been preserved.[18]

The train fleets have a working life far longer than the length of a passenger franchise contract, and therefore are not owned by the train franchisees but by private-sector rolling stock leasing companies (ROSCOs).[19] The ROSCOs have invested more than £4.2 billion since 1996 to bring 4,500 new vehicles into service, which the franchisees lease at a cost of more than £1 billion annually.[20] The government plays a role by guaranteeing the ROSCOs that rolling stock will be required beyond the end of a specific franchise contract.

One franchise in particular did not work out well. The SRA terminated the Connex South Eastern franchise in 2003 because SRA Chairman Richard Bowker was "not convinced that the financial management processes [were] sufficiently robust to allow them any more taxpayer's money."[21] The number of passenger complaints about overcrowding at peak times and poor on-time performance also contributed to the franchise cancellation.[22] Connex's chief executive of the franchise, Olivier Brousse, disputed the allegations of financial mismanagement and argued that service would have improved over time.[23] The franchise was transferred to South Eastern Trains, a subsidiary of the SRA, which is operating the line until a private company is awarded the contract. Thirteen private-sector companies expressed interest in the franchise;[24] a final selection is expected early in 2005.[25]

Government regulation contributed to problems at Connex South Eastern and other franchised lines through excessive regulation of fares. As difficult as it is to believe, the government required rates to be lowered when on-time performance faltered. Cheaper fares naturally sparked a rise in demand, which in turn caused more delays because more passengers getting on and off trains meant trains dwelled longer at stations. A maddening circle of events ensued, whereby fares were lowered again, which in turn caused still greater demand and more crowding. This foolish cycle, which caused operating costs to increase, was finally abandoned in 2003.

In another way, regulations hampered all franchisees. The government's financial penalties for service interruptions made it incredibly costly for a franchisee to resist labor demands and "take a strike." The labor organizations repeatedly exploited this flaw, and operators had little choice but to cave in to labor's demands. Hence, wages for train drivers have doubled since privatization.

Despite these drawbacks, the private operators have demonstrated more initiative, imagination, and visionary planning than state-run British Rail did in its prime or Amtrak does today. But it is difficult for these companies to get the credit they deserve because of the failings of Railtrack— the company formed to own and maintain tracks, signals, bridges, tunnels, level street-railroad crossings, and stations. Unfortunately, under Railtrack, track repairs were not undertaken in a timely manner, and costs increased.

The pivotal event that contributed to Railtrack's demise was a train derailment at Hatfield on October 17, 2000, which killed four people and injured seventy. The immediate cause of the accident was the fracture and subsequent fragmentation of a rail. Britain's Health and Safety Executive will not issue a final report on the accident until legal proceedings have been completed.[26]

According to the Department for Transport, the accident implicated Railtrack's maintenance shortcomings and revealed the degree to which the network had deteriorated under Railtrack.[27] In the accident's aftermath, Railtrack imposed new safety measures across the network, which caused a steep decline in reliability and required Railtrack to make penalty payments to the train-operating companies.[28]

Defenders of the Amtrak status quo generally point to Britain's Railtrack as a reason not to privatize Amtrak, but the argument is hollow because reformers do not suggest incorporating that part of the British model into the American system.

Railtrack was flawed from its creation as essentially a utility monopoly, the kind of organization least able to respond quickly to its customers— in this case the fast-moving managements of the train franchises. Moreover, government regulation required Railtrack to be privatized as a "virtual company" that retained few engineering skills. The government "compulsorily outsourced" engineering to maintenance companies, which became responsible for project specifications, carrying out the work, and follow-up inspections. This strategy allowed costs to increase even as the track deteriorated.[29]

Other factors contributed to Railtrack's poor performance, the primary one being that it inherited a railway the Department for Transport said was "suffering from historic under-investment stretching back for decades."[30] Socialistic spending practices had funded British Rail based on political whims instead of clearly defined capital needs. Hence, the railroad deferred maintenance for many years, and deterioration of assets was widespread. By the time Railtrack came along, there was an enormous amount of catch-up work to do. For example, an estimated 85 percent of the cost of upgrading the heavily used West Coast Main Line—the route between London and Scotland via Birmingham—was attributed to overcoming deferred maintenance.[31]

In October 2002, the government replaced Railtrack with Network Rail, a not-for-dividend company obligated to reinvest its operating surplus in maintaining and upgrading the rail network.[32] Its funding comes from a mixture of grants from the Strategic Rail Authority, access charges paid by franchisees, and borrowing. One of Network Rail's first actions was to bring maintenance in-house to better handle the daunting task of caring for 21,000 miles of track, 2,500 stations, and 40,000 bridges and tunnels, while also being responsible for the signaling and track paths of 25,000 trains a day.[33] (Amtrak's infrastructure and operational responsibilities are exceedingly modest compared with Network Rail's.) Over the next five years, Network Rail plans to spend about £26 billion on railway infrastructure.[34]

In one respect, Network Rail faces the same challenge that Railtrack did—major increases in trains utilizing capacity-constrained tracks. From the time of the first franchise to 2003, an average of 20 percent more train-kilometers has been added to the timetable each year. But that average masks some dramatic increases. The five intercity operators (Virgin West Coast, Virgin CrossCountry, Midland Mainline, GNER, and First Great Western) have increased train kilometers by 60 percent. No one would expect a highway to cope with that increased use without some detrimental impact on performance, especially while work is simultaneously underway to catch up on the backlog of thirty to forty years of underinvestment.[35]

In mid-1993, U.K. Transport Minister Alistair Darling said, "There are 1,300 more weekday scheduled train services than there were in 1997."[36] Yet, train frequencies continued to intensify, even though capacity remained virtually unchanged. One year after the minister's speech, the private operators ran 19,091 trains on an average weekday, an increase of 366 trains compared to the earlier year.[37] By Amtrak standards, the growth is astonishing because the one-year *increase* alone is greater than the 265 daily trains Amtrak operates.[38]

Network Rail is improving existing lines to allow higher speeds and faster journeys. The London–Manchester and London–Glasgow routes are the first to see results. Also, Network Rail is adding tracks to increase capacity and permit more train frequencies, upgrading the overhead electrical-supply system on lines where the new Desiro trains will run, and enhancing safety by installing a new train protection and warning system.[39] Initial reports about Network Rail's level of efficiency are encouraging.[40]

Substantial private financing is underwriting the first major railways to be built in Britain in more than a century. British airport operator BAA helped finance the construction of a $396 million rail line to Heathrow Airport and is investing more to initiate a local service to complement the express service.[41] A new high-speed line linking London with the Channel Tunnel—the first part of which opened in September 2003—is under construction in a public-private partnership between the government and the London & Continental Railways. The infrastructure enables Eurostar trains to travel at 186 miles per hour, resulting in quicker journey times, and doubles the capacity for the trains at peak hours. The first section was completed on time and on budget, and the second section is expected to be completed by 2007.[42] On a related point, a new speed record of 208 mph was set by the Eurostar on July 30, 2003.[43]

Amtrak and its labor-union allies would have the public believe that privatizing British rail service has jeopardized safety, but that simply is not true. While unfortunately there have been five fatal train accidents between 1997 and 2002, the overall safety record on Britain's privatized railways has shown steady improvement since their state-run days. Counting either the total number of fatalities or the number of fatal accidents, the rates since privatization are below British Rail's rates in the 1980s and 1970s.[44] The UK Rail Safety and Standards Board has found that the railroads' safety "performance is the best ever, with a further improvement over the previous best performance of 2001/02. The current [significant accident] rate is one third of the rate that existed immediately before privatisation and less than one fifth of the average rate that existed in the 1980s."[45] (See figure 8-1.)

This remarkable progress has come with varying degrees of public cost. In the first full year of franchising, 1997–98, the British government paid £1.425 billion to the train-operating companies. By 2002–3, the figure had dropped to £908 million—the net cost after the Strategic Rail Authority collected £169 million in payments from nine franchisees.[46] How significant are these payments? A similar situation would be if Amtrak sent money to the U.S. Department of Transportation because parts of its system were profitable, instead of Congress continually giving subsidies to Amtrak because all of its services are unprofitable.

Unfortunately, costs and subsidies have risen from 3.3 pence per passenger-kilometer in 2002–3 to five pence per passenger-kilometer

FIGURE 8-1
BRITISH RAIL SAFETY IMPROVES, 1975–2003
Significant Train Accident Rates

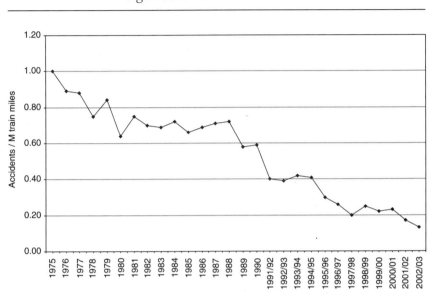

SOURCE: *Annual Safety Performance Report 2002/03* (London: UK Rail Safety and Standards Board, 2003), 22.

in 2003–4.[47] The loss of five pence per passenger-kilometer pales in comparison to Amtrak's loss in 2003 of nineteen cents per passenger-mile. Taking into account the exchange rate and the conversion of kilometers to miles, Amtrak's loss is nearly 50 percent greater.[48]

The British are taking action to restrain subsidy growth, and provisions in future franchise transactions will vary depending on route and traffic considerations. Even though tougher new terms will be negotiated, private-sector interest remains high.[49]

The overwhelming evidence is that privatization of British Rail has benefited the traveling public and taxpayers, while positioning the railways to make meaningful contributions to mobility in the future. Rail service today includes private-sector skills and commercial discipline, as well as access to private finance that has enabled an unprecedented program of investment to take place.

Franchising successes are sparking similar efforts. Officials are considering "micro-franchising" on stand-alone, smaller routes, provided they are backed by local governments and are part of a competitively bid process.[50] Franchising has moved to the transit arena in London, with a 24 percent reduction in the public subsidy to the urban Docklands Light Railways Limited being implemented during the franchise period running from 1997 to 2004. In addition, responsibility for the London Underground was transferred to private contractors on July 15, 2003, in a thirty-year concession.[51]

The British Rail privatization holds four lessons for the United States as it contemplates the future of Amtrak:

- *Franchising provides great flexibility:* Disappointing as the Connex experience was, it demonstrated that privatization, while not a flawless process, is capable of responding to problems. It also demonstrated the government's ability to protect the taxpayers' interest and make a smooth transition to a new operator without service disruptions to the passengers.

- *Do not reward failure:* When a British train operator begins to fail financially, it expects it will have to surrender the franchise, rather than receive any additional government support. Compare that with Amtrak's perennial threats to shut its system down because of funding shortfalls.

- *Be clear when outsourcing:* Even though Railtrack had problems with contractors, Iain Coucher, deputy chief executive of Network Rail, said there is nothing wrong with outsourcing: "I think that you have got to be very precise about how it can be delivered, and there needs to be a greater degree of input specification."[52]

- *Take care with infrastructure privatization:* This is particularly true when tracks are in disrepair and are expected to host increased train traffic. Based on the British experience, it was not surprising that the Amtrak Reform Council proposed placing Amtrak's Boston–Washington tracks under new public ownership. Since Amtrak trains elsewhere operate on tracks that the private freight railroads own and maintain to high standards, disrepair is not an issue in most of the United States.

Despite challenges, Great Britain's privatization experience has been remarkably successful. Private contractors have taken over decaying rail services, revitalized them, and financed the acquisition of new trains and new rail lines. Britain, in reviewing the structure of the privatized system, will abolish the Strategic Rail Authority and will move functions to the Department for Transport.[53] It also is considering other institutional changes, future investments, and revisions to regulations needed to fine tune the new system.[54]

Ronald Utt at the Heritage Foundation observes that even with Britain's early mistakes, "The Labor Party government, which inherited the newly privatized system from Conservative Party privatizers, has shown no inclination to reverse course."[55] That is no wonder, considering the amount of progress taking place and with passenger traffic setting a new half-century record.

Japan's Stunning Rail Efficiency Gains

On April 1, 1987, the Japanese government privatized Japan National Railways (JNR) by splitting it into six regional passenger companies and a nationwide freight carrier. The result has been a positive, indeed stunning, effect on passenger service. The Japan Transport Economics Research Center reported in 1992 that traffic on the former JNR had peaked at 215.6 billion passenger-kilometers in 1974. The record was quickly exceeded by the new companies in only their second year of operation, as service frequencies increased, employee attitudes improved, and trains became cleaner.[56] The number of passengers has continued to increase, and freight traffic has remained stable despite route-shedding, a recessionary economy, continuing motorization, and airline deregulation and expansion.

The three largest privatized railroads report dramatic results:

- The East Japan Railway Company, the largest passenger railway in the world, serving about 16 million riders daily, now has around 48,500 employees in railway operations, a dramatic reduction from the 72,000 who worked there when JR East was established in 1987.[57]

- The Central Japan Railway Company has seen a steady growth, from the 321 million passengers carried under the old Japanese National Railway regime in 1982 to 529 million carried on the privatized system in 2002—an increase of 64.7 percent.[58]

- Privatization of the West Japan Railway Company has enabled it to conduct business in a more flexible manner. It has cut costs by reducing its workforce from 50,000 employees to 41,000 in 2001, and plans to bring that figure down to 32,000 by 2006.[59]

The companies were free to succeed as the burden of financing money-losing lines was lifted. Japan's central government ceased funding for eighty-three local lines—more than half were changed to bus operations, and the remainder receive local subsidies.

Privatization has had another benefit: Impractical government proposals were stopped by the new franchises, which recognized these money-losing ideas for what they were. As JR East President Masatake Matsuda said, the new private operators were determined "never again to return to the dark memories of JNR's final years, when the organization was, in effect, bankrupt." Matsuda has said that government-owned corporations and national agencies have only vague objectives, while JR East's reorganization into the private sector has given management extremely well-defined goals.[60] Another benefit has been an explosion in research and development of advanced train technologies, with many train designs reaching new performance standards. For example, three companies built test trains designed to carry out a series of experiments to lead to faster bullet train services based on the conditions of their respective lines—JR West built the WIN 350, JR Central the Series 300X, and JR East the STAR 21. Each train set speed records between 1992 and 1996.[61] Since, each railroad has put new models into commercial service. Today, JR Central and JR West are jointly developing the Series N700, a train that will become the fastest yet on the Tokaido–Sanyo Bullet Train line when it starts commercial service in 2007.[62]

Rocky Mountaineer Trains Boost Canadian Tourism

Americans accustomed to Amtrak's dismal performance can hardly imagine a train receiving the kind of ringing endorsement the London *Daily Telegraph* reported in 2003. Twenty thousand people in Great Britain were asked to list fifty things they'd like to do before they died. Among the items chosen was a ride on the Rocky Mountaineer train in Canada.[63] Such is the power of an accomplished private operator—the ability to take over a lackluster operation and turn it into a worldwide hit.

The transformation started in 1990, when Canada's federal government decided to reduce the subsidized operation of VIA Rail (the country's equivalent to Amtrak) and privatize the daylight service running through the Rocky Mountains. In the competition that followed, the Great Canadian Railtour Company was awarded the rights to the service, named, appropriately enough, the Rocky Mountaineer. Peter Armstrong, a former motorcoach operator and tourism leader, had created the company; he brought aboard travel-industry experts and former railroad executives to plan the service along the Canadian Pacific and the Canadian National lines. Armstrong has said of his train:

> Generally speaking, rail is no longer a cheap, efficient way to transport people over long distances. However, this kind of rail experience where the scenery, service, and history are the attractions—more of an enjoyable excursion rather than a means of transportation—can still be marketed successfully.[64]

The Rocky Mountaineer, which bills itself as "The Most Spectacular Train Trip in the World," has sales representation in eighteen countries and a sterling reputation in the travel industry. It has become the largest privately owned passenger rail service in North America, with eighty-seven passenger cars and locomotives. Company officials initiated innovations by contracting with Colorado Railcar to build luxury, bilevel dome coaches, with seating for seventy-two guests in a panoramic environment on the upper level and a dining lounge, fully equipped galley, and observation platform on the lower level. The Rocky Mountaineer also appeals to the business market with a "rolling retreat" specialty car outfitted like a boardroom, where companies hold executive conferences or product launches. As an example of how the company is sparking a railway renaissance, it set the record for the longest passenger train in Canadian history, consisting of thirty-four cars and three locomotives, in September 1996. It carried more than 650,000 passengers through late 2003.[65]

I rode the Rocky Mountaineer in September 2003, and found its employees cheerful, enthusiastic, and attentive. The train was exceptionally clean—including the oversized windows in the bilevel dome car. In the dining section, the gourmet menu items were served with flair. The trains ran on time even though they share tracks with freight trains. The off-train experiences also were impressive. The train's two-day trip through the mountains is punctuated by an overnight stay in Kamloops, British Columbia, to permit travel through the scenic vistas in daylight. The company did a masterful job of handling the complicated logistics involved with bringing 1,000 travelers into a town, busing people to and from hotels and evening entertainment, and routing trains to different destinations.

Not surprisingly, given how well run it is, the Rocky Mountaineer is expanding. In 2004 it plans to:

- Launch a new tourist train along a popular Skeena River route to Prince Rupert. The three-hour trip aboard the North Coast Explorer train will be available as a shore excursion to more than sixty thousand Alaskan cruise ship passengers who visit Prince Rupert in the summer.[66]

- Start work on a new Vancouver station, scheduled to open by 2007.

- Put its twelfth $3.5-million custom-built dome coach in operation, responding to rising demand.[67]

- Run a test train over another spectacular rail route in British Columbia through Cranbrook, Creston, Nelson, Castlegar, and Trail, near the Washington state border, to determine feasibility of future service.[68]

- Include the Rocky Mountaineer as a pre- or postcruise vacation choice on four major cruise lines—Celebrity Cruises, Royal Caribbean, Holland American Line, and Princess Cruises.[69]

Firm plans for expanding privatized rail service in British Columbia even include restoring passenger train operations over routes that lost such service in the past. By 2006 the company will introduce the Whistler Mountaineer between North Vancouver and Whistler, and launch an additional Rocky Mountaineer route from Whistler to Prince George and continuing to Jasper, Alberta. The Canadian National Railway selected the company to operate the trains, concluding after a nine-month competitive bidding process that Rocky Mountaineer Railtours "best met its criteria for the new tourism service, including product quality, prospects for financial success, economic development benefits for British Columbia, and value to CN."[70]

Officials in Canada who argue to end subsidies to VIA Rail point to the success of this venture. Jim Gouk, a member of Parliament, said the Rocky Mountaineer replaced "an unsuccessful VIA Rail operation, and, with significant private-sector investment, turned it from a subsidized failure carrying 4,500 passengers a year to a tax-paying success with 70,000 passengers a year."[71] The profitable operation is a testament to the leadership, skills, and perseverance exhibited by Rocky Mountaineer's people—from executives to dining-car cooks to station personnel. The Rocky Mountaineer is a sparkling entrepreneurial venture worthy of replication in the United States.

America's Success with Conrail and the Alaska Railroad

Some question whether publicly owned rail systems in the United States can be privatized or devolved to the private sector. In fact, they already have been.

The federally owned Consolidated Rail Corporation (Conrail), successor to the bankrupt Penn Central, was sold to shareholders for $1.6 billion on March 26, 1987. At the time, it was the largest initial public stock offering in the nation's history.[72] While a similar outright sale is impractical for Amtrak, the Conrail experience nonetheless proves that it is possible to privatize a bulky government-sponsored railroad. Under private ownership, Conrail became much more efficient and profitable. Later it was purchased by the CSX and Norfolk Southern railroads, split into two, and incorporated into their systems. In 2004, most ex-Conrail freight lines are carrying record amounts of freight, and CSX and Norfolk Southern are profitable.

Devolvement of rail services has also been successfully tried in the United States with the Alaska Railroad, which was transferred to state control in 1985.[73] The railroad's performance today is outstanding. With a motivated local management attuned to market forces, it entered into partnerships with cruise ship companies to serve the leisure market. In 2003, the railroad transported more than 480,000 passengers—a higher passenger count on its highly seasonal trains than Amtrak carried on most of its short-distance routes through more heavily populated states.[74] More passengers traveled on the Alaska railroad than on thirty-one of Amtrak's forty routes.[75] (See table 5-1 for Amtrak ridership by route in 2001.)

Examples of devolvement exist in other modes of transportation. The federal government transferred operations of Washington's Dulles and National airports to a local authority. Federal gasoline taxes financed construction of interstate highways, but the roads have always been owned by the states. Cities such as Indianapolis and Las Vegas outsource some of their transit bus operations and maintenance to outside contractors; many school systems contract their school-bus operations to private operators; and most of the nation's dial-a-ride services for the elderly and handicapped are competitively contracted. The federal government does not run an airline or bus company; running a national passenger railroad is a costly aberration.

9

Creative Approaches to
Rail Transportation

In planning for America's passenger rail service, we can no longer afford to consider Amtrak a likely or reasonable part of the picture. We must not allow our vision of the future to become intertwined with questions about Amtrak. As Kenneth Mead has said, "That has not been a fruitful focus in the past and all parties, the public, the Congress, and the Administration will be better served by focusing on what we want intercity passenger rail service in this country to be, how we are going to produce and govern it, and how we are going to fund it."[1] Instead, we must consider:

- How do we reorganize Amtrak so that it maintains existing services while a new model is planned and implemented?

- Which public agencies would be the most appropriate new owners of Amtrak stations, tunnels, tracks, and other infrastructure?

- What entity should be put in charge of planning market-sensible capital expenditures, such as improved tracks in heavily populated corridors?

- Of the privatization and devolvement arrangements around the world, which are most suitable for implementation in the United States?

- What laws need to be modified to permit an effective franchising system to be implemented and to ease concerns of the private freight railroad industry about new entities operating over its tracks?

- How do we stop looking for the "one simple answer"—more federal funds to Amtrak—and begin looking for sound alternatives? Increasing Amtrak's subsidies is unimaginative and stifles creativity within the marketplace where others could propose alternatives to the Amtrak status quo.

The Amtrak Reform Council recommended that Amtrak be restructured into two companies. One would be a small federal agency responsible for conducting train operations. The other would own, operate, maintain, and improve the Northeast Corridor property and infrastructure. All services would be provided under contractual arrangements with performance requirements. After a transition period, competition to operate trains would be introduced through a bidding process, and the Northeast Corridor line would be placed in a separate corporation to be controlled by the states through which it runs.[2]

Eventual transfer of the Boston–Washington line from Amtrak ownership makes sense, considering that more commuter trains use the corridor than Amtrak trains. For example, Amtrak ran only 10 percent of the intercity and commuter trains operated on the Boston–New York line in 2002; commuter agencies operated the other 90 percent.[3] A similar situation exists south of New York. It is simply common sense to allow the agencies that operate the vast majority of traffic on these lines to assume responsibility for their maintenance, safety, and efficient operation.

Proposed changes in Northeast Corridor ownership bear no resemblance to the way the British transferred infrastructure to Railtrack, making that part of the British experience irrelevant to the debate about Amtrak.

Amtrak Undermines Emerging Competitors

Privatization would improve train service for travelers, enhance efficiencies, and lower Amtrak's need for subsidies. Regardless, Amtrak fights it tooth and nail. Amtrak continues to hold a de facto monopoly on intercity rail passenger service, which has stifled competition in several states.

In 2003, Amtrak asked states for a substantial increase in their subsidies. Missouri responded by soliciting competitive bids from the private sector to take over operation of a passenger train between Kansas City and St. Louis. What happened next was described by Alan Landes of Herzog Transit Service:

> We learned that under current conditions a private company cannot bid against Amtrak's uncooperative government-subsidized monopoly and win. In the case of Missouri, Amtrak's refusal to negotiate access to facilities and services essential to operating the route made it impossible to prepare a compliant bid. Further, once Herzog announced its interest, Amtrak dramatically and artificially lowered its subsidy requirement from $8.9 to $6.4 million. Amtrak succeeded in keeping competitors out of the bid process. They did not bother to put in a bid themselves, perhaps not wanting to give the competitive process any credibility. Herzog has learned a hard lesson. But we are not discouraged. We intend to press on and are continuing discussions with Missouri and other states on creating a mechanism to put the bid procedure on a level playing field. . . . We know many states are frustrated and want to introduce the element of competition into state subsidized intercity passenger service. . . . We believe a fair competitive bid procedure, to be directed by the states, but with DOT oversight, should be implemented immediately.[4]

When it was apparent Missouri officials would extend the Amtrak agreement, the company asked the state to do so for the shortest possible time and ultimately reopen the competitive process.

The Missouri experience, although extraordinary, was hardly unique. In Massachusetts, Bay State Transit Services was forced to file suit against Amtrak and rail labor organizations in 2001 for restraint of trade in violation of antitrust laws. Amtrak had been operating and maintaining trains for the Massachusetts Bay Transportation Authority. Citing Amtrak for inefficiency, and at the urging of the Federal Transit Administration, MBTA opened the equipment maintenance contract out for bid. Four companies bid, three of which came in between $175 million and $195 million for the five-year contract; Amtrak's bid was a staggering $291 million. Bay State Transit was initially selected to do the maintenance work under the contract. Nonetheless, Amtrak received a contract renewal.[5] (These events are described more fully in chapter 6.)

Bay State's complaint outlines the coordinated action of Amtrak and its unions to undermine the award process and force MBTA "to terminate its agreement with Bay State despite Bay State's vastly superior bid and enter into another contract with Amtrak."[6] That occurred even though Bay State's bid was $116 million less than Amtrak's and judged to be of higher quality.

In Pennsylvania, Amtrak has used its ownership of the railroad tracks and its monopoly powers to thwart private-sector innovation in rail service. For instance, on the Philadelphia–Harrisburg line, the Railway Service Corporation (RSC) offered to take over all local Amtrak trains several years ago. It would offer faster and more frequent service and restore direct train service to one of Philadelphia's centrally located train stations. The company estimated that traffic would double and Amtrak operating deficits for the line would be reduced.[7] But Amtrak was unhappy that the proposal brought to light its decline in business on the route, which had brought it down to about half of the million-plus passengers it had served in the late 1970s. Amtrak also was not pleased that another operator could step forward and show more promising results. Amtrak succeeded in blocking the private-sector proposal through the standard bureaucratic stonewalling technique of refusing to respond to RSC's communications and initiatives.[8]

U.S. Capabilities Exist to Replace Amtrak

Amtrak defenders allege it is impossible to franchise Amtrak routes to companies through a competitive bidding process and devolve them to regional or state agencies, despite significant legal and historical precedents that exist in the United States to carry out such changes.

Amtrak President David Gunn believes that franchising is unrealistic, and has said that only Amtrak has the "gene pool" to run U.S. passenger trains, particularly on the electrified Boston–Washington line. "We are the only game in town," he has declared, "when it comes to an electrified railroad."[9] The fact is, Amtrak's expertise is not so rare. Four other electrified railroads in the Northeast (the Long Island Rail Road and Metro North in New York, the Southeastern Pennsylvania Transit Authority in Philadelphia, and New Jersey

Transit) move a far greater number of passengers than Amtrak does, and they do so on complex systems. Chicago has two electrified commuter railroads.[10] These intensely used systems are managed successfully in the face of the challenges of maintaining electrification systems, upgrading signal systems, maintaining tracks, and building new bridges—all the components necessary on a mainline railroad. Moreover, engineering firms like Bechtel are qualified to install or upgrade electrification systems, and high-volume foreign franchise operators such as National Express and Virgin Rail experienced with electrified railroads in other countries—some far more intensely used than Amtrak—are interested in competing for U.S. franchises.

And some freight railroads have significant experience with managing some aspect of passenger train operations. For instance, millions of commuters are carried on Chicago's Metra trains under contract with railroads known primarily for carrying freight—the Union Pacific, Burlington Northern Santa Fe, and Canadian National. A similar arrangement exists on a few other systems where freight railroads operate trains or maintenance companies perform work under outsourcing contracts.

Private operators are ready to bid on franchised Amtrak operations. Alan Landes, senior vice president for Herzog Transit Services, said in Senate testimony in April 2003,

> By this time next year, nearly 40 million passengers a year will be riding on trains operated by private companies in the United States. The Herzog operations move 2.5 million passengers per year in Southern Florida, 1.4 million per year on the Trinity Railway Express in Dallas–Fort Worth, and 922,000 per year in California. The Connex operation in Boston will move 37 million passengers annually.[11]

Diversity of Alternative Operators

Around the world, literally millions of passengers are carried daily on thousands of privately run trains operated under contract to government authorities. The pool of private operators is large, with more than seventy-five companies running passenger rail systems. To induce them to compete for contracts in the United States, however, the government must establish a clear framework. In 2002, railroad consultant William Rennicke sent an inquiry to transportation companies about possible private participation in U.S. passenger rail service and found ten companies responding within forty-eight hours. According to Rennicke, companies qualified to participate in U.S. rail franchising include:

- Angel, a U.K. rolling stock lessor that operates internationally.

- Arriva, a British train and bus operator with concessions in the United Kingdom, the Netherlands, Denmark, and Portugal.

- Connex, a French train and bus operator that is a partner in the Boston commuter rail contract and has concessions in Germany, Sweden, and Australia.

- First Group, a train and bus operator with concessions in England and the Netherlands, and in the United States with school buses.

- National Express Group, the largest train operator in the United Kingdom, which carries more than 1 billion passengers a year worldwide on train, light rail, bus, and express coach operations, and operates thousands of school buses in the United States and Canada.

- Stagecoach/Virgin Rail, a train and bus operator with concessions in Britain, Sweden, Portugal, New Zealand, and Hong Kong.

- Sea Containers/GNER, a train and ferry operator that operates a rail concession in Britain, the famed Orient Express in Europe, and tourist trains in Australia and Peru.[12]

Various other companies have examined the potential to replace Amtrak, including British train operators Great Western Trains and GB Rail.[13] The largest privately owned bus company in the United States, Peter Pan Bus Lines, headquartered in Springfield, Massachusetts, informed the Amtrak Reform Council that it would be interested in a train franchise.[14]

During talk of an Amtrak bankruptcy in 1997, Guilford Rail System, a Massachusetts-based freight carrier, offered to purchase or lease Amtrak's Northeast Corridor line. It said it would operate private passenger service as a "reasonable approach to the inevitable failure of Amtrak." The Clinton administration simply ignored Guilford's offer. Later, when the Amtrak Reform Council proposed divestiture of the Boston–Washington line, Guilford Rail left the door open for possible involvement, depending on the council's recommendations.[15]

Amtrak is experiencing mounting competition for commuter rail contracts for new systems. For example, in Minnesota, the Burlington Northern Santa Fe Railroad is negotiating a contract to run a proposed Minneapolis commuter system; planning officials have noted the railroad's optimism and its willingness to be flexible on costs.[16] Georgia is planning to start a line to serve Atlanta and has entered negotiations with the Norfolk Southern railroad, rather than Amtrak.[17] And in a major shift regarding intercity passenger service, the Norfolk Southern has begun negotiations with Virginia to operate a train between Roanoke and the nation's capital.[18] Amtrak's role would likely be limited to permitting the train to stop at Washington Union Station.

Service to the Nostalgia Market

A small segment of American travelers want the option of getting aboard a long-distance train for a relaxing experience similar to a cruise ship environment. Others want to rekindle nostalgic moments by having dinner in a dining car as the countryside rolls by the window. These experiences are available now in a multitude of venues that have nothing to do with Amtrak.

North America is home to operators offering "experience" rail trips to leisure travelers. The American Orient Express operates trains on various itineraries, such as an eight-day trip through Salt Lake City, Yellowstone National Park, Grand Teton National Park, Great Falls, Missoula, and Portland, Oregon. Travelers wanting a blend of train and motorcoach tours through spectacular scenery can opt for one of the sixty packages offered in conjunction with the Rocky Mountaineer train in western Canada.

Cruise ship passengers to Alaska at layover points can select from the Rocky Mountaineer out of Vancouver, the North Coast Explorer train from Prince Rupert, British Columbia, or trips aboard the privately owned and managed rail cars (organized by Holland America Westours and Princess Tours) pulled along with general public coach cars by the Alaska Railroad. Passengers also can be carried aboard a privately owned railroad in Alaska, the White Pass and Yukon Route, a subsidiary of Tri-White Corporation based in Toronto. The line, which serves ship passengers arriving at Skagway, set a new one-day record in 2003 by carrying 4,888 passengers. Without relying on federal subsidies, the company is building additional passenger cars for next year's season.[19]

Tourist-oriented trains also serve local markets throughout the United States. The Tourist Railway Association is a good resource to find a service catering to a specific interest, whether it is a wine train in California, a leisurely trip to the Grand Canyon, a train pulled by a steam engine in Pennsylvania, or a visit to one of a number of museums that have restored and operate heritage railroad equipment. It is not necessary to preserve Amtrak to keep nostalgic rail trips alive.

Air and Bus Developments

Decisions about future rail service should not be made in a vacuum. Dynamic changes are underway in passenger travel in general, and they should be factored into the equation. Air travel, of course, has been rail's chief competitor for long-distance travel for more than fifty years now, and in various ways it is a more innovative and vibrant sector of the economy. Secretary of Transportation Norm Mineta noted the renewed growth in air travel in 2004, saying, "We are seeing different passengers traveling on new and different airlines, using different types of aircraft, flying in and flying out of different airports."[20] His acknowledgment of these market changes was reinforced by Federal Aviation Administrator Marion Blakey, who said,

> We're seeing smaller planes enter our system in record numbers—with regional and commuter carriers more than

doubling since 2000. These planes now account for nearly half of all commercial activity and point-to-point flying is becoming a reality.[21]

This means that in a growing segment of aviation, travelers are avoiding delay-prone airline hubs and reaching their destinations faster. Aviation innovation is creating new travel options for Amtrak passengers—and the millions of Americans not served by railroads.

Specialized buses are difficult to find in North America outside of the tour market. Nonetheless, the bus market is relevant to the future of railroads because the majority of passengers on long-distance trains are not, in fact, on for the full route—they're riding short segments where travel by bus is a reasonable option.

Recent innovations are worth noting, as entrepreneurs launch extraordinary services to compete with Amtrak and air travel. New starts include the LimoLiner, running on a four-hour, ten-minute schedule between Boston and New York. The upscale motorcoach service was founded in 2003 by Fergus McCann, the former owner of Scotland's Celtic football team, who with his travel industry background decided an upscale motorcoach could compete with the Acela Express and air shuttles. The LimoLiner offers roomy, comfortable leather recliner seats, unlimited Internet access, constant cell phone reception, live television reception, worktables for meetings, and an onboard attendant serving complimentary snacks.[22]

Similarly, in Oklahoma and Texas, Chris Gorman's transportation experience spurred him to create a luxurious bus service for people traveling 250 miles or less as an alternative to flying. Buses run by his company, The Coach, provide captain's chair seating to fifteen passengers, who are served meals by an attendant. Routes link Dallas with Oklahoma City, Tulsa, and Austin.[23]

No one knows exactly what would happen if these startup companies were able to compete with Amtrak on a level playing field—without Amtrak's heavily subsidized ticket prices. But even with Amtrak's subsidies now, these bus services are competing in certain markets. In Canada, Red Arrow Motorcoach has been operating luxury coaches between Calgary and Edmonton for twenty-five years.[24]

Effective Legislative Remedies

Congress is faced with stark choices over Amtrak. Keep pouring in billions, or do something serious to stop the bleeding. Every member of Congress who agrees to pour billions of dollars into Amtrak without stopping its fiscal hemorrhaging is committing policymaking malpractice by following a strategy that is certain to fail. Scaling back and restructuring Amtrak to make it more relevant is our only hope for the future.

Michael P. Jackson, when serving as deputy secretary of the Department of Transportation, has said that when it comes to Amtrak, money alone is not the answer because "Amtrak's core business design suffers from structural rot."[25] Unfortunately, the reform laws that have been enacted to date have not taken direct aim at Amtrak's unalterable structural rot. The Amtrak Reform and Accountability Act, unfortunately, did not serve as the foundation for meaningful change from within the railroad that it was intended to. Sadly, the failure to enact strong reforms is more illustrative of Congress's bias in favor of preserving even the most ineffective programs than a reflection of any public outcry in support of Amtrak.

Still, some in Congress recognize that Amtrak's system must be cut back. (See appendix D for a summary of legislative proposals.) Several bills have been introduced to establish a new agency to take over Amtrak facilities, continue to provide subsidies needed during the transition period, and restrain the railroad's out-of-control spending. Fortunately, Amtrak-related legislation is starting to reflect lessons learned overseas in rail-franchising, privatization, competitive contracting, and devolvement. The leading champions for effective reform are Senator John McCain of Arizona; Representative John Mica, a Republican from Florida and a member of the House Committee on Transportation and Infrastructure; and Representative Ernest Istook Jr., a Republican from Oklahoma who sits on the House Committee on Appropriations and serves as the chair of the Transportation, Treasury and Independent Agencies Subcommittee.

Conclusion

Creating real change is an uphill battle in Washington, D.C., where government programs, once begun, hardly ever end. Public agencies request higher appropriations each year, and Congress usually adds on still more for favored hometown projects. The Citizens Against Government Waste reported that the number of pork-barrel projects in fiscal year 2004 increased by 384 percent over the previous six years; the latest one-year cost is a record $22.9 billion.[1]

Amtrak is a prime beneficiary of that culture, and Congress has tolerated and coddled it for more than thirty years now. Preserving the status quo will do nothing to reverse Amtrak's high costs, increase its labor productivity, improve its response to market demands, or reduce the likelihood of its spending billions of dollars on grandiose, politically inspired rail projects. Congress's history regarding Amtrak has been counterproductive to the interests of taxpayers and travelers.

After the Amtrak Reform Council closed its doors in 2002, its executive director, Thomas Till, reflected on the meaning of the agency's call to restructure the railroad. Paraphrasing Winston Churchill, he noted that "Great, judicious, and well-considered steps are sometimes at first received with public incomprehension." No longer. The debate is changing—after decades of policy debates limited largely to annual haggling over how much money Amtrak should receive, the council's groundbreaking recommendations are beginning to be reflected in proposed reform measures. Policymakers, the press, and the public are beginning to pay attention to proposed alternatives to Amtrak.

Amtrak has treated its biggest customers—the commuter agencies and the states—with disdain, while disparaging successful rail privatization and devolvement that are occurring throughout the world. Part of the reason for Amtrak's attitude is that it is a calcified organization that resists change. Amtrak's poor attitude extends to customer service, where the lack of enthusiasm can be seen aboard trains and at many ticket windows.

A visit to Britain's privatized railroads shows what a difference market forces can make on the quality (and cost) of service. When Richard Bowker, chairman of Britain's Strategic Rail Authority, spoke to an industry conference in 2004, he acknowledged his audience by saying,

> This room is a snapshot of a wider industry "jam packed" with people who are passionate; passionate about being the best contractor; about giving the best customer service; about being the best train builder or running the best-kept station. About being the best in each of their fields.[2]

It is difficult to describe Amtrak management and personnel as "passionate" about anything except their belief that the government owes Amtrak higher subsidies. Amtrak also is passionate about taking little or no responsibility for failures, especially its most abhorrent mistakes, such as failing to perform needed safety work on the most important infrastructure it owns—the New York tunnels. Amtrak epitomizes Milton Friedman's observation that public agencies often eschew accountability: "It blames all problems on external influences beyond its control and takes credit for any and all favorable occurrences."[3]

Congress, unfortunately, has bought into Amtrak's myths, promises, and alibis. Even the chronology of warnings regarding Amtrak's financial condition listed in appendix A understates the admonitions Washington has received about Amtrak because it only covers the period since passage of the Amtrak Reform and Accountability Act of 1997. Warnings started much earlier; the GAO, for example, observed more than a quarter of a century ago that "Amtrak has made few route adjustments to improve its economic performance and/or reduce its requirement for operating subsidy."[4] The situation remains the same today.

The myths that support Amtrak were examined earlier, but one is worth repeating here—the idea that Amtrak is somehow essential. If providing essential transportation were a genuine objective of public policy, then Congress would write laws to award competitive franchises to whatever mode—airline, bus, or passenger rail—could provide the service for the least amount of subsidy. Such a program would be based upon objective criteria, such as service to all communities exceeding a particular population threshold, or service with a subsidy-per-passenger limitation.[5]

Amtrak has repeatedly issued extravagant claims regarding ridership projections, high-speed rail development, operational performance, financial results, labor productivity, and the need for long-distance trains. Amtrak's lack of credibility is a major issue, and it is time for Washington to be as tough on Amtrak when it breaks the public trust as it is on corporations like Enron. For example, the congressional response should have been sharper in 2002 when Amtrak "discovered" a $200 million cash shortfall and threatened to shut down. Amtrak Reform Council member Wendell Cox believes Amtrak got off lightly, even though its accounting irregularities were as serious as those in the notorious Enron and WorldCom cases, saying,

> Amtrak-WorldCom shows that a double standard operates in Washington. Misreport private financial results and the consequences begin with subpoenas. Misreport public financial results and the rewards begin with photo-opportunities. But in a government of laws, not men, similar improprieties would be punished similarly. Both public *and* private misconduct should be sanctioned. Indeed, government agencies should be held to a higher standard than private companies, because their funds are compelled from the taxpayers, not provided voluntarily by private investors. . . . Director of the Office of Management and Budget Mitch Daniels noted that if Amtrak had been a private company, the directors would have been forced to resign and would be facing "severe" sanctions.[6]

Amtrak is, indeed, the Enron and the WorldCom of transportation, and future financial bailouts will prove to be as futile as prior bailouts have been. Keeping Amtrak running forever is wrong; indeed, doing so causes economic harm. Consider the view of Henry Hazlitt, who in his classic book, *Economics in One Lesson*, said it is a mistake to try to prevent any industry from dying in order to protect the employees or the capital already invested in it. He wrote:

> Paradoxical as it may seem to some, it is just as necessary to the health of a dynamic economy that dying industries be allowed to die as that growing industries be allowed to grow. The first process is essential to the second. It is as foolish to try to preserve obsolescent industries as to try to preserve obsolescent methods of production: this is often, in fact, merely two ways of describing the same thing. Improved methods of production must constantly supplant obsolete methods, if both old needs and new wants are to be filled by better commodities and better means.[7]

What does America do next? New thinking is required, because several strategies directed toward Amtrak have failed:

- Attempts to reform Amtrak have avoided hard choices, had little impact on efficiency, and ultimately failed. Reform is a dead end.

- Proposals to give Amtrak even more generous subsidies ignore the railroad's irresponsible spending patterns, would not improve efficiency, and would divert funds that could be directed toward higher national priorities. Hence, throwing more money at Amtrak is hopeless.

- Proposals to kill Amtrak outright have not gotten far because doing so is seen as too difficult, especially with opposition by labor unions. Hence, in this case the "perfect answer" of outright abolishment is unlikely to be implemented without a substitute structure in place.

The sensible solution is to separate the future of passenger rail from the future of Amtrak and focus on maximizing public investments through a franchising and devolvement process. A phase-out of Amtrak timed with a phase-in of more competent organizations would succeed in the United States as it has in so many other countries.

It is time for Washington to set a multiyear transition in motion that will create more competition in railroad passenger service. A carefully designed plan will give federal officials time to devolve or sell Amtrak's assets, give state and local officials breathing room to plan continuance of selected passenger services, and enable the private sector to complete the preparations necessary to bid on passenger-train routes, obtain the necessary rolling stock to run the trains, and start service.

Provided that disincentives are removed, rail passenger transportation in a post-Amtrak world would result in more financially viable trains in healthier transportation markets. Commuter rail services would benefit from greater independence by unlinking their operations from Amtrak's operations. Short-distance and regional trains could thrive under a competitive franchise system that induced private-sector participation. A reconfiguration of long-distance routes whereby salvageable short-distance portions remained could result in lower expenses and more market relevancy—provided they, too, were franchised. Planning for high-speed trains in the few markets where such trains are justified would have to include risk-sharing with the private sector to minimize chances that expensive train systems would be built in unsustainable markets. Tourist and land-cruise trains could be operated profitably, without subsidies—as they already are in many instances—with a plethora of services ranging from luxury cross-country trips to local museum and dinner trains.

Congress often throws billions of dollars at problems and can thus subsidize inefficient entities such as Amtrak, but not even the federal government can defy the laws of economics. After Conrail had used $2.1 billion of federal funding and was looking for an additional $1.2 billion from Washington, many critics characterized it as the next Amtrak. That proved not to be the case, because the legislation that authorized additional funding also allowed Conrail to act like a private-sector company and to make investment and operating decisions based on market-driven economic forces rather than political considerations. The Conrail labor unions went along with many reforms, since the alternative was the likely loss of thousands of jobs. For rail passenger service to prosper, the federal government similarly needs to establish an environment that makes operators accountable through market forces, rather than a political process that gives Amtrak increasing amounts of public funding.

It is fitting to give the last word to a figure who was instrumental in Amtrak's creation—Anthony Haswell. He has concluded that

> Amtrak does not have a commitment to excellence. It has no interest in living up to its statutory mandate to provide "modern" passenger service. Its overriding concern is to assure its institutional survival. It is a sick and failed organization which should be put out of its misery.[8]

He is correct. The public interest would best be served by eliminating disincentives to private-sector involvement in rail passenger service, replacing Amtrak with more sensible alternatives, and providing useful rail transportation at a cost the public can afford.

Appendix A

Chronology of Warnings about Amtrak's Financial Condition

Washington policymakers have been warned time and again about Amtrak's misleading accounting practices, substandard performance, and poor prospects for the future. Below is a 1998–2003 chronology of such warnings:

1998

March 2. U.S. General Accounting Office (GAO): Issues a report examining the possible consequences of an Amtrak liquidation, including uncertainties in estimating potential costs associated with a liquidation, possible financial impacts on creditors, possible financial impacts on participants in the railroad retirement and unemployment systems, and possible impacts on intercity, commuter, and other rail services.[1]

March 24. GAO: Warns Congress that "We are here today to report that Amtrak continues to be in a very precarious position and will remain so for the immediate future. . . . Amtrak's financial condition continues to deteriorate. . . . Federal funding and recently enacted reforms will not solve Amtrak's financial problems.[2]

March 24. U.S. Department of Transportation inspector general (DOT IG): Testifies before Congress that Amtrak plans to use federal capital funding for the maintenance of equipment, infrastructure, and facilities, and that such costs "have generally been considered operating expenses, and generally have not been paid with federal capital assistance."[3] Amtrak's bookkeeping maneuver appears designed to obfuscate how operating and capital funds are defined to ease the manner in which the railroad could reach self-sufficiency. In effect, this is an attempt to "move the goal posts" after the game has started.

May. GAO: Publishes a report about the bleak performance of Amtrak's routes, stating that the railroad "spends almost $2 for every dollar of revenue it earns in providing intercity passenger service. . . . [and] is in a very precarious financial position. Amtrak's expenses were at least two times greater than its revenues for 28 of its 40 routes in fiscal year 1997. In addition, 14 routes lost more than $100 per passenger carried."[4]

June 5. GAO: "During fiscal year 1997, fewer than 100 passengers, on average, boarded Amtrak intercity trains and connecting buses per day in 13 states. . . . the relatively large number of states with relatively low ridership, along with other financial performance data, is indicative of Amtrak's financial performance problems."[5]

November. DOT IG: In assessing Amtrak's financial needs through 2002 and reviewing its strategic business plan, revised in March 1998, the office concludes that "several of Amtrak's financial projections are at risk of not being achieved, and thus threaten to increase Amtrak's projected cash loss."[6]

1999

March 4. DOT IG: Addresses costs in the Northeast Corridor that have grown "as a result of increasing the number and scope of the projects included in the high-speed rail budget and cost overruns on the electrification project. All project reserves have been depleted and any further cost increases will need to be funded by diverting funds from other system-wide capital needs."[7]

July. GAO: Says Amtrak is borrowing money to pay for operating expenses, "including those for payroll, fuel, ticket stock, and food."[8]

July 21. DOT IG: "We are concerned that Amtrak is spending capital funds in 1999 and 2000 on projects that go beyond minimum needs, while a gap in meeting minimum needs exists for 2001 and 2002. We believe that Amtrak's strategy is shortsighted in its failure to anticipate and set aside currently available funds as a contingency for what it knows to be future funding shortfalls."[9]

October 28. GAO: Amtrak fails to engender significant ridership increases on long-distance routes, causing the GAO to observe: "In fiscal year 1997, fewer than 100 passengers, on average, boarded Amtrak intercity trains and connecting buses per day in 13 states."[10]

2000

February. GAO: Confirms that Amtrak's quarterly reports to the Amtrak Reform Council fall short of full disclosure, stating, "As a result, these reports are less useful than they could be in helping the Council comply with its responsibility to monitor Amtrak's use of Taxpayer Relief Act funds."[11]

May 31. GAO: Notes that Amtrak attempted to reduce its management staff in 1994 and 1995 by offering employees early retirement and buyouts to leave the company. As a result, Amtrak's management staff declined by a total of about 15 percent between 1994 and 1995. But, by 1999, the number of management employees was almost the same as it was in 1994. Union-represented employment declined 7 percent from 1994 through 1996. But union-represented employment has also grown since then, and in 1999, Amtrak had more union-represented workers than in 1994.[12] Moreover, "Amtrak's operating costs increased from 1995 to 1999, and future increases are expected. Although Amtrak's business plans have attempted to keep annual cost growth at no more than the rate of inflation, Amtrak's total operating costs during the period increased about 12 percent above the rate of inflation and, in total, were about $150 million (nominal dollars) more than planned."[13]

September 19. DOT IG: A wide-ranging report finds many areas of concern, including the possibility that Amtrak's cash loss will be about $1.4 billion more than it projected for 2000–2004 and that revenues for the Acela Express were possibly overstated by $304 million. The inspector general's office noted that its earlier predictions of Amtrak's capital needs turned out to be more accurate than Amtrak's forecasts, and that the largest sources of growth in operating expenses in 1999 were due to labor costs.[14]

September 26. GAO: Testifies that "while Amtrak has 'spent money to make money,' it has realized little benefit from the expenditures it has made."[15]

2001

March 9. DOT IG: Alerts Congress to concerns with safety and accident risks in the Amtrak tunnels leading into New York.[16] (See chapter 6.)

March 19. Amtrak Reform Council: "Amtrak's performance in FY2000 was approximately $100 million short of its goal. Revenues were lower than expected, costs were higher than planned, and productivity improvements did not produce measurable financial gain."[17]

March 21. GAO: Tells Congress, "Amtrak has made minimal progress in reducing its budget gap in order to reach operational self-sufficiency."[18]

March 21. DOT IG: Warns that "Amtrak's overall financial results have not improved significantly since 1999. . . . Our assessment of Amtrak's 2000 business plan identified a number of elements that are unlikely to perform as Amtrak had expected. If no corrective action were taken to compensate for them, Amtrak's cash loss would be about $1.4 billion more than it projected over the four-year period 2001 through 2004."[19]

July 25. DOT IG: Reports Amtrak costs rising faster than revenues and a fiscal year 2000 operating loss of $944 million, the largest in history. As of September 2000, Amtrak's long-term debt and capital lease obligations totaled $2.8 billion, an increase of $1 billion over 1999. "Four years into its mandate for operating self-sufficiency, Amtrak should be showing signs of significant improvement, not standing in place or, worse, moving backwards."[20] [Note: At this time Amtrak offers 2,900 employees a voluntary separation through early retirement and other incentives.[21] Later results show this effort to reduce costs to be unsuccessful.]

November 9. Amtrak Reform Council: Issues a preliminary finding that Amtrak will not achieve operational self-sufficiency by the statutory deadline of December 2, 2002—despite repeated Amtrak assurances to the contrary—or by any reasonable later date.[22]

2002

January 24. DOT IG: Issues a major review of Amtrak, finding that despite the passage of the Amtrak Reform and Accountability Act of 1997, which gave Amtrak freedoms to improve performance, "Amtrak has not succeeded in implementing enduring financial improvements of the magnitude necessary to attain and sustain self-sufficiency in and beyond 2003. . . . For every $1 Amtrak realized in additional revenue [since December 1997] cash expenditures increased by $1.05. . . . Amtrak's operating loss in 2001 of $1.1 billion was $129 million higher than the 2000 loss and the largest in Amtrak's history."[23]

February 4. Excerpts from the proposed fiscal year 2003 federal budget: "[Amtrak] recently mortgaged Pennsylvania Station in New York over a 16-year period to cover approximately three months of operating expenses, a financial absurdity equivalent to a family taking out a second mortgage on its home to pay its grocery bills. . . . Amtrak is clearly in desperate financial condition."[24]

April. GAO: Reveals the financial performance of Amtrak routes and high losses per passenger carried, in particular noting that the amount per passenger was $347 on the Orlando–Los Angeles Sunset Limited. Such losses do not include depreciation and certain unallocated train labor costs.[25]

June 20. DOT IG: Informs Congress that "Between 1997 and 2001, Amtrak's total debt grew by about $2.7 billion, from $1.7 billion to $4.4 billion, representing an overall increase of 155 percent. Amtrak faces formidable challenges in meeting its rapidly growing debt service requirements. . . . By this fiscal year, nearly all available assets have been collateralized and Amtrak has nearly exhausted its long-term, secured debt capacity."[26]

July 15. GAO: Alerts Congress to Amtrak changes in route "profitability statements" for fiscal years 1999 and 2000. The agency concludes that "The clarity and usefulness of the schedules provided to congressional staff were impaired because there was limited explanation of how these schedules were prepared, why they changed, and how they correlated to the audited financial statements. . . . Amtrak allocated certain profits from its other business activities to its routes as a reduction in route net cost. According to Amtrak, it allocated these profits to partially offset the losses incurred on scheduled Amtrak routes. Prior to November 2001, Amtrak allocated these profits to all Amtrak routes in proportion to their share of total operating costs. In November 2001, Amtrak began allocating these profits only to routes with losses. Amtrak's allocation of these profits from its other business activities undermines the ability to assess whether or not individual routes are operated profitably."[27]

September. GAO: Finds while examining liabilities that Amtrak had concealed some costs by not revealing to congressional auditors that the interest of the preferred stockholder (the U.S. government) would be about $6 billion more than the $10.9 billion previously discussed. Says the GAO: "We noted that this $6 billion was not expressly disclosed in Amtrak's financial statements, and we brought this to Amtrak's, and its external auditor's, attention for possible future disclosure."[28]

2003

April 29. DOT IG: "As a consequence of Amtrak's external financing of its cash losses as well as new train equipment and related maintenance facilities, total debt and capital lease obligations increased by $3.1 billion, from $1.7 billion in 1997 to $4.8 billion in 2002, representing an overall increase of 178 percent. . . . Amtrak's heavy debt load was acquired during a period when Amtrak received federal operating and capital grants, as well as other federal assistance totaling $5.27 billion, or more than $1 billion annually." He also warns that debt continues to climb, saying Amtrak is "awash in debt, nearly $5 billion worth . . . which will consume more than $250 million in annual federal funding merely to service that debt."[29]

September. Congressional Budget Office: "Today, having received a total of about $27 billion in federal subsidies over 32 years, Amtrak is still teetering on the edge of bankruptcy."[30]

October 2. DOT IG: Declares the "current model is broken" while addressing Amtrak's cash operating loss, growing debt service, and declining on-time train performance: "What is not commonly understood is that these results have developed in an environment in which Amtrak has had access to external funding of $8.4 billion over the last six years (1998–2003). This is an average annual amount of $1.4 billion per year—more than twice the average $670 million in appropriated funds during this period."[31]

Appendix B

Chronology of Acela Express Development

1993

January. Amtrak begins testing and later places in commercial service the X2000 between New York and Washington. The European-designed tilting train can take curves at higher than normal speeds and could be the prototype for future Amtrak high-speed trains.[1] The train is to prove popular with passengers and operate with a high degree of reliability.

May 19. Amtrak initiates the high-speed train procurement even before it concludes testing foreign train designs. Amtrak states it will require manufacturers to "deliver two complete train sets by April 1996 and the remainder of the train sets within two years thereafter."[2] Hence, all trains are to be delivered by May 1998.

October 4. Amtrak begins trial runs in commercial service of the German-made InterCity Express, or ICE Train, between New York and Washington.[3] Passenger response is highly favorable.

November 3. Amtrak announces it "plans to award a contract by the middle of 1994 with the first trains being delivered two years later."[4]

1994

March 17. The first hint of trouble arises as Amtrak no longer refers to a 1996 delivery date and informs Congress that "two advance versions of the train sets are expected in early 1997 for testing. The remaining 24 train sets will then go into production, with the final train set arriving in 1999."[5]

Little additional public notice occurs during the year as an Amtrak design team works on specifications for the train.

1995

An Amtrak design team continues to develop specifications for the train. Little public notice occurs during the year.

1996

March 16. Amtrak no longer refers to its trains as "new Metroliners"; it now calls a desktop model the "American Flyer." Amtrak names a consortium of Bombardier Inc., of Canada and GEC Alstom of France to build eighteen American Flyer high-speed trains at a cost of $754 million. Amtrak says the trains will go into service by 1999, a two-year slip from the 1997 start previously announced.[6] Amtrak projects net income of $110 million to $150 million a year by 2002 from the service, after debt service and expenses are paid. This causes *Crain's New York Business* to observe, "To meet revenue targets, Amtrak is counting on doubling its ridership on [the route] within three years of starting the service—a huge increase that may be unrealistic. . . . Amtrak officials estimate that ridership on the Washington-to-Boston route would double to about 4 million riders a year, up from 2 million now, by 2002. They're anticipating 5 million riders by 2010, mostly business travelers."[7] Clinton administration Transportation Secretary Federico Peña says, "These trains will be the safest ever built in the world. They'll set the standards."[8]

May 1. The Bombardier-Alsthom consortium executes $1.1 billion in contracts with Amtrak to manufacture twenty Acela Express trains, construct maintenance facilities to support the trains, build fifteen "high-speed loco-motives" to pull existing Amtrak rolling stock, and provide certain man-agement services on an ongoing basis.[9]

Little other public notice occurs during the year. Preparations for manufacturing begin.

1997

April 22. Amtrak suggests that the train will be part of the solution to its financial problems, in that the railroad plans to pocket $150 million a year after paying previous debts.[10]

Little other public notice occurs during the year as manufacturing proceeds.

1998

March 18. Amtrak informs Congress that "five train sets will be delivered in late 1999, with the remaining 13 by July 2000."[11] The first train sets are now three and one-half years behind the original schedule (as announced in 1993) and two years behind the revised delivery date of trains for testing in "early 1997" (as announced in 1994).

Little other public notice occurs during the year as manufacturing proceeds.

1999

January 7. The *Washington Post* reveals that the new trains were built four inches too wide and an Amtrak official concedes that railroad officials had known about the problem since April 1997. The result is that the wider trains "cannot tilt the planned 6.5 degrees maximum without violating what is called the 'clearance envelope.' Under what is essentially a disaster scenario, there must be enough room between adjacent tracks that two passing trains could have a total suspension breakdown and lean the wrong way while still passing safely." Also, Amtrak has minimized reports that the problem would add twenty minutes to the New York–Boston schedule and instead predicts, "All else being equal, this will have a three-minute trip-time impact."[12]

March 9. At a display of the train in New York's Penn Station, Amtrak announces it is discarding "American Flyer" and, in a rebranding effort, naming the trains "Acela Express."[13] Acela is a contraction of the words "accelerate" and "excellence."

June 29. A prototype Acela Express is put on display at a maintenance base in Washington, D.C., where Amtrak President George Warrington says, "The introduction of high-speed rail later this year will add further momentum to our business plan which already is running $10 million ahead of target."[14]

August 30. Startup of the Acela Express will be delayed until next spring because of excessive wheel wear, which requires some redesign. Amtrak President Warrington says, "That slippage is one-time, and it is short-term, and it is in no way consequential to our long-term revenue or our absolute commitment to operational self-sufficiency by 2003."[15]

September 9. Amtrak will proceed with a $7 million advertising campaign to promote the Acela service, even though equipment problems have delayed the start of high-speed train service until the spring of 2000.[16]

2000

February 1. Launch of the Acela Express may be delayed until summer because, under a slow-moving testing schedule, the first train will not be available until then.[17]

March 18. A newspaper reveals loans to Amtrak, possibly totaling $1 billion, from the Canadian Export Development Corporation—loans that had previously not been disclosed in Canada—for purchases of high-speed rail equipment and maintenance facilities. The loans, some of which occurred in

1996, helped Bombardier Corporation win over two competing companies that were offering other train designs. As of August 2004, Amtrak and Canadian officials have yet to reveal terms of the loans. (See chapter 3.)[18]

May 27. Officials from the Connecticut Department of Transportation, which owns tracks between New Haven and the New York state line, along with officials from Metro-North, a commuter train operator, and Amtrak confirm that conditions between New Haven and New York prohibit use of the Acela Express tilting mechanism because of safety considerations. Among the concerns are that a tilting train could strike a platform at a train station or tilt too closely to a passing train.[19]

May 31. For the first time, Amtrak admits the Acela Express will not connect Boston and New York in three hours or less but will take "about" three hours and fifteen minutes. Amtrak says the time will be reduced to three hours "definitely within the next year or two, and hopefully sooner than that."[20]

June 20. Amtrak halts Acela Express test runs because of cracked or missing bolts in the wheel assemblies discovered during endurance testing. The problem will delay start of service until perhaps mid-August.[21]

June 30. Acela Express testing resumes following modifications to bolts in the locomotive undercarriages.[22]

July 6. Amtrak officials won't predict a date for service startup except to say the train will start carrying passengers by late August or early September.[23]

July 27. Testing is halted again after loose and broken bolts are found in another location, on antisway bars that help steady the ride of the coaches. Amtrak attributes the problem to human error.[24]

September 17. Amtrak suggests that if all goes well, service will start on October 29.[25]

October 18. Amtrak announces that the Acela Express will begin regularly scheduled trips serving passengers on December 11. Train fares will be lower than weekday walk-up airline fares but somewhat higher than some airfares on weekends or with advance purchase. Amtrak President George Warrington says value, *not price,* will be the appeal of the Acela Express (emphasis added).[26]

December 11. The first Acela Express trains begin commercial service with a Washington–Boston run.[27] Although its top speed is billed at 150 mph, the train reaches that speed on only eighteen miles of track in Rhode Island and Massachusetts. The biggest time savings comes between New York and Boston, where the new three-hour-and-twenty-three-minute schedule is faster by about forty-five to ninety minutes than current Amtrak trains.[28]

December 12. The debut of the Acela Express is marred as trips are canceled on the second day of service. Inspectors have found that the train has suffered damage to its pantograph, the metal device that connects the train to overhead electrical wires, and a second Acela Express held in reserve is also found to be inoperable.[29]

2001

January 11. Amtrak announces that in late February it will increase Acela Express schedule frequency, including adding a "non-stop super-express connecting New York and Washington in 2 hours, 28 minutes."[30]

February 22. The schedule additions are delayed, and Amtrak announces they will be put in place on March 5.[31]

April 29. Amtrak begins four daily round trips between New York and Boston and additional weekend service along the entire route.[32]

July 13. Malfunctions of Acela Express equipment have occasionally been highly visible, as in the case of a train that today loses power and coasts into the Stamford train station. Passengers are delayed for about three and a half hours.[33]

August 21. Acela Express problems become still more visible as on-time performance suffers, passenger complaints rise to three times the number of those associated with the Metroliner service it is replacing, and Amtrak concedes that ridership and revenues have not met projections. Amtrak had projected that once all trains were in service, Acela Express would post annual revenues of $300 million and net $180 million. Thomas Till, executive director of the Amtrak Reform Council, says those projections are in doubt. Also, the nonstop Acela Express between Washington and New York has not lured as many airline passengers as Amtrak had hoped it would; the nonstop is dropped and replaced by a train that stops along the way. Amtrak declines to state when full Acela Express service using all twenty trains will be in place, giving as an estimate "sometime this winter."[34] Deirdre O'Sullivan of the Amtrak Reform Council says, "The fact that Acela isn't doing what Amtrak expected is an enormous problem. Amtrak has definitely hitched its star to the Acela Express."[35]

September 11. Terrorists attack the United States by hijacking airliners and crashing them into buildings. The Federal Aviation Administration shuts down the national air system. Trains are temporarily prohibited from entering or leaving New York.

September 15. First press reports show stranded and terrified air travelers flocking to Amtrak, Greyhound, and other ground-transportation companies. Amtrak honors airline tickets of those grounded during the chaos.[36]

September 17. Amtrak says it experienced at least a 36 percent increase in riders nationally and will increase the number of Acela Express trains between Boston and Washington to ten by the end of the year.[37]

September 27. The acting chairman of Amtrak's board of directors, Michael Dukakis, says ridership in the Northeast is up 35–40 percent since the terrorist attacks.[38]

September 28. Amtrak states that traffic on the Acela Express has surged 40 percent since the terrorist attacks. Observes one journalist: "Careful to avoid appearing gleeful in the wake of the attacks, Amtrak officials say they are nevertheless delighted by their newfound popularity, which arrives as Amtrak nears a 2003 deadline to reach fiscal independence or risk dissolution by Congress."[39]

October 4. Ronald Reagan Washington National Airport reopens—the last U.S. airport to reopen following a nationwide shutdown. A Zogby International poll shows American confidence in airline security has grown, with nearly 70 percent of those surveyed saying they are confident about the air transportation system, compared with about 50 percent a week earlier.[40]

October 6. Amtrak says ridership has increased 25 percent on the Acela Express since the terrorist attacks.[41]

November 5. The US Airways shuttle between Boston and Washington's Reagan National Airport, which resumed with just four daily flights, now runs fourteen, and many are oversold. The Delta Shuttle is running seventeen times each weekday between Boston and New York, a normal schedule.[42]

November 8. Bombardier Corporation, the manufacturer of the Acela Express, files a lawsuit against Amtrak for $200 million, saying that the railroad has disrupted its ability to produce the train efficiently. In turn, Amtrak accuses the company of having a record of failure that is "staggering" and claims it is trying to shift blame for program mismanagement onto the railroad. Bombardier President Peter Stangl says the relationship with Amtrak has sullied the name of his company.[43]

November 30. The Amtrak Reform Council reports ridership figures that contradict Amtrak's projections that traffic would boom in the weeks following the September 11 attacks. Nationwide ridership was actually lower each day in the week after the attacks compared to the week before. Overall, Amtrak's ridership was down 6 percent in September and 1 percent in October, compared with a year earlier. Amtrak says its projection of a 17 percent boost in traffic the week following the attacks was based on an established formula based on tickets sold, but many passengers canceled their train travel plans.[44] Asks Paul Weyrich, a member of the

Amtrak Reform Council, "If they couldn't get a spike in ridership where the airlines were shut down, where thousands of people were afraid to fly, when are they going to get it?"[45]

2002

January 17. Amtrak and Continental Airlines enter into an arrangement whereby travelers between Newark International Airport and certain cities can book train travel to and from the airport as part of their flight reservation.[46]

January 29. Amtrak expands Acela Express service by adding six weekend trains between New York and Boston and seven additional round trips between New York and Washington; it also launches a Guest Rewards points incentive program to lure additional travelers.[47]

April 11. In congressional testimony, railroad consultant William Rennicke reveals that he recently distributed to a number of companies a blueprint for possible private participation in U.S. passenger rail service, and among those that responded to express interest was France's Alstom Ltd., part of the consortium building the Acela Express.[48]

April 26. David L. Gunn is appointed Amtrak president and chief executive officer, effective May 15.[49]

August 1. Competition increases in the Northeast. Delta Air Lines and US Airways have long operated shuttle flights in the region, and today American Airlines begins shuttle service between Reagan National Airport in Washington, LaGuardia Airport in New York, and Logan International Airport in Boston. The airline's affiliate, American Eagle, will use Embraer regional planes for the service.[50]

August 6. The Acela Express is breaking down so often and its on-time record is so bad—the worst of any Northeast Corridor train—that older Metroliners may begin substituting on some trips. "This train is causing us a lot of trouble," David Gunn tells the *Washington Post*. "I'm not going to order any more of those." He says the next generation of high-speed train is more likely to be a modified version of an already successful European train.[51] Bombardier Corporation issues an unusual defense in which it points out the customer's shortcomings. The company remarks that several of the train's defects "were the direct result of the customer's specifications," and that when the manufacturer "repeatedly warned" Amtrak about deficiencies, Amtrak nonetheless insisted on the designs.[52]

August 13. Amtrak suspends operation of all eighteen Acela Express trains after discovering cracks and breaks in the wheel assemblies of eight of the trains. The defects could cause a derailment.[53]

August 15. Previously undetected defects in shock-absorbing equipment cause Amtrak to cancel plans to return some Acela Express trains to service today.[54]

August 19. Amtrak says nine of its eighteen Acela Express trains will be restored to service today as repairs are moving more quickly than expected.[55]

August 20. Amtrak suffers another delay in restoring Acela Express service as new cracks are found in shock-absorbing assemblies on four of the eight trains Amtrak had intended to operate. [56]

October 28. For the first time since mechanical problems arose in August, Amtrak is running a full Acela Express schedule between New York and Boston, while service remains at reduced levels between New York and Washington.[57]

November 22. Amtrak countersues the Canadian-French consortium that built the Acela Express, asking for more than $200 million in damages. Among other issues, Amtrak says all the trains were delivered a year later than originally stipulated, some more than two years late.[58]

December 20. On the Acela Express's second birthday, the service still is not running at full strength, some trains remain under repair, and one train has yet to be delivered by the builders. Modifications were made in the manufacturing process as each train was built, so each train is different. An Amtrak spokesman refers to the design and mechanical flaws as "kinks."[59]

2003

March 29. Amtrak cancels nine of forty-four Acela Express trains after inspectors find indications of substandard maintenance practices by the Northeast Corridor Management Service Consortium, a unit of the Bombardier-Alstom consortium whose managers oversee Amtrak employees in the work.[60]

April 23. Amtrak says it will reduce fares 22 percent on Acela Express Service between New York and Boston, to $99, with off-peak tickets at $85.[61] The action contradicts Amtrak's October 18, 2000, statement that "value, not price will be the appeal of the Acela Express."

April 28. Amtrak begins permitting Connecticut commuters on cheap monthly passes to ride the Acela Express at no extra charge.[62] The action boosts ridership but does virtually nothing for revenues. The action is also another violation of Amtrak's October 18, 2000, assertion that "value, not price will be the appeal of the Acela Express."

August 10. Reuters News reports that airlines have regained New York–Washington business lost to Amtrak after the 2001 terrorist attacks. Train traffic eroded during late 2001 and through 2002, and by January 2003 airlines had overtaken Amtrak. Both US Airways and Delta have restored their full schedules of shuttle flights. Between New York and Washington for April through June 2003, traffic on the Acela Express and Metroliner trains was off a combined 17 percent.[63]

September 10. Amtrak launches low-fare deals where a traveler takes only two Acela Express round trips and earns a free companion ticket for use on a future trip to anywhere in Amtrak's system, with no limit on the number of certificates earned and no restrictions on to whom they may be transferred.[64] Amtrak's yield per passenger carried is lowered.

September 28. David Gunn admits what his predecessors at Amtrak had not about the high-speed rail program: "The truth is this thing went off the rails in terms of time and cost."[65]

October 15. Amtrak acknowledges that Acela Express ridership is down from 2,473,921 in fiscal year 2002 to 2,363,454 in fiscal year 2003, a 4.5 percent decline. Combined Acela Express–Metroliner traffic fell in the same period from 3,213,981 to 2,936,885, a reduction of 8.6 percent.[66]

October 27. With Acela Express trains late nearly 30 percent of the time, Amtrak will boost reliability by cutting weekend service in half to allow more time for maintenance, and several stops will be eliminated to enhance prospects for on-time performance.[67]

2004

January 27. Amtrak has billed itself as an alternative to airports during bad weather. However, although airport delays are expected because of a snow and ice storm, Amtrak cancels eleven Acela Express trains, seven Metroliners, and several regional trains.[68]

February 25. Amtrak's first publication about accepting the twentieth and last Acela Express, which had occurred in June 2003, is buried in a note in its consolidated financial statements for the 2003 fiscal year.[69] Considering Amtrak's assertion to the media that it will receive its final train in 1998, and before Congress that it will receive its final train in 1999, this delivery is between four and five years late.[70]

March 8. The GAO holds Amtrak accountable for failure to operate Acela Express trains between Boston and New York in three hours. The GAO concludes that Amtrak did not comprehensively plan or manage improvements to Boston–Washington infrastructure. The agency also finds that Amtrak stated it was relying on the three-hour goal to help it attract the ridership and revenue necessary to achieve ARAA-mandated self-sufficiency. As recently as 2000, Amtrak's chairman testified before Congress that Amtrak would achieve the three-hour goal between Boston and New York City. Continues the GAO, "Such statements indicate that, rather than abandoning the 3-hour trip-time goal, Amtrak continued to publicly represent until at least 2000 that it would attain this goal—a goal established by the 1992 Amtrak Authorization and Development Act."[71]

March 17. Amtrak and the Bombardier-Alstom consortium announce an out-of-court settlement regarding all Acela Express legal disputes. The consortium will be entitled to receive up to $42.5 million against approximately $70 million that Amtrak previously withheld.[72] Neither party receives the large settlements they had sought. When the Acela Express deliveries were delayed, Amtrak had said that the holdups would not affect profitability or Amtrak's ability to attain financial self-sufficiency, because Amtrak anticipated recovering substantial liquidated damages from Bombardier due to the late delivery of the equipment. The appearance that Amtrak has come out ahead by $27.5 million ($70 million less $42.5 million) is misleading because the consortium will terminate its Acela Express maintenance role in October 2006, about seven years earlier than called for in the prior agreement. Amtrak prepaid for maintenance oversight as part of Acela Express's acquisition cost. With the contract term being reduced, Amtrak's maintenance expenses will increase in ways that had not been anticipated when the program began. Thus, the value of Amtrak's total "award" is likely lower than it appears to be.

April 26. Amtrak adds four weekday Acela Express trains between New York and Washington, bringing to thirty (fifteen in each direction) the number of weekday trains south of New York. The new schedule calls for fifteen train sets to be in commercial service on a typical weekday, up from fourteen.[73]

Appendix C

The Breadth and Depth of Worldwide Rail Privatization

See table 8-1 for a listing of rail privatization and devolvement efforts in fifty-five nations throughout the world. Other rail privatization experience, intended to illustrate the scope of such activity, is summarized below.

North America

In addition to the Conrail, Alaska Railroad, and Rocky Mountaineer experiences described in chapter 7, the following North American experiences are noteworthy:

Canada. Rail reform began in 1988 when B.C. Hydro Railway was privatized. Now known as the Southern Railway of British Columbia Limited, it operates under a long-term licensing arrangement with the provincial government that is in effect until 2064. The railroad's president, John van der Burch, has reported that fifteen years after privatization, carloads have increased by 47 percent. He has said that the railroad is a "great example" of how a government-owned asset can perform under private-sector management.[1]

That experience was followed on a transcontinental scale with the privatization of the Canadian National Railway (CN). The sale of nearly 84 million shares brought proceeds of $2.1 billion, making CN one of the largest initial public offerings in the North American market in 1995.[2]

Since then, the CN has performed exceptionally well, with a 2003 operating ratio below 70 percent. Since the company's initial public offering through 2004, the cash dividend has increased annually eight times for a total of almost 200 percent, and the share price has increased by more than 500 percent.[3]

Meanwhile, British Columbia moved to privatize BC Rail as a method of obtaining additional capital investment in the railroad without incurring new public debt. In the fifteen years leading up to 2003, BC Rail cost taxpayers C$857 million in asset write-offs and accumulated a debt of C$502 million. Under the model, BC Rail's rights-of-way and tracks would remain publicly owned while the private sector would operate and manage the freight service and provide improvements.[4]

Competition became intense with bids from the Canadian Pacific Railway, Canadian National Railway, and OmniTRAX, in partnership with the Burlington Northern Santa Fe Railroad and RailAmerica. The winner was CN, which will spend C$1 billion to lease BC Rail for sixty years.[5] CN has announced it expects to earn an annual $100 million profit by luring more freight as it cuts travel time to railroad freight centers like Chicago. A government-commissioned report said, "The financial value obtained by the province was above what might be expected," and municipalities along the rail line will benefit from receiving new property tax payments substantially above the amount BC Rail paid as an annual grant in lieu of taxes.[6] The transaction was completed on July 14, 2004, and CN began a step-by-step integration of BC Rail into its system.[7]

Mexico. The old National Railways of Mexico had a legacy of poor service and high government subsidies. By the early 1990s, it needed hundreds of millions of dollars in capital improvements, which the government found unaffordable. Officials recognized that the private sector had to be enlisted to improve efficiency, especially with growing shipper demands resulting from the North American Free Trade Agreement (NAFTA). Mexico's constitution was modified to permit railway privatization, and, starting in 1996–97, the government sold portions of the railway as fifty-year concessions.[8]

Privatization eliminated freight subsidies and brought in more than $2.5 billion as assets were sold to the private sector. Over the five-year period leading up to 2000, private-sector investments totaled $1.3 billion, and freight traffic grew by 49 percent.[9] Results for 2003 were mixed because of negatives that had nothing to do with the rail system (for example, reduced automobile production and a 12 percent peso devaluation from the prior year), and positives that had everything to do with railroad management (such as a significant conversion of truck shipments to rail, which was one of the objectives of privatization).[10]

Unfortunately, the process for granting concessions created cost disparities and made it difficult for companies to reach agreements on shared use of tracks.[11] Although the issue has proved thorny, there has been no movement to bring back a nationalized rail system and its inherent inefficiencies.

Latin America

Argentina. Privatization has improved passenger service in Argentina's heavily populated areas. The number of commuter passengers has grown from 212 million under state ownership in 1993 to 476 million under concessionaire operations in 2000, a 125 percent increase. As a measure of efficiency, the number of commuter passengers jumped from 17,670 per employee to 62,300 per employee in the same period, a 253 percent increase. Prior to privatization, subsidies reached $1.3 billion on revenues of $500 million; afterward, subsidies were eliminated for intercity passenger and freight services, and the amount for commuter and metro services declined from $300 million to $50 million.[12]

Prior to major reforms, the rail system represented the worst of a nationalized system—it operated lightly used passenger trains in rural territories at a tremendous financial loss and kept redundant tracks. Facilities were kept open more to create employment than to serve a transport need, and management showed little innovation. In 1990, according to Jorge H. Kogan and Louis S. Thompson, privatization experts at the World Bank,

> There was no further hope for a company that was mainly a provider of surplus employment and uneconomic services, subject to political pressure, and strongly influenced by workers'

unions, suppliers, and local authorities. There were two options: let the situation continue until the railroad collapsed, or do something drastic.[13]

In 1991 Argentina received a $300 million World Bank loan to invest in rail facilities and make severance payments, actions designed to attract buyers. The railroad was separated into thirty-year concessions for those willing to pay fees to the government and provide capital for improvements to revive freight traffic. A concession process that included subsidies was used for local passenger service. As most long-distance passenger trains incurred large deficits, the national government stopped subsidizing them, and about 70 percent were discontinued. The freight railroads retained some passenger trains after provinces agreed to provide subsidies.

Other Latin American Countries. A total of thirteen Latin American countries have privatized railways from the early 1990s to the present, namely Argentina, Bolivia, Brazil, Chile, Colombia, Costa Rica, Ecuador, Guatemala, Panama, Paraguay, Peru, Uruguay, and Venezuela.

Europe

European Union. Any country with membership in the European Union is prohibited from having profitable rail freight operations cross-subsidize passenger service that is operating at a loss. This regulation, along with higher passenger-train deficits and rail's continuing loss of market share to air and roadway systems, is causing railroads throughout Europe to move from all-public operations to include private-sector involvement. The exception is eastern Europe, where many passenger trains are simply being discontinued.[14]

Germany. Germany started the privatization process when it regionalized thirty-nine routes in the mid-1990s and gave local authorities the right to decide rail issues for which they held financial responsibility.[15] Since then, the railroad has been split into commercial and public-sector functions. The commercial portion became a joint-stock company, Deutsche

Bahn AG (DBAG). While the government owns all the stock, privatization will follow after the railroad becomes financially self-sufficient and able to enter the capital markets as a full-fledged commercial business.[16] Plans are to put the state-owned railway on the market piecemeal, with a stake of 15–20 percent to be offered initially. The railway is experiencing increased losses on long-distance passenger trains because of competition by Europe's influx of low-cost airlines, and it saw a sales decline in the early part of 2003.[17] In mid-2004, the German Railway Advisory Council recommended listing DBAG on the German stock market in 2006. Meeting that date may be difficult because a new study has been initiated to determine the potential of privatizing the railroad without selling off the infrastructure.[18] Meanwhile, the British rail and bus operator, Arriva, has purchased Prignitzer Railway Group to position itself to bid on Germany's upcoming passenger rail franchising opportunities.[19]

Norway. In the emerging rail privatization program, limited private-sector competition began in 2003 as a new company, Ofotbanen AS, began running passenger services on the Ofoten–Narvik line. Both Connex and Arriva have expressed interest in bidding for future Norwegian rail passenger contracts.[20] In the longer term, for operations starting in 2008, Norway is set to approve private participation in railroad capital projects whereby a concession company would finance, design, and build facilities and then operate them for twenty-five years, earning annual fees from the states.[21]

Poland. The restructuring and privatization process of the Polish State Railways (PKP) was set in motion with the passage of laws in 2000 and 2001.[22] The World Bank followed that action with a $101 million loan to help PKP ease restructuring by providing early retirement and severance packages to up to 37,000 workers. The Polish government intends to restructure PKP to be more responsive to the needs of a market economy, reduce its burden on taxpayers, and make subsidiary units more viable for privatization.[23]

Russia. Privatization in the purest capitalist sense is not yet on the agenda in Russia, but startling reforms are, including breaking up the Rail Ministry's monopolistic control of the far-flung rail system and injecting some market-based principles. The restructuring plan may include devolvement of commuter and long-distance passenger trains so that they no longer remain responsibilities of the national government.[24]

Spain. The Public Works Ministry has announced that it will end a sixty-two-year exclusive franchise held by the government operation, *Red Nacional de Ferrocarriles Españoles* (RENFE), and by 2005 permit private contractors to run passenger and freight services in a competitive concessionaire program.[25]

Sweden. Swedish State Railways is the long-distance passenger train operator; its monopoly will likely be erased in the future as passenger services are franchised.[26]

Other European Countries. Other nations in various stages of studying or planning the privatization of railroads include Austria, the Czech Republic, Estonia, Latvia, Lithuania, the Netherlands, and Romania.

Middle East

The Iranian Islamic Republic Railways is in the process of privatizing the majority of its track maintenance.[27] In Israel, the transport ministry launched a competition that will be decided in 2004 for a thirty-two-year concession to build and operate a transit line in Tel Aviv.[28] Jordan plans to split the Aqaba Railway Company into a government-owned property with operations sold to the private sector, an effort that is moving forward under World Bank guidelines.[29] The Saudi Railways Organization is seeking private participation in constructing two new lines—a land bridge linking the Red Sea port of Jeddah to the Arabian Gulf port of Dammam via Riyadh and a rail link between the holy cities of Makkah and Madinah via Jeddah. Bids will be sought in 2005 for concessions, which will be granted to the private sector for a term ranging from twenty-five to fifty years. Passenger train service will be part of the concession package.[30]

Africa

Privatization of rail freight and passenger services is underway in Africa. The nations that have implemented privatization at least in part are Ivory Coast, Mozambique, and Zimbabwe. Other countries that will award concessions in 2004 and 2005 and are in the phase of advertising for expressions of interest are Congo, Djibouti-Ethiopia (joint concession), Ghana, Madagascar, Tanzania, and Zambia.

Asian Pacific

Australia. Regional passenger rail services in Melbourne are now operated under a concessioning arrangement with Connex, which in turn has awarded a contract to Alstom to maintain tracks, overhead electrification, and more than two hundred stations.[31] That is one outgrowth of rail privatization, which started in 1977 when the Australian National was sold to private-sector interests.[32] The government's next step was to sell its majority stake in National Rail, a freight operator.[33] Efforts to increase rail usage included constructing a long-proposed railroad line linking Alice Springs with Darwin across Australia's Outback. Approximately 70 percent of the cost of building the north–south railway came from private investments in a "boot" (build–own–operate–transfer) arrangement, while the remainder came from public expenditures. A consortium invested in the line, and Freight Link now operates its trains over it in a fifty-year concession from the federal government.[34] The line opened in January 2004 for freight, but it is also used by the famous passenger train, The Ghan.[35]

South Korea. The private sector is leading the construction of a major rail project. A consortium has won a thirty-year concession to build and operate the rail link between central Seoul and Inchon Airport; construction has begun and the line is expected to open in stages in 2007 and 2010. The Korea Development Bank will arrange debt financing for part of the cost for the $3.5 billion project. The line will have a dual role in carrying airport passengers and local commuters. Trains serving airport passengers will offer baggage stowage areas, while trains designed for commuters will be equipped with double doors for faster loading and unloading.[36]

New Zealand. The Auckland Regional Council conducted a competition to award a concession to operate the city's commuter trains, and three companies—Stagecoach, Serco, and Connex—competed for the award. Connex was declared the winner. It will operate the trains and stations, but the public agency will continue to own both.[37]

From a national standpoint, rail privatization is undergoing change. Burdened by debt, the government sold New Zealand Rail in 1993 to the Tranz Rail Limited, a consortium, for $220 million.[38] Tranz Rail's initial years of operation were praiseworthy, but service deteriorated as ownership within the consortium changed. New arrangements are being put in place that will result in renewed public ownership of infrastructure while Tranz Rail is taken over by Toll Holdings of Australia. The outcome is viewed as positive by the *New Zealand Herald*, which observed, "For all this risk, there is the potential for considerable gain. Toll will bring capital, an efficient IT system, and a reputation for good service. It also appears confident it can repeat events in Australia by doubling the freight carried by rail."[39] Toll has assumed control of Tranz Scenic, which operates the intercity passenger trains, and Toll also now operates the suburban passenger trains in Wellington.[40]

Appendix D

Legislation Reflecting Reform Attempts

The Amtrak Reform and Accountability Act (ARAA) fell far short of the mark in bringing about true reforms. It is instructive to review other legislation proposed in recent years to gain a sense of what some members of Congress have attempted to accomplish. This is not an exhaustive list:

I. *1997:* Republican representative Frank R. Wolf of Virginia introduces the Amtrak Route Closure and Realignment Act, which would create a commission patterned after the military base-closing commission. Named the Total Realignment of Amtrak Commission, it would be empowered to terminate Amtrak routes and authorize the continued operation of promising routes.[1]

II. *1997:* Representative Joel Hefley, Republican from Colorado, introduces the Amtrak Privatization Act, designed to put Amtrak on a more business-like footing, permit discontinuance of money-losing routes, limit any employee-protection payment to six months, and decrease subsidies over a four-year period.[2]

III. *1997:* The Amtrak Reform and Accountability Act is passed (see chapter 2). Because of the ARAA's reforms and the substantial cash infusion from the Taxpayer Relief Act of 1997, other, more stringent legislation is not enacted into law.

IV. *1998–2001:* The introduction of new legislation is at a low ebb as many legislators take a wait-and-see approach and monitor Amtrak's performance under the ARAA.

V. *2001:* Republican representative John Mica of Florida, in response to Amtrak's impending financial collapse, introduces the Systemic

Passenger Infrastructure and Network Overhaul through Financial Freedom Act (aka SPINOFF), which seeks to transfer the Northeast Corridor and the Auto Train to the Transportation Department to operate on an interim basis while a competitive selection process is launched to award operating rights to a contractor.[3]

VI.   *2002:* Senator John McCain, Republican from Arizona, introduces the Rail Passenger Service Improvement Act, a comprehensive proposal to restructure Amtrak by creating a franchising office within the Department of Transportation, along with an Amtrak Control Board to oversee financial plans, budget, and privatization, and by requiring that states play a greater role in route decisions and financial contributions.[4]

VII.   *2003:* At the request of the Bush administration, Senator McCain introduces the Passenger Rail Investment Reform Act, which creates three separate corporations, including a commission to manage operations between Boston and Washington under a ninety-nine-year lease from the federal government. It also schedules a five-year phaseout of operating subsidies to Amtrak's long-distance routes; transfers certain real estate assets such as Chicago Union Station and Penn Station in New York to appropriate state authorities; liquidates unneeded real estate and other facilities; and cancels more than $10 billion in accrued (but unpaid) dividends on preferred stock that Amtrak owes the United States. Capital grants would be issued to improve rail facilities on a matching basis with state governments. A remnant Amtrak organization would exist to lend to other operating entities its right to operate passenger trains on freight railroads.[5]

VIII. *2004:* Senator McCain introduces the Rail Passenger Service Restructuring, Reauthorization, and Development Act. It adopts the core concepts for reform advanced by the Bush administration's bill, above, but it modifies allowable times and some terms for certain reforms; it also terminates authority for the General Services Administration to provide services to Amtrak, a cost-saving luxury that no private-sector company has and which poses a handicap to companies that want to compete with Amtrak.[6]

Notes

Introduction

1. David W. Kendall, letter addressed to "American Traveler," Amtrak Nationwide Schedules of Intercity Passenger Service, effective May 1, 1971, inside front cover.

2. Wendell Cox, "Amtrak, Passenger Rail and Federal Policy: A Return to the Basics," remarks prepared for "All Aboard? A Private Solution for Amtrak," Heritage Foundation Forum, Washington, D.C., April 28, 1998, 2.

3. Steve Jordon and Virgil Larson, "U.P. Executive Criticizes Subsidies for Amtrak," *Omaha World-Herald*, April 19, 2003, 1a.

4. On July 7, 2004, the General Accounting Office changed its name to the Government Accountability Office; references are to what the agency's name was at the time it issued the particular report being cited.

5. Joseph Vranich, testimony before the Senate Committee on Commerce, Science, and Transportation, *Oversight Hearing on Amtrak*, 106th Cong., 2nd sess., September 26, 2000.

6. Senator John McCain, "Senate Approves Amtrak Reform," press release, November 7, 1997, 1.

7. Leslie Miller, "Homeland Security to Test Rail Screening," Associated Press, March 22, 2004.

8. Jonathan Rauch, *Demosclerosis: The Silent Killer of American Government* (New York: Times Books, 1994).

9. Brian Tracy, *Maximum Achievement* (New York: Simon and Schuster, 1993), 87.

10. The quote is from Amtrak Chairman and Wisconsin Governor Tommy G. Thompson in Richard P. Jones, "Amtrak to Serve Lake Geneva," *Milwaukee Journal Sentinel*, June 12, 2000.

11. Amtrak Chief Financial Officer Elizabeth Reveal, quoted by Jackie Spinner, "Amtrak's CFO Is Well Acquainted With Fiscal Chaos," *Washington Post*, July 31, 1995, F9.

Chapter 1: A Brief History of Amtrak

1. George W. Hilton, *Amtrak, The National Railroad Passenger Corporation* (Washington, D.C.: AEI Press, 1980), 13. See also 3–4 for a statistical table that details the decline in traffic from 1920 through 1970.

2. *Rail Passenger Service Act*, Public Law 91-518, *U.S. Statutes at Large* 84 (1970): 1327.

3. U.S. Congressional Budget Office, *Budget Options* (Washington, D.C.: Congressional Budget Office, February 2001), Option 400-01. at www.cbo.gov/showdoc.cfm?index=2731&sequence=0.

4. Press accounts and official documents in 1970 referred to the planned railroad as "Railpax," which was discarded when the railroad's incorporators settled on the name Amtrak.

5. James Beggs, under secretary of transportation, letter to John D. Ehrlichman, White House, February 18, 1970, 8, exhibit C.

6. Anthony Haswell, "Amtrak: The Reality Tarnishes the Crusade," *Journal of Commerce*, January 7, 2000.

7. Readers wanting to know more about Amtrak prior to 1997 are encouraged to examine my book, *Derailed: What Went Wrong and What to Do About America's Passenger Trains*, published that year by St. Martin's Press. Also, an excellent review of Amtrak's first decade is in Hilton's *Amtrak: The National Railroad Passenger Corporation*.

8. See Hilton's discussion of elasticity of demand and related conditions in ibid., 36–42, where he cites internal Amtrak memoranda.

9. "Amtrak Under the Gunn," *Wall Street Journal,* June 24, 2002, A16.

Chapter 2: The Failure of Amtrak Reform Efforts

1. John Volpe quoted in Robert Lindsey, "Nixon Drafts Bill for Body to Run Passenger Trains," *New York Times*, January 19, 1970, 43; Mr. Volpe is quoted again to that effect in "Railroad Mercy Killing," *New York Times*, December 6, 1970, 10.

2. Robert Lindsey, "For Generations, Railroads Gauged the Nation's Growth," *New York Times,* May 1, 1971, 34.

3. National Railroad Passenger Corporation and Subsidiaries (Amtrak), *FY 05 Grant and Legislative Request* (Washington, D.C.: Amtrak, February 10, 2004), 1.

4. National Railroad Passenger Corporation (Amtrak), KPMG auditor's letter, *Consolidated Financial Statements, September 30, 2003 and 2002*, February 25, 2004 (Washington, D.C.: Amtrak, 2004).

5. House Committee on Transportation and Infrastructure, Working Group on Inter-City Passenger Rail, *A New Vision for America's Passenger Rail*, 105th Cong., 1st sess., 1997. Statements are summarized from various pages.

6. Ibid., appendix D, 3.

7. Anick Jesdanun, "Panel Urges Competition for Amtrak's Franchise," Associated Press, June 26, 1997, quoting panel member Patrick Cleary.

8. HR 1788, 104th Cong., 1st sess., 1995.

9. HR 2247, 105th Cong., 1st sess., 1997.

10. David Field, "Amtrak Rolls Toward Strike Oct. 22," *USA Today*, October 14, 1997, 1B.

11. Overview of the essential points regarding the Amtrak Reform Council are found in Amtrak Reform and Accountability Act of 1997, Public Law 105-134, Title II—Fiscal Accountability, secs. 201–5 and sec. 209(a)(2)(b), *U.S Statutes at Large* 111 (1997): 2570.

12. Senator John McCain, Hearing of the Committee on Commerce, Science, and Transportation, *Amtrak Nomination Hearing*, 105th Cong., 2nd sess., September 22, 1998, 2.

13. Anthony Haswell, "Which Way for Amtrak?" *Washington Post*, July 24, 1998, A19.

14. Gilbert Nicholson, "Birmingham-to-Dallas Train Starts in Spring," *Birmingham Business Journal*, December 29, 2000.

15. Gilbert Nicholson, "Amtrak's Dallas Route Sidetracked by Money," *Birmingham Business Journal*, March 9, 2001.

16. See White House, "Personnel Announcement," press releases of September 12, 2003, 1, and February 6, 2004, 1. Also see Don Phillips, "3 Eyed for Amtrak Panel," *Washington Post*, September 13, 2003, E1.

17. See White House, "Personnel Announcement," press releases of July 1, 2004, 1, and July 30, 2004, 1.

18. W. Graham Claytor Jr., "A Penny for Amtrak," *Washington Post*, April 28, 1992, A15.

19. National Railroad Passenger Corporation (Amtrak), *Strategic Business Plan FY 1999–2002* (Washington, D.C.: Amtrak, October 12, 1998), 3.

20. Don Phillips, "Warrington Named Amtrak President," *Washington Post*, December 22, 1998, A21.

21. National Railroad Passenger Corporation (Amtrak), *Strategic Business Plan FY 2000–2004* (Washington, D.C.: Amtrak, 1999), 2.

22. Tommy G. Thompson, "Amtrak Is on Track to Get Rid of Federal Subsidies," letter to the editor, *Business Week*, October 18, 1999.

23. House Committee on Transportation and Infrastructure, Subcommittee on Ground Transportation, *Oversight of Amtrak*, 106th Cong., 1st sess., October 28, 1999, 1–2.

24. The quote for Thompson as well as Moody's appeared in "Amtrak Surpasses Business Plan Target, Remains on Track To Become Operationally Self-Sufficient," Amtrak press release, ATK-00-06, January 23, 2000, 1–2.

25. Larry Sandler, "Thompson Disputes Report Criticizing Amtrak," *Milwaukee Journal Sentinel*, January 25, 2000.

26. Senate Committee on Commerce, Science, and Transportation, *Oversight Hearing on Amtrak*, 106th Cong., 2nd sess., September 26, 2000, 1, 6.

27. Tim Dobbyn, "Amtrak Seen Facing Huge Task to Meet 2003 Deadline," Reuters, September 26, 2000.

28. House Committee on Appropriations, Subcommittee on Transportation and Related Agencies, *Hearing on FY2000 appropriations for National Railroad Passenger Corporation (Amtrak)*, 106th Cong., 1st sess., March 4, 1999, 1; see also Tim Dobbyn, "Amtrak Chief Seeks Decision on Rail's Direction," Reuters, May 24, 2001.

29. U.S. General Accounting Office, *How Much Federal Subsidy Will Amtrak Need?* GAO/RED-76-97 (Washington, D.C.: Government Printing Office, April 21, 1976), 5.

30. David Keating, National Taxpayers Union, letter to members of the U.S. House of Representatives, November 13, 1997.

31. Senator John McCain, press release, July 18, 1997, 1–2.

32. Amtrak, untitled press release, ATK-97-162, July 30, 1997.

33. National Railroad Passenger Corporation (Amtrak), *Quarterly Report on TRA Expenditures* (Washington D.C.: Amtrak, July 1998), 1; ibid., December 1998, 1.

34. Taxpayer Relief Act of 1997, sec. 977(e)(1).

35. National Railroad Passenger Corporation (Amtrak), *Making Investments in America's Passenger Rail System: Amtrak's Quarterly Report on TRA Funding* (Washington, D.C.: Amtrak, July 31, 1998), 1.

36. Ibid., 2.

37. Stephen J. Thompson, *Amtrak and the 105th Congress* (Washington, D.C.: Congressional Research Service, updated August 18, 1998), CRS-2.

38. Amtrak Reform Council, *A Preliminary Assessment of Amtrak* (Washington, D.C.: Government Printing Office, January 24, 2000), v.

39. Amtrak Reform Council, *Intercity Rail Passenger Service in America: Status, Problems, and Options for Reform* (Washington, D.C.: Government Printing Office, March 19, 2001), 4.

40. The $300 million loan was arranged without informing the Amtrak Reform Council until it was awaiting approval by the secretary of transportation.

41. Senate Committee on Appropriations, Transportation Appropriations Subcommittee, *Hearing to Examine the Status of Intercity Transportation*, 107th Cong., 1st sess., June 28, 2001, 2.

42. Joint letter from the senators to Transportation Secretary Norman Mineta, June 22, 2001.

43. House Committee on Transportation and Infrastructure, Subcommittee on Railroads, *The Congress Faces Critical Decisions about the Role of and Funding for Intercity Passenger Rail Systems*, 107th Cong., 1st sess., July 25, 2001, 1.

44. Don Phillips, "The View From the Ground; Amtrak: The Boost That Began September 11 May Not Be Temporary," *Washington Post*, September 23, 2001, H01.

45. Amtrak Reform Council, "Resolution," in *An Action Plan for the Restructuring and Rationalization of the National Intercity Rail Passenger System: Report to Congress* (Washington, D.C.: Government Printing Office, February 7, 2002), 80.

46. Ibid., 3.

47. Ibid., 4.

48. Amtrak Reform Council, letter to President George W. Bush, November 14, 2001, 1.

49. This is a sample of examples cited in an eight-page summary, *Statutory Factors Considered in Finding*, issued by the Amtrak Reform Council (Washington, D.C.: Government Printing Office, February 7, 2002).

50. Amtrak Reform Council, letter of transmittal, *An Action Plan for the Restructuring and Rationalization of the National Intercity Rail Passenger System*, 1.

51. Infrastructure includes railroad tracks, bridges, tunnels, signaling and communications systems, electrical power distribution systems, and associated stations and other buildings needed to support rail passenger service.

52. Amtrak Reform Council, *An Action Plan for the Restructuring and Rationalization of the National Intercity Rail Passenger System*, summarized from 29–37.

53. Ibid., ii.

54. Amtrak Reform and Accountability Act, Public Law 105-134, Title II, Fiscal Accountability, sec. 204(c)(2), *U.S. Statutes at Large* 111 (1997): 2570.

55. U.S. General Accounting Office, *Issues Associated with a Possible Amtrak Liquidation*, GAO/RCED-98-60 (Washington, D.C.: Government Printing Office, March 2, 1998), 2.

56. Robert P. Murphy, general counsel, General Accounting Office, letter to Representative Bud Shuster, chairman, House Committee on Transportation and Infrastructure, October 20, 1997, 6.

57. U.S. General Accounting Office, *Potential Financial Issues in the Event That Amtrak Undergoes Liquidation*, GAO/RCED-02-871 (Washington, D.C.: Government Printing Office, September 2002), 4.

58. Douglas G. Baird, "The Hidden Virtues of Chapter 11: An Overview of the Law and Economics of Financially Distressed Firms," *Chicago Working Papers in Law and Economics*, no. 43 (second series) (Chicago: University of Chicago Law School, March 1997), 20–21.

59. S. Daggett, *Railroad Reorganization* (Chevy Chase, Md.: Beard Books, 1999), v.

60. U.S. General Accounting Office, *Issues Associated with a Possible Amtrak Liquidation*, 14.

61. Bankruptcy Reform Act of 1978, as amended, USC 11 (1978), sec. 101 et seq.

62. Laurence Arnold, "A Democratic Foe Returns to Challenge Whitman, This Time on Amtrak," Associated Press, July 31, 1998.

63. Mark Murray, "Amtrak's Bumpy Ride," *National Journal*, October 30, 1999, 3136.

64. Amtrak, "Amtrak Response to the Final Report of the Amtrak Reform Council," press release ATK-02-030, February 7, 2002, 1.

65. Wendell Cox, "Derailed: The Amtrak Problem," *National Review Online*, February 5, 2002, www.nationalreview.com (accessed February 5, 2002).

66. Wendell Cox, "No Bailout for Amtrak; Board Members Should Resign," *Heritage Foundation WebMemo no. 108*, June 6, 2002, www.heritage.org/Research/Budget/WM108.cfm (accessed July 28, 2004).

67. Tom Ramstack, "Amtrak Reaches End of the Line," *Washington Times*, February 24, 2002.

68. Don Phillips, "Amtrak President Ready to Depart," *Washington Post*, March 7, 2002, E01.

69. This was Amendment No. 2458 to H.R. 3338, the Department of Defense Appropriation Act, 2002, passed by the Senate on December 7, 2001, and agreed to in a House-Senate conference on December 20, 2001. See also John Fund, "Railing Against Reform," *Wall Street Journal, Online Opinion Journal*, January 3, 2002.

70. Wendell Cox, "Derailed: The Amtrak Problem," *National Review Online*, February 5, 2002, www.nationalreview.com (accessed February 5, 2002).

71. Kevin Horrigan, "Chugging Along on the National Rathole," *St. Louis Post-Dispatch*, February 10, 2002, B3.

72. Stephen Moore, "No Way to Run a Railroad," *Washington Times,* February 11, 2002, A17.

73. Kenneth L. Bird, "A Rolling Enron," *Washington Post*, June 13, 2002, A36.

74. Senate Committee on Appropriations, Transportation Appropriations Subcommittee, Hearing to Examine the Status of Intercity Transportation, 107th Cong., 1st sess., June 28, 2001, 2.

75. Joseph Vranich, letter on behalf of the Amtrak Reform Council to Amtrak, August 31, 1998, followed by subsequent requests for meetings.

76. The council's senior financial analyst, Michael Mates, told the council during a public presentation that there was no logical reason for Amtrak to begin allocating non-core profits largely earned from utility easements and construction on the Northeast Corridor to trains in other parts of the country. In examining the new methodology, it became clear that most of the non-core revenues and profits were being allocated to trains with the greatest losses, generally overnight trains that did not even run on the Northeast Corridor. After time, when Mary Phillips, the council's transportation analyst, and Mates met with Amtrak financial staff, Amtrak confirmed that non-core profits were being allocated based on train losses, not based on where the trains operated.

77. Linda M. Calborn, General Accounting Office, letter to Senator John McCain, July 15, 2002, 1–2; this is more fully identified in Appendix A; see the entry for July 15, 2002.

78. The council's paid staff, while never exceeding five at any one time, included Thomas A. Till, executive director; Michael A. Mates, senior financial analyst; Kenneth P. Kolson, legal counsel; Mary B. Phillips, transportation analyst; Deirdre O'Sullivan, public affairs specialist; and Dee R. Gray, followed by Felton Jones, administrative specialist.

79. Mark Murray, "Is Amtrak Spinning More Than Its Wheels?" *National Journal*, October 14, 2000.

80. *Anthony Haswell v. National Railroad Passenger Corporation*, U.S. District Court for the District of Columbia, Civil Action No. 1:01CBO1643, filed July 30, 2001.

Chapter 3: Amtrak's Present Condition

1. Amtrak, auditor's cover letter, *Consolidated Financial Statements, September 30, 2003 and 2002*, 5.

2. U.S. Congressional Budget Office, preface, *The Past and Future of U.S. Passenger Rail Service* (Washington, D.C.: Congressional Budget Office, September 2003), 1.

3. William W. Millar, president, American Public Transportation Association, testimony before the Senate Committee on Commerce, Science, and Transportation, *Passenger and Freight Rail Security*, 108th Cong., 2nd sess., March 23, 2004, 1.

4. Rosalyn A. Wilson, *Transportation in America 2001*, 19th ed. (Washington, D.C.: Eno Transportation Foundation, 2002), 46, as cited in U.S. Congressional Budget Office, *The Past and Future of U.S. Passenger Rail Service*, 17.

5. Stephen J. Thompson, *Amtrak and the 105th Congress* (Washington, D.C.: Congressional Research Service, November 14, 1997), CRS-2.

6. Amtrak issued nine press releases between August 25, 1999, and April 26, 2001, with headlines such as "Amtrak's Bottom Line Continues to Improve" and "Another Month of Record-Setting Revenue." Not one mentioned cost growth. The newspapers that reprinted the information apparently did not ask Amtrak about expenses, seeing as their stories also failed to mention cost growth.

7. Robert P. Murphy, letter to Representative Bud Shuster; see also U.S. Government Accounting Office, *Issues Associated with a Possible Amtrak Liquidation*; and U.S. Government Accounting Office, *Potential Financial Issues in the Event That Amtrak Undergoes Liquidation*.

8. The agencies that produced most of the information included the now-defunct Amtrak Reform Council and two longstanding institutions—the inspector general of the Department of Transportation and the U.S. General Accounting Office. For the most part these organizations have met their responsibilities to evaluate Amtrak

fairly, provide factual evidence to support their findings, and examine options to the status quo. For examples of these reports, see *An Action Plan for the Restructuring and Rationalization of the National Intercity Rail Passenger System* (Washington, D.C.: Amtrak Reform Council, February 7, 2002); *2001 Assessment of Amtrak's Financial Performance and Requirements*, CR-2002-075 (Washington, D.C.: Office of Inspector General, U.S. Department of Transportation, January 24, 2002); and *Potential Financial Issues in the Event That Amtrak Undergoes Liquidation*, GAO-02-871 (Washington, D.C.: General Accounting Office, September 20, 2002).

9. William J. Rennicke, vice president of Mercer Management Consulting Inc., testimony before the House Committee on Transportation and Infrastructure, *Restructuring of America's Intercity Passenger Railroad System*, 107th Cong., 2nd sess., April 11, 2002, 55.

10. Haswell, "Which Way for Amtrak?" A19.

11. *Rail Passenger Service Act*, Public Law 91-518, *U.S. Statutes at Large* 84 (1970): 1327.

12. Amtrak Reform Council, *A Preliminary Assessment of Amtrak*, 22.

13. Edward C. Burks, "Amtrak Announces Rail Cutbacks in Northeast and Plan for Higher Fares," *New York Times*, September 1, 1977.

14. Associated Press, "Secretary Lewis Urges Amtrak Funding Be Cut Substantially," February 23, 1981, and Dow Jones News Service, "Amtrak Would Cut Service if Reagan Budget Is Adopted," March 23, 1981.

15. Associated Press, "Amtrak President Says Reduced Subsidy Will Kill The System," March 14, 1985.

16. James R. Norman, "The Featherbed Express," *Forbes*, August 28, 1995.

17. Stephanie Nall and William L. Roberts, "Turf War Could Doom Amtrak, Official Says Rail's President Fears Bankruptcy," *Journal of Commerce*, June 26, 1995.

18. Laurence Arnold, "Amtrak Head Says Service May Stop," Associated Press, June 6, 2002.

19. Christine Richard, "Amtrak Ratings Cut To Near Junk As Rail Muddle Worsens," *Dow Jones Capital Markets Report*, June 21, 2002.

20. Ronald Utt, "A Gunn to Their Head," *National Review Online*, July 1, 2002, www.nationalreview.com (accessed July 1, 2002).

21. "Amtrak under the Gunn," *Wall Street Journal*, June 24, 2002.

22. Susan Milligan and John Aloysius Farrell, "$100m Loan Keeps Amtrak Rolling for Now," *Boston Globe*, June 29, 2002; also, the Transportation Department approved the loan under the Railroad Rehabilitation and Improvement Financing (RRIF) program.

23. John Crawley, "Amtrak Threatens Another Shutdown Over Funding," Reuters, January 15, 2003.

24. Associated Press, "Amtrak Facing Shutdown Again," January 22, 2003.

25. Don Phillips, "Funding Battle Threatens Survival of Amtrak," *Washington Post*, July 11, 2003.

26. Patrick Crow, "Amtrak Threatens October Shutdown If Funding Not Doubled," *Public Works*, September 1, 2003.

27. Leslie Miller, "Amtrak Unions Plan One-Day Work Stoppage," Associated Press, September 17, 2003.

28. John Crawley, "Court Sides with Amtrak in Strike Dispute," Reuters, July 2, 2004.

29. Mark Helm, "Amtrak Chief Says More Aid Needed," *The Day* (New London, Conn.), October 1, 2003.

30. Senate Committee on Commerce, Science, and Transportation, *Hearing: Amtrak*, 108th Cong., 1st sess., October 2, 2003, 2.

31. Leslie Miller, "Amtrak President Derides Funding Proposal," Associated Press, February 10, 2004.

32. Jere Downs, "Amtrak, Pennsylvania to split cost of upgrading Philadelphia–Harrisburg line," *Philadelphia Inquirer*, July 21, 2004.

33. Joshua Green, "The Quasi-Governmental Official Who Cried Wolf," *Slate*, February 11, 2004, www.slate.com/id/2095339 (accessed August 1, 2004).

34. This issue is not entirely new. Historically, if a railroad shut down, the Interstate Commerce Commission would issue a directed service order and have another railroad maintain critical rail services. Arguably, commuter authorities could be given directed service orders by the Surface Transportation Board, allowing them to run critical Amtrak rail assets and services.

35. U.S. General Accounting Office, *Financial Performance of Amtrak's Routes*, GAO/RCED-98-151 (Washington, D.C.: May 1998), 2.

36. Robert W. Poole Jr., "Only Bankruptcy Will Force Changes," *Orlando Sentinel*, June 30, 2002, G-1.

37. Ronald D. Utt and Wendell Cox, "Amtrak Gets More Than Its Fair Share of Federal Funding," *Heritage Foundation WebMemo*, No. 118, June 25, 2002. www.heritage.org/Research/Budget/WM118.cfm

38. Congressional Budget Office, *Federal Subsidies for Passenger Rail Service* (Washington, D.C.: Government Printing Office, July, 1982), xvi, as cited in *Derailed*, 42.

39. Senator Wayne Allard of Colorado, speaking against amendment number 3958 to the Agriculture, Rural Development, Food and Drug Administration, and Related Agencies Appropriations Act, 2001, an amendment to correct a termination of the authority of Amtrak to lease motor vehicles from the General Services Administration that results from previously enacted legislation, on July 20, 2000, on the floor of the U.S. Senate. *Congressional Record* S7341-S7342, 106th Cong., 2nd sess., July 20, 2000.

40. Phyllis F. Scheinberg, General Accounting Office, testimony before the House Committee on Transportation and Infrastructure, Subcommittee on Ground Transportation, *Amtrak Faces Challenges in Improving Its Financial Condition*, 106th Cong., 1st sess., October 28, 1999, 3.

41. Amtrak Reform Council, *A Preliminary Assessment of Amtrak*, 6.

42. National Railroad Passenger Corporation (Amtrak), *Annual Report 1983* (Washington, D.C.: Amtrak, 1984), notes to financial statements, 25n4.

43. U.S. General Accounting Office, *Northeast Rail Corridor: Information on Users, Funding Sources, and Expenditures*, GAO/RCED-96-144 (Washington, D.C.: Government Printing Office, June 1996), 2–3.

44. Frank Cozzoli, "Rail Line Secures HATS Backing," *Harrisburg Patriot*, February 24, 2001, B1; "Train Station Shines after Years of Neglect," *Daily Sentinel* (Rome), June 4, 2004; "State Funds Amtrak Station Renovation," *Business Journal* (Milwaukee), July 12, 2000.

45. Jere Downs, "$145 Million Boost Set for Amtrak Route to Harrisburg," *Philadelphia Inquirer,* July 21, 2004.

46. For a sample of grade-crossing expenditures see U.S. Department of Transportation, Federal Railroad Administration, "Federal Railroad Administrator Announces Funding for Grade Crossing Hazard Elimination Programs," press release FRA 05-03, September 4, 2003; for a sample of unreimbursed security-related work, see Greg Bischof, "Railroad Official Checks Local Station's Security," *Texarkana Gazette*, March 16, 2004.

47. PR Newswire, "Amtrak to Site One of Three National Reservation Sales Call Centers to Philadelphia," February 2, 1998.

48. Andi Esposito, "Mission Remains Clouded, Challenges Remain for Union Station," *Worcester Sunday Telegram,* December 10, 2000, E1; Joelle Babula, "All Aboard for Las Vegas," *Las Vegas Review Journal*, December 15, 1999; Luke Klink, "Sturtevant Railroad Depot Approved," *Milwaukee Journal Sentinel,* April 22, 2001, 4.

49. Cynthia J. Burbank, program manager, Planning and Environment, Federal Highway Administration, memorandum regarding guidance on CMAQ under TEA-21, April 28, 1999.

50. Kenneth M. Mead, inspector general, Department of Transportation, letter to Representative Frank Wolf, December 18, 2000, 3, 13, 15–16.

51. Thomas J. Lueck, "Pact Reached on New Penn Station and Post Office," *New York Times*, March 5, 1998.

52. Dennis Buckley, fire chief of Beech Grove, quoted in Katie DeFreese, "Beech Grove Oks $7.73 Million Budget," *Indianapolis Star-News*, September 24, 1998.

53. U.S. Congressional Budget Office, *Cost Estimate on Amtrak Reform and Privatization Act of 1997* (Washington, D.C.: Congressional Budget Office, September 16, 1997), 4.

54. CONEG Policy Research Center, preface, *The Northeast and MidAtlantic States: Investors in Intercity Passenger Rail That Serves the Region and the Nation* (Washington, D.C.: CONEG Policy Research Center, June 2002), 2. CONEG is the Coalition of Northeastern Governors, and the report reflects investments

from 12 states—Connecticut, Delaware, Maine, Maryland, Massachusetts, New Hampshire, New Jersey, New York, Pennsylvania, Rhode Island, Vermont, and Virginia.

55. *Newark* (N.Y.) *Courier-Gazette,* "Lyons Amtrak Station Would Help Tourism," April 8, 2004.

56. Other states that help to finance Amtrak include Illinois, Michigan, Wisconsin, Missouri, Oregon, Washington, Oklahoma, and North Carolina.

57. Eric Durr, "CDTA Calculates Its Share Of Rail Station Cost at $1.5M," (Albany) *Business Review,* December 12, 2003.

58. Joan Kent, "City to Sell North Side Amtrak Depot," *La Crosse Tribune,* May 13, 2004.

59. Susan Nolan, "Town Liable for Station Insurance," *Exeter News-Letter,* July 22, 2004.

60. Bill Stewart, "Amtrak CEO Tours Nation to Get Officials, Staff on Board," *Portland Oregonian,* October 13, 2003.

61. Paul McKay, "EDC Backed Bombardier Bids by Loaning Amtrak $1-Billion," *Ottawa Citizen,* March 18, 2000.

62. Mark Murray and Louis Jacobson, "Critics Question $1B in Canadian Loans to Amtrak," *Congress Daily,* April 4, 2000.

63. Matthew L. Wald, "2 Builders Chosen for Speedy Trains on Northeast Run," *New York Times,* March 16, 1996, 48.

64. Anthony Haswell, personal correspondence with the author, November 22, 2000.

65. The most recent information about Canadian loans appeared in National Railroad Passenger Corporation (Amtrak), *Consolidated Financial Statements, September 30, 2003 and 2002,* 15: "Under separate financing arrangements, Amtrak was allowed to borrow up to $870 million toward the construction and acquisition of high-speed locomotives and trainsets, and related maintenance facilities. As of September 30, 2003 and 2002, the Company had borrowed a total of $761 million and $749 million, respectively. Upon delivery of the locomotives and trainsets, and the completion of the maintenance facility, Amtrak has been refinancing the related outstanding advances under capital leasing arrangements. As of September 30, 2003 and 2002 outstanding advances made on Amtrak's behalf under these arrangements totaled $500,000 and $10,404,000, respectively. The final two trainsets were delivered during fiscal year 2003, one in October 2002 and the last in June 2003. All outstanding advances at September 30, 2003, are secured by the final two trainsets and have not been refinanced under capital leasing arrangements. Interest charged is based on the London Interbank Offered Rate (LIBOR) and was capitalized during the construction phase."

66. Claytor, "A Penny for Amtrak," A15.

67. Neil Gray, "The Bus Is Better," *Washington Post,* May 11, 1992, A16.

68. Thomas M. Downs, "Capital Will Get Amtrak Back on Track," *Wall Street Journal*, May 20, 1997.

69. Don Phillips, "Amtrak Proposes Trust Fund," *Washington Post*, October 17, 2002, E03.

70. Ronald D. Utt, "FAA Reauthorization: Time to Chart a Course for Privatizing Airports," *Heritage Foundation Backgrounder*, No. 1289, June 4, 1999, 2–3, www.heritage.org/Research/Budget/BG1289ES.cfm (accessed August 16, 2004).

71. Ronald Utt, "End of the Line?" *National Review Online*, February 9, 2001, www.nationalreview.com (accessed February 9, 2001).

72. James C. May, president and chief executive officer, Air Transport Association, "State of the Industry," remarks, Federal Aviation Administration Forecasting Conference (Washington, D.C., March 25, 2004), 2.

73. In 2002, the railroad freight industry generated $36.9 billion in revenue and set a new high for freight traffic with more than 1.5 trillion revenue ton-miles (a unit of measurement that incorporates both weight and distance). This is cited in Federal Railroad Administration, "Freight Railroads Background," undated, 1, www.fra.dot.gov/downloads/policy/freight5a.pdf (accessed August 4, 2004).

74. The story of railroad freight growth is well told by Cathy Booth Thomas, "On a Faster Track," *Time*, March 8, 2004; see also Eric Wahlgren, "Railroad Stocks: Ready to Roll?" *Business Week*, February 11, 2004.

75. Seven major freight railroads operate in the U.S.—CSX Transportation, Burlington Northern Santa Fe Railway, Union Pacific Railroad, Norfolk Southern Railway, Kansas City Southern Railway, Canadian National Railway, and Canadian Pacific Railway—and more than 500 short line and regional railroads.

76. Associated Press, "Union Pacific Declines Business; Crew Shortage," April 2, 2004.

77. Daniel Machalaba, "Woes at Union Pacific Create a Bottleneck for the Economy," *Wall Street Journal*, July 22, 2004, 1. See also Rip Watson, "Rail Delays Disrupt Shipments, Business," Bloomberg News, as published in *Pittsburgh Tribune-Review*, July 13, 2004; and William C. Vantuono, "Can We Handle It?" *Railway Age*, July 2004, 31–35.

78. Jordon and Larson, "U.P. Executive Criticizes Subsidies for Amtrak," 1a.

79. U.S. Congressional Budget Office, *The Past and Future of U.S. Passenger Rail Service*, Appendix: Amtrak's Interconnections with Freight and Commuter Railroads, 39.

80. David Randall Peterman, *Amtrak: Overview and Options* (Washington, D.C.: Congressional Research Service, January 25, 2001), appendix, CRS-12.

81. John Crawley, "Watchdog Concerned About Growing Rail Traffic," Reuters, December 15, 2003.

82. Complications also ensue when trains are heading in the same direction because passenger trains generally operate at higher speeds than freight trains.

Amtrak can overtake a multitude of freight trains moving in the same direction and cause dispatching problems and slower freight train movement over hundreds of miles of lines. Amtrak does not compensate the railroads for adding to operational complexity or restraining swifter freight train movements. There are times when the Amtrak train waits for the freight train. Passengers notice when their train is sitting idle on a siding while a freight train passes by, a practice usually derided by the Amtrak crew, generally with the explanation, "Well, that's the way freight railroads treat us." What passengers are not told is that operating conditions often make it impossible for the freight railroad to give Amtrak priority. For example, when a one hundred–car freight train and an eighteen-car Amtrak train are heading toward each other on a single-track line and the passing siding is too short for the freight train, the Amtrak train must take the sidetrack and wait for the other to pass. This is an operational fact that train dispatchers live with every day in many parts of the nation.

83. As referenced in Andrew Gillies, "Making Nice With Big Rail," *Forbes*, April 14, 2004.

84. Information provided by Robert Turner, Union Pacific senior vice president for corporate relations, in Don Phillips, "U.S. Rail Crunch Could Snarl Asia Trade," *International Herald Tribune*, March 29, 2004.

85. John Tierney, "Amtrak Must Die," *New York Times Magazine*, June 16, 2002, 56.

86. Senate Committee on Commerce, Science, and Transportation, *Hearing: Amtrak*, 107th Cong., 2nd sess., April 29, 2003, 9n6.

Chapter 4: Myths about the Value of Amtrak

1. Barrie McKenna, "Gunn's Amtrak learns from TTC," *Toronto Globe and Mail*, August 22, 2002, B3.

2. The "essential" nature of Amtrak service was betrayed by Amtrak itself when it suspended the Downeaster, a Portland, Maine–Boston train, for a week during the 2004 Democratic National Convention. Amtrak said security concerns at the Fleet Center, which is above Boston's North Station, drove its decision. Amtrak could have followed MBTA's plan whereby commuter trains kept operating, although trains stopped short of the station and passengers transferred to transit lines. Also, Concord Trailways bus service and all airlines kept to normal schedules. See David Sharp, "Downeaster to Shut Down during DNC," Associated Press, June 2, 2004; "Concord Trailways To Continue Service During DNC," Associated Press, June 10, 2004; and Anthony Flint, "T to Suspend Shuttle Near Fleet Center Next Week," *Boston Globe*, July 21, 2004.

3. Don Phillips, "Bill Would Leave Amtrak Short," *Washington Post*, September 25, 2002, A04.

4. Laurence Arnold, "Amtrak Usage Swells after Attack," Associated Press, September 14, 2001.

5. Raphael Lewis, "Travelers Use Ground Routes," *Boston Globe*, September 15, 2001, A-14.

6. Liz Kowalczyk and Jeffrey Krasner, "Sudden Drop in Air Travel Strains Rail and Bus Service," *Boston Globe*, September 17, 2001.

7. Sonja Isger, "Train, Bus Ridership Tapering Off after Post-Disaster Peak," *Palm Beach Post*, September 20, 2001, 3A.

8. Stuart Silverstein, "Response to Terror: Amtrak's Post-Attack Ridership Surge Is Ebbing," *Los Angeles Times*, September 27, 2001, C-1.

9. Amtrak Reform Council, *An Action Plan for the Restructuring and Rationalization of the National Intercity Rail Passenger System*, 85.

10. The period September 1–10 represented 33.3 percent of the month, with September 11–30 representing 66.7 percent of the month. The number of passengers carried in the month was 34.4 percent for the days prior to the terrorist attacks and 65.6 percent for September 11 through the end of the month, illustrating that there was no "big surge" in ridership, as Amtrak had claimed.

11. The new Amtrak fare was posted on its website; the 1953 fare is from the "New York Central Railroad Timetable," Form 1001, April 1953, 44; the inflation calculation is based on the Consumer Price Index for April 1953 and March 2004. (Use of a 2004 comparison is justified because Amtrak has extended such fares into the year.)

12. The new Amtrak fare was posted on its website; the 1971 fare is from "Amtrak Nationwide Schedules," Sample Fares, May 1, 1971, 27; the inflation calculation is based on the average annual Consumer Price Index for 1971 and March 2004. (Use of a 2004 comparison is justified because Amtrak has extended such fares into the year.)

13. Terry Horne, "Attacks Shift Focus of Federal Workers," *Indianapolis Star*, September 30, 2001.

14. *Bombardier Corporation v. National Railroad Passenger Corporation*, U.S. District Court for the District of Columbia, CA: 01-2335(RCL), "Bombardier's Memorandum in Opposition to Amtrak's Motion to Dismiss," December 17, 2001, 6.

15. U.S. General Accounting Office, *Amtrak's Management of Northeast Corridor Improvements Demonstrates Need for Applying Best Practices*, GAO-04-94 (Washington, D.C.: Government Printing Office, February 27, 2004), 20.

16. Amtrak, untitled press release, ATK-93-24, May 19, 1993.

17. Amtrak included the news about accepting the last Acela Express in June 2003 in a footnote under "Equipment Obligations" in National Railroad Passenger Corporation (Amtrak), *Consolidated Financial Statements, September 30, 2003 and 2002*, 8.

18. Summarized quite well in two stories by Janice D'Arcy in the *Hartford Courant*, "Acela: A Poor Track Record" on September 28, 2003, and "Acela: Lessons Learned Too Late" on September 29, 2003.

19. *Bombardier Corporation v. National Railroad Passenger Corporation*, U.S. District Court for the District of Columbia, CA: 01-2335(RCL), November 8, 2001, 5.

20. Arguments are sometimes made that proven European designs would have been easier to put into use in the United States had Amtrak asked for and received waivers from certain Federal Railroad Administration safety regulations. Convincing arguments are made that FRA standards are outdated and result in passenger trains being unnecessarily heavy, in turn contributing to more accident damage than if the trains were lighter and crumple-zone standards were revised. It may be time to review FRA safety standards, but that is outside the scope of this book.

21. The X2000 was chronicled in a positive way numerous times. See David Field, "Leaning Closer to Implementation, Amtrak Gives Tilt Train a Dry Run," *Washington Times*, January 28, 1993; Tom Belden, "Superfast Train Takes Smooth Final Test Run," *Philadelphia Inquirer*, January 28, 1993; Rose DeWolf, "Amtrak Rolls Into the Future—at 155 mph," *Philadelphia Daily News*, January 28, 1993; James Harney, "Techno-Train Turns Corner on the Future," *USA Today*, January 28, 1993, 3A; and Martin Tolchin, "Amtrak Picks Up Fans with High-Speed X-2000," *New York Times*, February 2, 1993.

22. Dan Machalaba, "Much-Hyped as Super-Fast Train, Acela Creeps Along Certain Routes," *Wall Street Journal*, August 2, 2001.

23. Amtrak System Timetable, effective October 27, 2003, to April 2004, 40–46.

24. The New York, New Haven and Hartford Railroad Co., Time Table No. 180, September 26, 1954, 18, 41.

25. Trains on various lines in Japan, France, Belgium, Germany, Spain, Sweden, England, and Italy run faster than the Acela Express. An authoritative listing can be found in *Railway Gazette International*, "World Speed Survey 2003," October 2003, 661–64.

26. Brad Foss, "Amtrak to Overhaul Acela Express," Associated Press, October 5, 2003.

27. U.S. General Accounting Office, *Amtrak's Management of Northeast Corridor Improvements Demonstrates Need for Applying Best Practices*, highlights page, unnumbered.

28. Telephone interview with the author, April 8, 2004.

29. Amtrak support for faulty planning is exemplified by its praise for legislation that will fund incremental improvements to existing freight-choked rail lines and fail to bring about marketable high speeds. See Amtrak, "Amtrak Applauds Bill to Fund the Development of High-Speed Rail Corridors Nationwide," press

release ATK-99-173, October 28, 1999, and Jenny Price, "Midwest Rail Plan Would Cost $4.1 Billion," Associated Press, February 22, 2000.

30. The U.S. Census Bureau considers Texarkana, Arkansas, and Texarkana, Texas, a unified Metropolitan Statistical Area (MSA), whose estimated population on July 1, 1999 (the latest available) was 122,886. Information from http://eire.census.gov/popest/archives/metro/ma99-01.txt (accessed August 4, 2004).

31. For one example of an Amtrak promise to relieve airport congestion, see Michael Dukakis, "A Down-to-Earth Solution to Airport Gridlock," *New York Times,* September 1, 2001.

32. A useful role for rail is to provide links to crowded airports. One of Amtrak's busier stops is BWI Airport, Maryland, as travelers take the train to enjoy cheap airfares out of BWI. Continental Airlines has a joint ticket program in effect with Amtrak with passengers connecting to or from its flights at Newark, New Jersey.

33. The current federally designated high-speed rail corridors pursuant to section 1103(c) of the Transportation Equity Act for the 21st Century (TEA-21) are: California Corridor (Sacramento–Bay Area–Los Angeles–San Diego); Chicago Hub Corridor (Chicago to Milwaukee, Minneapolis, Detroit, and St. Louis, connecting to Cleveland, Columbus, and Cincinnati); Empire State Corridor (New York–Albany–Buffalo); Florida Corridor (Miami–Orlando–Tampa); Gulf Coast Corridor (Mobile–New Orleans–Houston, connecting to Birmingham, Alabama); Keystone Corridor (Philadelphia–Harrisburg–Pittsburgh); Pacific Northwest Corridor (Eugene–Portland–Seattle–Vancouver, B.C.); Southeast Corridor (Washington, D.C.–Richmond, with connections to Newport News, Raleigh, Atlanta, and the Southeast and Gulf Coast Corridors); South/Central Corridor (San Antonio–Austin–Dallas, with connections to Oklahoma City and Texarkana, Arkansas, and Little Rock); Southeast/Gulf Coast Connection (Birmingham–Atlanta–Macon–Savannah–Jacksonville); New England Corridor (Boston to Montreal and Maine), as cited in National Railroad Passenger Corporation (Amtrak), *Amtrak 2001 Strategic Business Plan* (Washington, D.C.: Amtrak, undated), 15.

34. Phyllis F. Scheinberg, General Accounting Office, testimony before the House Committee on Appropriations, Subcommittee on Transportation, *Hearing on FY2002 Appropriations for AMTRAK,* 107th Cong., 1st sess., March 21, 2001, 1.

35. Paul Gessing, "High-Speed Rail: Making Tracks at Taxpayer Expense," National Taxpayers Union, NTU issue brief 130, October 18, 2001, 2.

36. Larry Bivins, "High-Speed Rail to Atlanta Ticket for Savings, TDOT says," *Tennessean,* December 24, 2003.

37. For an analysis of how Amtrak has little impact on highway congestion, see the report by economists Wendell Cox and Jean Love, *Amtrak's Negligible Impact on Congestion,* Highway Users Federation, September 1995.

38. The argument that Amtrak's involvement in high-speed rail is a hopeless endeavor is made well by Ryan H. Sager in "Air Terror Saves Amtrak?" *American Enterprise,* December 1, 2001, 52–53.

39. "Trop Peu, Trop Tard, Trop Amtrak," *Economist*, August 11, 2001.

40. "Last Stop for the Gravy Train," *Chicago Tribune*, editorial, November 30, 2001.

41. "Amtrak Overview," *Congressional Digest* 80, no. 12 (December 2001): 291.

42. *International Railway Journal*, "DB Celebrates 1 Year Of Rail Reform," March 2004, 14; "Dutch Travel Less By Rail," *International Railway Journal*, April 2004, 2.

43. Senate Commerce, Science, and Transportation Committee, *Hearing: Amtrak*, 108th Cong., 1st sess., October 2, 2003, 2.

44. U.S. Department of Transportation, Bureau of Transportation Statistics, *National Transportation Statistics 2003* (Washington, D.C.: U.S. Department of Transportation, March 2004), table 1-3: Number of U.S. Airports; table 1-7: Number of Stations Served by Amtrak and Rail Transit.

45. Mike Dennison, "Study: Empire Builder Carries Life Blood of Northern Montana," *Great Falls Tribune*, August 6, 2003, 1A.

46. Anthony Haswell, filing before the Surface Transportation Board, Application of the National Railroad Passenger Corporation Under 49 USC sec. 24308(a)—Union Pacific Railroad Company and Southern Pacific Transportation Company, Finance Docket 33469, November 10, 1997.

47. C. Kenneth Orski, "Reinventing Amtrak—Commentary," *Innovation Briefs*, September/October 2003, 2.

48. Tierney, "Amtrak Must Die," 55.

49. Senate Committee on Commerce, Science, and Transportation, Surface Transportation and Merchant Marine Subcommittee, *Intercity Passenger Rail Finance*, 108th Cong., 1st sess., June 5, 2003, 1.

50. National Railroad Passenger Corporation (Amtrak), introduction and executive summary, *Market Based Network Analysis*.

51. Tommy G. Thompson, chairman, Amtrak, testimony before the House Committee on Transportation and Infrastructure, Subcommittee on Ground Transportation, *Oversight of Amtrak*, 106th Cong., 1st sess., October 28, 1999, 3.

52. Tommy G. Thompson, testimony before Senate Appropriations Committee, Transportation Appropriations Subcommittee, *Oversight of Department of Transportation Programs*, 106th Cong., 2nd sess., March 9, 2000, 3.

53. National Railroad Passenger Corporation (Amtrak), *Market Based Network Analysis*, 29.

54. Amtrak, "Amtrak Unveils Market-Driven Route Strategy," press release, ATK-00-19, February 28, 2000, 1; this announcement based upon National Railroad Passenger Corporation (Amtrak), *Strategic Business Plan, Update, FY 2000–2004* (Washington, D.C.: Amtrak, undated), 2.

55. In fiscal year 2001, the new trains lost money. The Kentucky Cardinal's deficit was $6.2 million and the Lake Country Limited's deficit was $1.9 million;

cited in U.S. General Accounting Office, *Amtrak Needs to Improve Its Decision-making Process for Its Route and Service Proposals*, GAO-02-398 (Washington, D.C.: Government Printing Office, April, 2002), appendix 1, 18.

56. *Rail Passenger Service Act,* outlined at 49 USC 24101 (a)(1)(b).

57. Amtrak, "Kentucky Cardinal Brings Amtrak Passenger Service to Louisville Metro Area," press release ATK-99-192, December 2, 1999.

58. Amtrak Jeffersonville–Chicago schedule, Train 851, August 2, 2001.

59. Pennsylvania Railroad through and local service, Chicago–St. Louis–Pittsburgh Timetable, Train 317, 1925, 53–54.

60. Anthony Haswell, cover letter to parties interested in Amtrak documents released as a result of his Freedom of Information lawsuit, October 25, 2002; also, conversation with the author, November 13, 2002.

61. *Trains* magazine newswire, January 28, 2002.

62. Larry Sandler, "Amtrak Critic Wants Thompson Ousted," *Milwaukee Journal Sentinel*, July 12, 2000.

63. Amtrak Janesville–Chicago schedule, Train 344, August 5, 2001.

64. National Railway Publication Company, *The Official Guide of the Railways* (New York: National Railway Publication Company, June 1952), 811–12.

65. Larry Sandler, "Amtrak Critic Wants Thompson Ousted," *Milwaukee Journal Sentinel*, July 12, 2000.

66. Fred Francis, "Amtrak: A Great Train Robbery?" Fleecing of America, *NBC News*, May 2, 2001.

67. Larry Sandler, "Amtrak to Drop Janesville Route," *Milwaukee Journal Sentinel*, March 16, 2001.

68. Larry Sandler, "Amtrak Cancels Fond du Lac plans," *Milwaukee Journal Sentinel*, September 10, 2001.

69. Chris Youngquist, "Amtrak to Forgo Chicago-to-Des Moines Route," *Quad City Times*, August 18, 2001.

70. Nancy deWolf Smith, "Letter From America: All Aboard Acela; Or Not," *Wall Street Journal Europe*, March 16, 2000, 11.

Chapter 5: Fallacies about the Cost of Amtrak

1. Senate Committee on Commerce, Science, and Transportation, *Hearing: Amtrak*, 108th Cong., 1st sess., April 29, 2003, 2.

2. Amtrak, "'Julie' Nets Major Travel Industry Award," press release ATK-03-179, November 6, 2003.

3. The new connections are in Baltimore, Boston, Chicago, Dallas, Fort Worth, Fullerton, Los Angeles, Miami, New Carrollton, New Haven, New York, Philadelphia, Richmond (California), San Bernardino, San Diego, San Francisco, San Jose, Seattle, Silver Spring, Trenton, and Washington, D.C.

4. Amtrak, "Unprecedented Investment in Service Will Bolster the Corporation's Growing Revenues and Continue Its Business Turnaround," press release, PR Newswire, June 17, 1999.

5. For a contrast between Amtrak and the American Orient Express, see Tierney, "Amtrak Must Die," 54, 57.

6. Telephone interview with the author, April 8, 2004.

7. See Amtrak, "Amtrak On-Time Performance Reaches New High," press release ATK-98-14, February 5, 1998; Tommy G. Thompson, chairman, Amtrak, letter to Amtrak Reform Council, June 14, 1999.

8. For a comprehensive analysis of sixty-three instances of Amtrak schedule padding, see Joseph Vranich and Edward L. Hudgins, *Help Passenger Rail by Privatizing Amtrak* (Washington, D.C.: Cato Institute, November 1, 2001), 16–17.

9. "Japanese Bullet Trains Beat Punctuality Record With 12 Seconds 'Delay,'" Agence France-Presse, March 24, 2004.

10. Ed Ellis, "No, Really, Amtrak Can Be Profitable," *Trains*, September 1995, 68–69; National Railroad Passenger Corporation (Amtrak), *The Market Based Network Analysis of the National Railroad Passenger Corporation: Report to Congress* (Washington, D.C.: Amtrak, February 29, 2000), 8; Lee W. Bullock, Amtrak intercity interim president, quoted in Amtrak, "Edwin E. Ellis Named Vice President at Chicago-Based Amtrak Intercity," press release ATK-97-209A, November 19, 1997.

11. "Amtrak Seeks New Freight Business," *Railway Age*, April 1997, 28.

12. Daniel Machalaba, "Amtrak Quietly Hauls Cargo on Its Trains, to the Horror of Rivals," *Wall Street Journal*, July 30, 1997, 1.

13. J. David Ingles, "Express First, People Second," News Wire, *Trains* magazine online, September 4, 1997, www.trains.com (accessed September 4, 1997).

14. Anna Wilde Matthews, "Amtrak Trims Freight Plan, Projects Huge Loss," *Wall Street Journal*, May 15, 1998.

15. Bob Johnson, "Amtrak Mail-and-Express Balancing Act," *Trains*, December 1998, 27.

16. National Railroad Passenger Corporation (Amtrak), *Building A Commercial Enterprise, Strategic Business Plan, FY01-05 Financial Plan Update* (Washington, D.C.: Amtrak, undated), 24.

17. Kenneth M. Mead, inspector general, Department of Transportation, testimony before the House Appropriations Committee, Transportation Appropriations Subcommittee, *Amtrak's Financial Performance and Requirements*, 107th Cong., 1st sess., March 21, 2001, 18.

18. National Railroad Passenger Corporation (Amtrak), *Building A Commercial Enterprise*, 48, 49.

19. Don Phillips, "Amtrak Chief Proposes More Cuts: Budget Plan for '03 Ends Freight Service," *Washington Post*, September 19, 2002, E1.

20. Tom Ramstack, "Amtrak Cancels Mail on Passenger Trains," *Washington Times*, August 31, 2004.

21. *2001 Assessment of Amtrak's Financial Performance and Requirements*, CR-2002-075 (Washington, D.C.: Office of Inspector General, U.S. Department of Transportation, January 24, 2002), 6.

22. Concurring statement of Wendell Cox, member, Amtrak Reform Council, published in *An Action Plan for the Restructuring and Rationalization of the National Intercity Rail Passenger System* (Washington, D.C.: Government Printing Office, February 7, 2002), 68.

23. U.S. General Accounting Office, *Amtrak Will Continue to Have Difficulty Controlling Its Costs and Meeting Capital Needs*, GAO/RCED-00-138 (Washington, D.C.: Government Printing Office, May 2000), summarized from 22–26.

24. Ibid., 27.

25. Ibid., 27.

26. "Rail Labor Victory!—ARC Funding Slashed," *Journal* (of the Brotherhood of Maintenance of Way Employes), August 1999.

27. Greyhound Lines Inc., "Greyhound Drivers and Mechanics Ratify New Contract," press release, March 26, 2004, 1.

28. Federal Railroad Administration, "Freight Railroads Background," 4.

29. U.S. Interstate Commerce Commission, *Railroad Passenger Train Deficit*, report proposed by Howard Hosmer, hearing examiner, docket no. 31954 (1958).

30. Hilton, *Amtrak, The National Railroad Passenger Corporation*, 11–12.

31. A Boeing 767 jetliner with a crew of nine can fly 244 passengers in four hours from Chicago to Los Angeles; the same crew can work the return flight carrying a similar passenger load. Adding two hours for equipment turnaround, the airline utilizes 90 person-hours to move 488 passengers. By contrast, an Amtrak train from Chicago to Los Angeles will have a crew of approximately twenty employees on a trip that will take forty-three hours, or 860 person-hours, to transport 250 passengers (under peak season conditions). Once crew trip preparation and check-out times are included, the airline labor efficiency rate per passenger is approximately twenty times Amtrak's rate for long-distance trains.

32. U.S. Government Accountability Office, *Commercial Aviation: Legacy Airlines Must Further Reduce Costs to Restore Profitability*, GAO-04-836 (Washington, D.C.: Government Printing Office, August 2004), summary page. The report defines legacy airlines as Alaska Airlines, American Airlines, Continental, Delta, Northwest Airlines, United Airlines, and US Airways.

33. Ibid.

34. Susan Carey, "Growing Heft Puts Budget Airlines In the Pilot's Seat," *Wall Street Journal*, March 29, 2004, A1.

35. The domestic carriers chiefly responsible for low air fares are ATA, AirTran Airways, America West Airlines, Independence Air, JetBlue Airways, Southwest Airlines, and Spirit Airlines; another low-fare airline, Virgin America, will launch in 2005.

36. U.S. Department of Transportation, "Transportation Secretary Mineta Says Passengers Rapidly Returning to the Skies," press release DOT 36-04, March 25, 2004.

37. Amtrak trains that generally operate with sleeping cars are the Auto Train, California Zephyr, Capitol Limited, Cardinal, City of New Orleans, Coast Starlight, Crescent, Empire Builder, Federal, Lake Shore Limited, Silver Star, Silver Meteor, Southwest Chief, Sunset Limited, Texas Eagle, and Three Rivers.

38. U.S. Congress, Special Study Group on Transportation Policies, *The Doyle Report: National Transportation Policy*, 87th Cong., 1st sess., June 1961, 322.

39. U.S. General Accounting Office, *Amtrak's Subsidy Needs Cannot Be Reduced Without Reducing Service*, CED-78-86 (Washington, D.C.: Government Printing Office, May 11, 1978), 53.

40. U.S. General Accounting Office, document resume, *Should Amtrak's Highly Unprofitable Routes Be Discontinued?* CED-79-3 (Washington, D.C.: Government Printing Office, November 27, 1978), 1.

41. Airlines measure efficiency in a number of ways, including calculating the break-even load factor, which is the percentage of seats that must be filled to cover the operating costs of a flight. The Amtrak Reform Council analyzed Amtrak trains using Amtrak Route Profitability System reports and the airline methodology for calculating break-even load factors. Even excluding all capital costs, Amtrak had—and no doubt still has—trains that need 110 percent to 140 percent of their seats filled for the entire trip (origin to destination) just to cover avoidable operating expenses. Such load factors are impossible unless American train riders begin sitting on each other's laps or standing in the aisles while paying fares no lower than they do now.

42. Amtrak, "Results In: First Quarter Ridership for Amtrak/Metrolink's 'Rail 2 Rail' Ticket Program Skyrockets," press release ATK-03-032, March 6, 2003.

43. Stephanie Reitz, "Amtrak Welcomes Shoreline Commuters," *Hartford Courant*, April 23, 2003.

44. Amtrak, "Amtrak Plans More Trains, Lower Fares on Springfield Line," press release ATK-03-041, April 15, 2003.

45. Amtrak, "Amtrak to Cut Acela Express Fares," press release ATK-03-052, April 22, 2003.

46. Daniel Machalaba, "Amtrak to Cut Aggressive Seasonal Fare Promotions," *Wall Street Journal*, October 7, 2003.

47. Amtrak, "Amtrak Cuts Fares on Keystone Line," press release ATK-03-172, October 16, 2003.

48. Amtrak, "Rail Sale—Weekly Specials Online," at www.Amtrak.com, displayed during December 2003.

49. Amtrak, "New Acela Ad Campaign to Launch With Buy-Two-Get-One-Free Offer," press release ATK-04-015, February 13, 2004.

50. Paul Sisson, "Rail 2 Rail Program Slated for North County," *North County Times*, March 19, 2004.

51. Based on examination of rail and bus fares on Amtrak's and Greyhound Bus Lines's websites on April 1, 2004.

52. Amtrak, "Amtrak To Offer More Off-Peak Departures on Northeast Trains," press release ATK-04-046, April 26, 2004, 1–2.

53. Amtrak, "Rail Sale—Weekly Specials Online," at www.Amtrak.com, displayed during April 2004.

54. Tom Mashberg, "Riders Rail On MBTA as Fare Hike Kicks In," *Boston Herald,* January 4, 2004, 8.

55. "New York MTA Proposes Fare, Toll Increases, Service Cuts," Associated Press, July 29, 2004.

56. John M. Roman, "Struggling SEPTA Mum On Fare-Hike Rumors," *Delaware County Daily Times,* March 17, 2004.

57. Edie Gross, "VRE Raising Rail Rates," *Fredericksburg Free Lance-Star,* April 17, 2004; also, Associated Press, "VRE Seeks Second Fare Hike in as Many Years," March 9, 2004.

58. Heather Lourie, "Commute Fares Rising," *Orange County Register,* June 23, 2004, Local 1.

59. Lola Sherman, "NCTD Considers Ways to Boost Funds," *San Diego Union Tribune,* April 1, 2004.

60. Melanie Trottman, "How a City Can Win By Losing Its Airport Hub Status," *Wall Street Journal,* April 28, 2004, B1.

61. Dennison, "Study: Empire Builder Carries Life Blood," 1A.

62. The ridership number is from Inspector General Kenneth M. Meade, Department of Transportation, testimony, U.S. Senate Committee on Commerce, Science, and Transportation, hearings, *The Future of Intercity Passenger Rail Service and Amtrak,* 108th Congress, 1st session, October 2, 2003. The analysis of segmented ridership is from U.S. Department of Transportation, Office of Inspector General's analysis of Amtrak's 2000 Origin/Destination station pair data.

63. The author performed this research in April 2004, comparing the comprehensive list of station stops published in Amtrak System Timetable, effective October 27, 2003 through April 2004, with U.S. Census Bureau online data, Table 1a, "Population in Metropolitan and Micropolitan Statistical Areas in Alphabetical Order and Numerical and Percent Change for the United States and Puerto Rico: 1990 and 2000," Internet Release Date: December 30, 2003, at www.census.gov/population/cen2000/phc-t29/tab01a.pdf.

Chapter 6: Defending against Terrorism: Can Amtrak Do the Job?

1. Different types of terrorist threats that Amtrak faces are explored by Chana R. Schoenberger, "Peace Train; Amtrak's Lack of Travelers May Make It Safer," *Forbes,* April 28, 2003.

2. U.S. Department of Transportation, Office of Inspector General, *2001 Assessment of Amtrak's Financial Performance and Requirements*, CR-2002-075 (Washington, D.C.: U.S. Department of Transportation, January 24, 2002), 60.

3. Kenneth M. Mead, inspector general, Department of Transportation, letter to Representative Frank Wolf, December 18, 2000, 3–4.

4. News retrieval systems show many stories through August 14, 2001, about this fire. One story about the widespread effect on the city was John Biemer, "Derailment, Fire Water-Main Break Leave Baltimore in Turmoil," Associated Press, July 19, 2001.

5. Senate Committee on Commerce, Science, and Transportation, *Passenger and Freight Rail Security*, 108th Cong., 2nd sess., March 23, 2004, 10.

6. Mead, letter to Wolf, 2, 5–6.

7. U.S. Department of Transportation, Federal Railroad Administration, "Transportation Secretary Announces Grant to Amtrak for New York Rail Tunnel Improvements," press release FRA 06-02, July 2, 2002; this document notes, "Funding for the grant was authorized through a $100 million appropriation contained in the FY 2002 Department of Defense and Emergency Supplemental Appropriations for Recovery From and Response to Terrorist Acts on the United States Act."

8. A review of some of the improvements underway and planned is found in Michael Luo, "Fixing Problems in Tunnels, but Keeping Trains Running," *New York Times,* June 2, 2004.

9. The most recent example can be found in Michael Weissenstein, "Effort Intensifies to Secure Penn Station," Associated Press, August 29, 2004.

10. Mead, letter to Wolf, 3.

11. Dean E. Murphy, "State Faults Amtrak for Neglect of Tunnels," *New York Times*, August 23, 2001.

12. Mead, letter to Wolf, 3.

13. Dee Wedemeyer, "Amtrak Will Vote on $2 Million Allocation For Fire Safeguards in L.I.R.R. Tunnels," *New York Times*, September 19, 1977.

14. Wendell Cox, "Derailed," *National Review Online*, February 5, 2002, www.nationalreview.com/comment/comment-cox020502.shtml (accessed August 27, 2004).

15. Peter F. Guerrero, director, physical infrastructure issues, and Norman J. Rabkin, managing director, homeland security and justice issues, General Accounting Office, testimony before the Senate Committee on Commerce, Science, and Transportation, *Passenger and Freight Rail Security*, 108th Cong., 2nd sess., March 23, 2004, 8.

16. Senate Committee on Commerce, Science, and Transportation, *Passenger and Freight Rail Security*, 108th Cong., 2nd sess., March 23, 2004, 4.

17. David Briginshaw, "Terror Attack Calls For Cool Heads And Vigilance," *International Railway Journal*, April 2004, 1.

18. Bill Bergstrom, "Transportation Secretary Mulls Metal Detectors in Train Stations," Associated Press, October 1, 2001.

19. Senate Committee on Commerce, Science, and Transportation, *Passenger and Freight Rail Security*, 108th Cong., 2nd sess., March 23, 2004, 4.

20. Ibid., 3.

21. "Rail Passenger Screening Test Ends in Maryland," Associated Press, June 4, 2004.

22. Transportation Security Administration, "TSA Begins 3rd Phase of Rail Security Experiment; Pilot Marks 1st Ever Passenger and Baggage Explosive Screening in a Moving Railcar," press release, July 15, 2004.

23. Summarized from U.S. Department of Homeland Security, "Fact Sheet: Rail and Transit Security Initiatives," undated, www.dhs.gov/dhspublic/display?content=3377 (accessed July 29, 2004).

24. Senate Committee on Commerce, Science, and Transportation, *Passenger and Freight Rail Security*, 108th Cong., 2nd sess., March 23, 2004, 5.

25. Ibid., 2.

26. "Operators Respond to Bomb Attacks," *Railway Gazette International*, April 2004, 181.

27. Dale Fuchs, "New Rail Bomb Was Nearly Complete," *New York Times*, April 2, 2004.

28. The sabotage to the Amtrak train is covered in detail in William Claiborne, "Amtrak Train Derailed by Sabotage In Arizona, Killing 1, Injuring 78," *Washington Post*, October 10, 1995, A1; also, Don Phillips, "110,425 Miles Cannot Be Secured; Until Monday, Railroaders Worried About Trespassers and Petty Vandals," *Washington Post*, October 12, 1995, A14.

29. The FBI's investigation into the 1995 Amtrak sabotage led to an examination of a railroad historical society magazine article that had appeared a week earlier detailing the 1939 wreck; see Don Phillips, "Tale of a 1939 Wreck Is Studied for Clues to Train Sabotage," *Washington Post*, October 12, 1995, A3.

30. Bill Geroux and Rex Springston, "FBI Joins Probe in Wreck of Train, Sabotage Possible in Switch Tampering," *Richmond Times-Dispatch*, August 14, 1992, A1.

31. Bob Simon, "Are America's Trains Safe?" *CBS News*, March 31, 2004.

32. Jennifer Lin, "Officials Straining to Secure Rail Lines as Threat of Attacks Grows," Knight-Ridder Newspapers, April 6, 2004.

33. Pierre Thomas and Richard Esposito, "Raised Suspicions: Could Terrorists Be Casing New York–Philadelphia–D.C. Rail Corridor?" *ABC News*, May 21, 2004.

34. Bill Gertz and Audrey Hudson, "Boston, New York Rail Lines Vulnerable," *Washington Times,* July 9, 2004.

35. Richard B. Schmitt and Josh Meyer, "Task Force Set Up to Ferret Out Plans for Terrorist Attack in U.S.," *Los Angeles Times*, May 27, 2004.

36. These incidents summarized from "Amtrak Police Search Three Trains," Associated Press, May 21, 2004; "Amtrak Train Searched After Report," Associated Press, June 7, 2004; "New Haven Train Station Shut Down Because of Bomb Threat," Associated Press, June 15, 2004; "Train to N.Y. Halted in Probe of Threat," Associated Press, July 3, 2004; and Wayne Parry, "Amtrak Train Searched in Newark Station after Threatening Note Found," Associated Press, July 22, 2004.

37. "Bomb Threat Prompts Search of Amtrak Trains in N.C., Fla., Pa.," Associated Press, March 30, 2004.

38. Amtrak's meaningless allocation of capital is reminiscent of what politicians did in Ayn Rand's classic novel *Atlas Shrugged*: People who were "good-hearted" financed the continuation of lightly used trains by shortchanging maintenance. When such policies contributed to the collapse of an important tunnel in Colorado, resulting in great loss of life, the railroad came to a halt. The story is fictional, but it conveys the consequences of a catastrophic tunnel event in New York—one that could bring America's single most important passenger railroad line to a halt for an indeterminate period.

39. Larry Sandler, "Milwaukee Route May Get First New Amtrak Trains," *Milwaukee Journal Sentinel*, October 8, 2003.

40. Associated Press, "Amtrak President Rides Through ND," October 10, 2003.

41. Three stories focusing on Gunn's visit ran in the *Havre Daily News*, as follows: "Amtrak President Will Take the Train Through Montana," October 6, 2003; "Amtrak's Gunn Stops Along the Hi-Line," October 10, 2003; and "Bush Plan Would Kill the Empire Builder," October 14, 2003.

42. Jo Dee Black, "Amtrak Vows No Service Cuts," *Great Falls Tribune*, October 10, 2003.

43. Stewart, "Amtrak CEO Tours Nation."

44. Senate Committee on Commerce, Science, and Transportation, *Passenger and Freight Rail Security*, 108th Cong., 2nd sess., March 23, 2004, 4.

45. Reuters, "U.S. Airlines Balk at Paying More for Security," April 28, 2004.

46. Associated Press, "US Ridge: Private Sector Must Help Fund Anti-Terror Effort," April 5, 2004.

Chapter 7: Escape from Amtrak: State and Local Governments

1. Senate Committee on Commerce, Science and Transportation, *Hearing: Amtrak*, 108th Cong., 1st sess., October 2, 2003, 3.

2. *Commuter Rail Transit Ridership Report, Fourth Quarter 2002* (Washington, D.C.: American Public Transit Association, May 21, 2004), www.apta.com/research/stats/ridershp/riderep/documents/03q4cr.pdf (accessed July 29, 2004).

3. Laurence Arnold, "Amtrak Warns About Looming Shutdown," Associated Press, June 22, 2002.

4. Justin Pope, "Amtrak Threat Worries MBTA," as published in the *Worcester Telegram*, with Saun Sutner contributing to the report, June 22, 2002.

5. Ridership statistic from Massachusetts Bay Transportation Authority, www.mbta.com/insidethet/taag_ridership.asp (accessed August 7, 2004).

6. For train delays, see Thomas C. Palmer Jr., "MBTA Eyes Amtrak for Rail-Delay Fines"; for maintenance problems, see Palmer, "Part Defect Forces Shutdown of Some Old Colony Train Cars"; for crew-scheduling problems, see Palmer, "2nd Delay Reported On Old Colony Rail Line," all in the *Boston Globe*, August 15, 2001, April 8, 1999, and October 10, 1997, respectively.

7. Charles D. Chieppo, "How the Labor Department Can Bring Common Sense to a Rail Contract," *Heritage Foundation Backgrounder*, No. 1552, May 23, 2003, 2, available at www.heritage.org/Research/Labor/BG1552.cfm, last visited July 29, 2004.

8. Palmer, "MBTA Awards Work To Private Company," and Palmer, "Contract Ends MBTA, Amtrak Link," *Boston Globe*, September 16, 1999.

9. Palmer, "Amtrak Workers Reject Commuter-Rail Plan," *Boston Globe*, December 16, 1999.

10. Senator Wayne Allard, testimony before the Senate Committee on Commerce, Science, and Transportation, *Oversight Hearing on Amtrak*, 106th Cong., 2nd sess., September 26, 2000, 15. Note that Senator Allard was on the Committee on Banking, Housing, and Urban Affairs as chairman of the Subcommittee on Housing and Transportation, which has jurisdiction over the federal mass transit program that subsidizes MBTA and other commuter rail systems.

11. For an overview of Senator Kerry's activities on behalf of rail labor, see Senate Committee on Commerce, Science, and Transportation, *Oversight Hearing on Amtrak*, 106th Cong., 2nd sess., September 26, 2000, 73–83. See also "Kerry Met Often with Mostly Unions in '03," Associated Press, April 23, 2004, for an account of Kerry's work with the AFL-CIO and his high approval ratings from organized labor.

12. Palmer, "Under Pressure, T to Give Up on Cost Saving, Pay $119m More," *Boston Globe*, May 8, 2000.

13. "Truth about the T Told by Strangers," *Boston Herald,* July 13, 2000, 22.

14. Palmer, "Firms Block T From Signing Contracts With Competitors," *Boston Globe*, May 12, 2000.

15. *Bay State Transit Services, LLC v. National Railroad Passenger Corporation, et al.*, U.S. District Court for the District of Columbia, CA: 01-CV01926, September 13, 2001, 4.

16. The quote is from Andrea Estes and Mac Daniel, "Family Seeks $25m in T Passenger's Death," *Boston Globe*, January 23, 2003; this event is also reported in Mac Daniel, "Probes Launched Into T Rider's Death," *Boston Globe*, August 1, 2002; Ron

DePasquale, "Amtrak Suspends Second Conductor," Associated Press, August 3, 2002; and Robert O'Neill, "Commuter Train Conductor Was Wrong to Continue Route While Passenger Was Having Heart Attack, Amtrak Report Says," Associated Press, August 3, 2002.

17. Reuters, "Bombardier, Connex Group Signs Boston Train Deal," February 25, 2003.

18. Massachusetts Bay Transportation Authority, "MBTA Introduces Massachusetts Bay Commuter Railroad As Its New Commuter Rail Service Provider," press release, July 1, 2003, 1.

19. "MBTA Raises Bar on Commuter Rail O and M," *Public Works Financing*, June 2003, 5–6.

20. "New Commuter Rail Operator Reaches Contact Deals With 14 Unions," Associated Press, June 20, 2003.

21. See Steve Bailey, "Blood on the Tracks," *Boston Globe*, November 12, 1999, for a cogent account of the unfairness of undermining cost-effective, private-sector bids in favor of Amtrak's higher bid.

22. Mac Daniel, "MBTA Move Could Put US Rail Service on New Track," *Boston Globe*, October 13, 2001.

23. Jason Penshorn, "Boston, Massachusetts: For MBTA General Manager Michael Mulhern, Ingenuity and Optimism Add Up to Big Changes in Boston," *Mass Transit*, February/March 2004.

24. Laura Brown and Stacey Urich, "Amtrak Strike Derailed, T Riders Thankful Commute Will Be On Track," *Boston Herald*, November 3, 1997, 5; Laura Brown, "Amtrak Workers Threaten Strike in Response to Layoffs," *Boston Herald*, June 11, 1999. For a sense of intractable union positions, see three stories by Thomas C. Palmer Jr., *Boston Globe*: "Amtrak Workers Reject Commuter-Rail Plan," December 16, 1999, which reported a union spokesman telling the public, "It's us or the bus"; "Rail Workers Confront Visiting Officials," December 1, 1999, which reported that officials from a company competing with Amtrak terminated a visit to a maintenance base after being confronted by angry Amtrak employees; and "Amtrak Workers in No Mood to Celebrate," January 20, 1999, which reported "About 100 Amtrak workers from several unions disrupted the 100th birthday celebration of South Station yesterday."

25. Leslie Miller, "Amtrak Unions Plan One-Day Work Stoppage," Associated Press, September 17, 2003.

26. Mac Daniel, "Riders Bear Brunt of Train's Rehab," *Boston Globe,* May 26, 2004.

27. Robert McCoppin, "Amtrak Funding Crisis Worries Metra," *Chicago Daily Herald*, June 21, 2002.

28. Larry Sandler, "Region's Officials Favor Metra Link," *Milwaukee Journal Sentinel,* September 30, 2003; also, Rich Rovito, "Money Slated for Metra Study," *Business Journal* (Milwaukee), April 30, 2004.

29. Dow Jones Newswires, "Bombardier Inc. Gets $40M Train Maintenance Pact," April 12, 1998.

30. William X. Lydon Jr. and Linda Ford-McCaffrey, memorandum to Southern California Commuter Rail Authority, June 24, 2002.

31. Kurt Streeter, "Metrolink Proposes Deal to Keep Train Operators," *Los Angeles Times*, July 3, 2002.

32. Nancy Luna, "Metrolink Will Keep On Track With Plan B," *Orange County Register*, January 5, 2003.

33. Larry Higgs, "NJ Transit Increases Service on NE Corridor Line," *Bridgewater Courier News*, September 22, 2001; also, "Good Move for NJ Transit," *Star Ledger* (Newark), May 6, 2004

34. Dean E. Murphy, "State Faults Amtrak for Neglect of Tunnels."

35. Richard Pérez-Peña, "Fight Over Amtrak State Aid Goes Public," *New York Times*, November 27, 2002.

36. Joshua Robin and Joie Tyrrell, "Officials: Amtrak Engineer Caused Train Crash," *Newsday*, April 20, 2004; also, Associated Press, "At Least 130 Commuters Hurt When Amtrak Train Bumps Their Train," April 19, 2004.

37. Tom Ramstack, "VRE Gives Amtrak Deadline for Questions on Service Pact," *Washington Times*, June 7, 2003.

38. Ibid.

39. U.S. General Accounting Office, *Commuter Rail: Information and Guidance Could Help Facilitate Commuter and Freight Rail Access Negotiations,* GAO-04-240 (Washington, D.C.: Government Printing Office, January 2004), 30.

40. VRE's situation is more fully discussed in Joseph Vranich, "Amtrak's Woes Shouldn't Derail VRE Riders," *Fredericksburg Free Lance-Star,* September 25, 2003.

41. National Railroad Passenger Corporation (Amtrak), "Note 2: Business Condition and Liquidity," *Consolidated Financial Statements, September 30, 2003 and 2002,* 1.

42. Kenneth M. Meade, U.S. Department of Transportation Inspector General, "Amtrak RRIF Loan," Memorandum to the Secretary, December 9, 2003, 2.

43. Operating subsidies come from California, Illinois, Maine, Michigan, Missouri, New York, North Carolina, Oklahoma, Oregon, Pennsylvania, Vermont, Washington, and Wisconsin. Capital funding that benefits Amtrak has come from most of the aforementioned states as well as Connecticut, Delaware, Florida, Maryland, Massachusetts, New Jersey, Rhode Island, and Virginia.

44. Senate Committee on Commerce, Science, and Transportation, 108th Cong., 1st sess., October 2, 2003, internet version, 3, available at www.fra.dot.gov/Content3.asp?P=1220.

45. Audrey Cooper, "State to Study Amtrak Pact," *Stockton Record*, March 29, 2003.

46. Jeff Morales, director, California Department of Transportation, testimony before the Senate Committee on Commerce, Science, and Transportation, Surface

Transportation and Merchant Marine Subcommittee, *Intercity Passenger Rail Finance*, 108th Cong., 1st sess., June 5, 2003, pages unnumbered.

47. See "Consumers, Taxpayers Hurt by Amtrak Arrogance" and "Better Deal on Trains," *Kansas City Star* editorials of April 18, 2003, and February 17, 2003, respectively.

48. Tim Hoover, "Company Decides Not to Pursue Passenger Service in Missouri," *Kansas City Star*, April 2, 2003.

49. Pérez-Peña, "Fight Over Amtrak State Aid Goes Public."

50. Melissa Mansfield, "Hevesi Criticizes Turboliner Delays, Cost Overruns," Associated Press, June 12, 2003.

51. See "Amtrak Should Keep the Promises It Makes," *Troy Record*, January 5, 2004, and "Turboliner Project Scaled Back," *Newsday*, March 7, 2004.

52. Cathy Woodruff, "State Sues Amtrak over High-Speed Rail," *Times Union* (Albany), August 14, 2004.

53. Cited in Department of Transportation, Federal Railroad Administration, "Notice of Funds Availability and Request for Comment To Assist in the Development and Implementation of a Procedure for Fair Competitive Bidding by Amtrak and Non-Amtrak Operators of State-Supported Intercity Passenger Rail Routes," *Federal Register* 69, no. 71 (April 13, 2004): 19613.

Chapter 8: Passenger Railroads: They Can Work

1. The topic is explored more fully at Privatization.org, a program of the Los Angeles-based Reason Public Policy Institute.

2. Robert W. Poole Jr., "Reason's 35th Anniversary Banquet Remarks," Reason Foundation Banquet, November 6, 2003, 3.

3. UK Department for Transport, *The Future of Rail*, Report Cm6233, July 2004, 21.

4. Emanuel S. Savas, *Privatization: The Key to Better Government* (Chatham, N.J.: Chatham House Publishers, 1987), 109–110, 262.

5. Amtrak Reform Council, *Intercity Rail Passenger Service in America*, 18.

6. Rennicke testimony, 4.

7. The efficiency savings are calculated as a decrease in operating costs in constant currency per unit of output (e.g., ton-miles); ibid., 7.

8. From 2001 through 2004, franchise operators were Anglia Railways, ARRIVA, c2c, Cardiff Railways, Central Trains, Chiltern Railways, Connex, FirstGroup, Gatwick Express, GNER, Island Line, Midland Mainline, ScotRail, Silverlink, South Central (renamed Southern Railway), South Eastern Trains, South West Trains, Thames Trains, Thameslink, TransPennine, Virgin CrossCountry, Virgin West Coast, WAGN, Wales & Borders Trains, Wales & West Railway, and Wessex Trains. This list according to UK Strategic Rail Authority, "Britain's Railway Properly

Delivered," *Annual Report 2003–2004* (London: Strategic Rail Authority, 2004), appendix 5, 8, www.sra.gov.uk/pubs2/ann_reps/ (accessed August 27, 2004).

9. Passenger trips and passenger-kilometers from UK Strategic Rail Authority, "National Rail Trends," table 1.1, "passenger-kilometers by ticket type (billions)," and table 1.2, "Passenger journeys by ticket type (millions)," June 2004, www.sra.gov.uk/pubs2/performance_statistics/nrt_june04/nrt0604 (accessed August 8, 2004).

10. Association of Train Operating Companies, "Britain Has Europe's Fastest Growing Railway," press release, July 1, 2004, 1.

11. Central Trains, "A Third of Passengers Say They Haven't Caught the Train in More than 20 Years," press release, July 21, 2004, www.centraltrains.co.uk/_popups/news/news_detail.asp?id=20040721130419-118 (accessed August 16, 2004); the surveyed passengers were traveling "long distance," which because of the length of Britain's routes would mean short distance in the United States.

12. UK Strategic Rail Authority, *Annual Report 2002–03* (London: Strategic Rail Authority, 2003), 4, www.sra.gov.uk/pubs2/ann_reps/ (accessed August 27, 2004).

13. Association of Train Operating Companies, "Rail Travel Is Changing for the Better," press release, July 22, 2004.

14. UK Strategic Rail Authority, "Britain's Railway Properly Delivered," *Annual Report 2003–2004* (London: Strategic Rail Authority, 2004), page unnumbered, www.sra.gov.uk/pubs2/ann_reps/ (accessed August 27, 2004).

15. The train operating companies with new equipment are Anglia Railways, Chiltern Railways, First Great Western, ScotRail, ARRIVA Trains Northern, South Eastern, First Great Eastern, Midland Mainline, South Central, South West Trains, Virgin CrossCountry, and Virgin West Coast.

16. South West Trains, "Your New Trains," www.swtrains.co.uk/ourservices/newtrains.asp (accessed August 10, 2004).

17. "On-Board Internet," *Railway Gazette International*, September 2003, 550.

18. Andrew Haldenby, "What Went Wrong with Railtrack?" *Reform Britain*, July 10, 2002, www.reformbritain.com/campaignnews.asp?article=229 (accessed August 11, 2004).

19. The ROSCOs are Angel Trains Ltd., GATX Capital Corp., GE Rail Services, HSBC Rail (UK) Ltd., and Porterbrook Leasing Company Ltd. List is from the Office of Rail Regulation, www.rail-reg.gov.uk/server/show/nav.001009005004 (accessed August 10, 2004).

20. UK Department for Transport, *The Future of Rail*, July 2004, 15.

21. Alistair Osborne, "Accountants Found No Black Hole at Connex," *Telegraph*, March 7, 2003.

22. Rebecca Bream, "Connex Chief Went From Hero to Zero in 10 Months," *Financial Times*, June 28, 2003, 3.

23. "Fail rail franchise 'needed time,'" BBC News, November 13, 2003.

24. "UK Franchises to Be Extended," *Railway Gazette International*, October 2003, 610.

25. UK Strategic Rail Authority, "Green Light for High Speed Services for Kent—Four Bidders Selected for New Kent Franchise," press release, December 22, 2003.

26. UK Health and Safety Executive, "Hatfield," July 7, 2004, www.hse.gov.uk/railways/hatfield.htm (accessed August 16, 2004).

27. UK Department for Transport, *The Future of Rail*, July 2004, 30, 37.

28. Ibid., 13.

29. Ibid.

30. Ibid., 9.

31. This estimate was reported by the Bechtel Corporation as follows: "About 85 percent of the work will be upgrades to existing track, electrical lines, and switches. In some cases, a wholesale replacement of tracks, ties, and the bed of rocks beneath the line is necessary. The remaining 15 percent of the project involved *enhancements* to track and signals" (emphasis added). See "Back on Track," *Bechtel Briefs*, August 2003, www.bechtel.com/Briefs/0803/Back_on_Track.htm (accessed August 11, 2004).

32. The company describes itself this way: "Network Rail is a company limited by guarantee. This means that, while we are a private organisation and operate as a commercial business, we have no shareholders. Instead we are accountable to members, who do not receive dividends or share capital. They have similar rights to those of shareholders in a public company, except they have no financial or economic interest in Network Rail. This means they have a duty to act in the best interests of the company without personal bias." From www.networkrail.co.uk/companyinformation/index.htm (accessed August 11, 2004).

33. Ibid.

34. Network Rail, "Network Rail Publishes 2004 Business Plan—A Clear Plan for a Better Railway," press release, March 31, 2004, 1.

35. Ibid.

36. Alistair Darling, UK transport minister, speech before the Railway Forum Conference, July 1, 2003, 1.

37. Association of Train Operating Companies, "Train Operating Companies Put on More Trains for New Summer Timetable," press release, May 21, 2004, 1.

38. Number of Amtrak trains from "Amtrak Facts," undated, www.amtrak.com/about/amtrakfacts.html (accessed August 8, 2004).

39. Network Rail Infrastructure Limited, "Annual Report and Accounts," June 2, 2004, 2, 6.

40. British Rail had estimated that 500 miles of track needed to be replaced each year just to stand still in quality. But in the lead up to privatization, less than 300 miles of track were renewed each year; after privatization, under Railtrack, it dropped to just 200 miles. Network Rail replaced 853 miles of track in 2003–4. UK Department for Transport, *The Future of Rail*, 32.

41. AP-Dow Jones, "BAA/Heathrow Express Sees Small Initial Operating Loss," August 20, 1997; "New Heathrow Stopping Service," *International Railway Journal*, July 2003, 4.

42. London & Continental Railways, "Prime Minister Opens First Section of Channel Tunnel Rail Link," press release, 1-2, www.lcrproperties.com/html/bodies/lcr/releases/prn062.html (accessed August 11, 2004).

43. "Train Smashes Speed Record," *BBC News*, July 30, 2003.

44. Information that confirms improved safety is reported in various ways by Her Majesty's Rail Inspectorate; one example is "Train accident fatalities 1975-2002/03," as posted on the UK Health and Executive website at www.hse.gov.uk/railways/.

45. UK Rail Safety and Standards Board, *Annual Safety Performance Report 2002/03*, 22–23.

46. The franchisees making payments were Anglia Railways, First Great Eastern, Gatwick Express, GNER, Midland Mainline, South Central, Thames Trains, Thameslink, and WAGN; from UK Strategic Rail Authority, "Franchise Net Payments: TOCs," *Annual Report 2002–03*, appendix 3, 140–41.

47. UK Strategic Rail Authority, "Britain's Railway Properly Delivered," *Annual Report 2003–2004* (London: Strategic Rail Authority, 2004), appendix 5, 8, www.sra.gov.uk/pubs2/ann_reps/ (accessed August 27, 2004)

48. Admittedly, fluctuating exchange rates make comparisons difficult. The 2003 rates were available at www.ozforex.com (accessed August 10, 2004). The calculation is charitable to Amtrak in two respects. First, Amtrak's fiscal year ends on September 30, and the British fiscal year ends on March 31; of the several options available, the calculation that put Amtrak in the best light was selected. Second, the comparison is based only on Amtrak's direct federal subsidy of $1,043,000 to its 5.5 billion passenger-miles; the many indirect federal, state, and local subsidies to Amtrak discussed earlier in this book were excluded from the calculation.

49. "UK Franchises to Be Extended," *Railway Gazette International*, October 2003, 610.

50. UK Department for Transport, *The Future of Rail*, July 2004, 89.

51. Ibid., 8; "Tube Transfers to TfL," *Railway Gazette International*, August 2003, 478.

52. "UK Brings Infrastructure Maintenance Back In-House," *Railway Gazette International*, June 2004, 345.

53. UK Department for Transport, *The Future of Rail*, July 2004, 74.

54. "Britain," World in Brief, *International Railway Journal*, February 2004, 3.

55. Ronald D. Utt, Herbert and Joyce Morgan Senior Research Fellow, Heritage Foundation, testimony before the House Committee on Government Reform, Subcommittee on Energy Policy, Natural Resources, and Regulatory Affairs, *How Can We Maximize Private Sector Participation in Transportation?* 108th Cong., 2nd sess., May 18, 2004, 16.

56. Japan Transport Economics Research Center, *Issues and Achievements in the Five Years Since the Japan National Railway Reform* (Tokyo: Japan Transport Economics Research Center, October 1992).

57. East Japan Railway Company, *Annual Report 2003* (Tokyo: East Japan Railway Company, 2003), 4, 10.

58. Central Japan Railway Company, *Annual Report, 2002* (Nagoya, Japan: Central Japan Railway Company, 2002), 7.

59. West Japan Railway Company, "An Interview with the President," *Annual Report, 2002*, www.westjr.co.jp/english/english/company/con02/ar/2002/c00.html (accessed April 18, 2004).

60. East Japan Railway Company, *Annual Report 1996* (Tokyo: East Japan Railway Company, 1996), 9.

61. "High Speed Trains Worldwide," *Japan Railway and Transport Review*, October 1994, 1, www.jrtr.net/jrtr03/pdf/photo_00.pdf (accessed August 12, 2004).

62. Central Japan Railway Company, "N700 Rolling Stock Design for the Tokaido–Sanyo Shinkansen," press release, June 16, 2004, 1, http://jr-central.co.jp/english.nsf/doc/n-04-0616 (accessed August 2, 2004).

63. "50 Things to Do Before You Die," *Daily Telegraph*, September 22, 2003.

64. This quote is from the Rocky Mountain Railtours, *Company History*, undated; for a more complete account of the creation of the Great Canadian Railtour Company and start of Rocky Mountaineer service, see Paul Grescoe, *Trip of a Lifetime* (Vancouver, B.C.: Hurricane Press, 2000).

65. Summarized from Rocky Mountain Railtours, "New Tourist Train" Backgrounder, undated, 4.

66. Rocky Mountain Railtours, "Great Canadian Railtour Company Announces the Launch of 'North Coast Explorer' Tourism Train," press release, January 26, 2004.

67. Rocky Mountain Railtours, "Rocky Mountaineer Railtours Celebrates Its 15th Anniversary Season With New Package Tours and a New Vancouver Station," press release, March 1, 2004.

68. Kate Skye, "Passenger Rail Tours Could Give Kootenays Tourism Boost, Says MP," *Trail Daily Times*, September 9, 2003.

69. Rocky Mountain Railtours, "Rocky Mountaineer Railtours Provides Perfect Vacation Add-On to Popular 2004 Alaska Cruises," press release, April 14, 2004.

70. See Canadian National Railway, "CN Selects Great Canadian Railtour Company to Introduce New Tourist Trains in B.C. and Alberta," press release, September 3, 2004, 1, www.cn.ca/news/newsreleases/2004/en_News20040903.shtml (accessed September 3, 2004); Rocky Mountain Railtours, "Great Canadian Railtour Company Wins Bid to Operate New Tourist Trains in British Columbia and Alberta," press release, September 3, 2004, www.rkymtnrail.com/media_center/news_releases/releases/2004/09-03.htm (accessed September 3, 2004); and Rocky

Mountaineer Vacations, "New Tourist Train Service" Backgrounder, undated, at www.whistlermountaineer.com/media_center/backgrounder-gcrc.htm#partnership (accessed September 3, 2004).

71. Jim Gouk, "Privatize Un-Via-ble Rail," *Globe and Mail*, November 6, 2003.

72. Conrail, *A Brief History of Conrail* (Philadelphia, 1996), 1.

73. Based on Alaska Railroad Transfer Act of 1982; see also *Alaska Railroad History*, undated, www.alaskarailroad.com/corporate/history.html (accessed August 27, 2004).

74. Alaska Railroad, *2003 Alaska Railroad Fact Sheet*, undated, 1, www.alaskarailroad.com/corporate/FactSheet.html (accessed August 27, 2004). The Alaska Railroad carried more passengers than these short-distance Amtrak routes based on ridership, as reported in Amtrak's Route Profitability System for 2001: Albany, New York–Rutland, Vermont; Albany–Montreal; Chicago–Champaign-Urbana, Illinois; Chicago–Detroit–Pontiac, Michigan; Chicago–Grand Rapids, Michigan; Chicago–Milwaukee; Chicago–Quincy, Illinois; Chicago–St. Louis; Chicago–Toronto; Kansas City–St. Louis; Oklahoma City–Fort Worth; Raleigh–Charlotte, North Carolina; Springfield, Massachusetts–St. Albans, Vermont. Amtrak short-distance routes carrying more passengers than the Alaska Railroad, based on traffic in the same RPS report, were two Northeast Corridor routes—Boston–New York–Washington, D.C., and New York–Philadelphia– Harrisburg, Pennsylvania—along with four routes that have received significant state subsidies over the years, namely, New York–Albany–Buffalo; Seattle–Portland, Oregon; Santa Barbara–Los Angeles–San Diego; Sacramento–Oakland–San Jose. On a head-count basis, only one Amtrak long-distance route carried more passengers than the Alaska Railroad—the Seattle–Los Angeles train, the Coast Starlight.

75. Amtrak Reform Council, *An Action Plan for the Restructuring and Rationalization of the National Intercity Rail Passenger System*, appendix 5, 96. In another example of this approach, part of the process in which Conrail became a success was the devolvement of its commuter rail operations to the northeastern states in 1981.

Chapter 9: Creative Approaches to Rail Transportation

1. Senate Committee on Commerce, Science, and Transportation, *Hearing: Amtrak*, 108th Cong., 1st sess., April 29, 2003, 1.

2. Summarized from Amtrak Reform Council, *An Action Plan for the Restructuring and Rationalization of the National Intercity Rail Passenger System*, i–vi.

3. U.S. General Accounting Office, *Amtrak's Management of Northeast Corridor Improvements Demonstrates Need for Applying Best Practices*, 7.

4. Ibid., 1.

5. Charles D. Chieppo, "T Reform Derailed, Thanks to Moakley," Pioneer Institute for Public Policy Research, April 24, 2000, www.pioneerinstitute.org/research/opeds/moakley.cfm (accessed August 27, 2004).

6. *Bay State Transit Services, LLC v. National Railroad Passenger Corporation, et al.*, U.S. District Court for the District of Columbia, CA: 01-CV01926, September 13, 2001, 4.

7. Associated Press, "Company Wants to Take over Philadelphia–Harrisburg Railroad Line," January 16, 1998; see also Joseph Vranich, "Phase Out Amtrak," *Harrisburg Sunday Patriot News*, February 22, 1998, B11, and Marilyn Wimp, "New Rider in the Rail Business," *Philadelphia Business Journal*, March 9, 1998.

8. Scott R. Spencer, president, Railway Service Corporation, revealed Amtrak's lack of cooperation in conversations with the author in 1998 and 1999. Amtrak publicly asserted that RSC had not provided a "viable business proposal," an ironic claim coming from a railroad that has not produced one proposal that could be considered "viable."

9. Phillips, "Amtrak Chief Proposes More Cuts," E1.

10. Further evidence that Amtrak's capabilities with electric rail systems are hardly unique is the engineering and maintenance expertise found on electrified "heavy rail" (subway) systems in Atlanta, Baltimore, Boston, Chicago, Jersey City, Los Angeles, Miami, New York, Philadelphia, San Francisco, and Washington, D.C.; such talent also keeps electrified "light rail" (streetcar-type) systems running in twenty-three U.S. cities.

11. Senate Committee on Commerce, Science, and Transportation, *Hearing: Amtrak*, 108th Cong., 1st sess., April 29, 2003, 5.

12. These are extracted from a long list of examples provided by Rennicke testimony, 15.

13. Stephen Aug, "Why New Corporate Investors Are Training Their Sites [sic] on Amtrak," *Nightly Business Report*, December 24, 2001, go to www.NightlyBusiness.org, then "Transcript Archive," then "2001," then "12/24/01" (accessed August 2, 2004). See also Tricia A. Holly, "Debate Swirls over Whether Amtrak Can Stand on Its Own," *Travel Agent*, July 24, 2000.

14. Revealed by Thomas Till, Amtrak Reform Council executive director, in Associated Press, "Oversight Panel: Let Amtrak Compete," January 11, 2002.

15. The 2003 expression of interest was by company spokesman David Fink, as quoted in John Crawley, "Rail Overhaul Would Strip Amtrak's Assets," Reuters, January 10, 2002. The earlier offer is referenced in "Guilford Makes Offer to Buy Northeast Corridor," *Progressive Railroading*, July 1997, 25.

16. Associated Press, "Hopes Brighten for Northstar Commuter Rail Plan," April 8, 2004.

17. Andy Peters, "Commuter Rail Plan Gains Steam," *Macon Telegraph*, March 18, 2004.

18. Lois Caliri, "NS Gets on Track for Passenger Rail," *Roanoke Times*, July 23, 2004.

19. Associated Press, "Skagway Railroad Sets Passenger Record," June 14, 2003.

20. Jon Hilkevitch, "FAA Report Sees Steady Growth in Air Travel," *Chicago Tribune*, March 26, 2004.

21. Marion C. Blakey, administrator, Federal Aviation Administration, "2004 Forecast Speech," at conference sponsored by the Airports Council International–North America (Washington, D.C., March 25, 2004), 1.

22. The press has covered LimoLiner from several perspectives. See Ken Gordon, "Boston to New York: Four Ways to Make the Trip," *New York Times*, January 20, 2004; Michael Conlon, "Don't Want to Fly? Take a Limo," Reuters, December 17, 2003; Vicky Hallett, "The Deals on the Bus," *U.S. News*, November 3, 2003; and Keith Reed, "Not Your Father's Magic Bus," *Boston Globe*, September 12, 2003; information also from www.limoliner.com.

23. Brian Brus, "Posh Bus Line to Offer Alternative to Air Travel," *Oklahoman*, December 29, 2001; also Motor Coach Industries, "Barry Switzer Directs J4500 to Get On the Field at The Coach," press release, July 29, 2003; information from https://www.ridethecoach.com.

24. "Luxury Bus Services Face Tough Road," *Bus and Motorcoach News*, September 24, 2003.

25. Senate Committee on Commerce, Science, and Transportation, *Hearing: Amtrak*, 108th Cong., 1st sess., April 29, 2003, 3.

Conclusion

1. Citizens Against Government Waste, "CAGW Identifies Record $22.9 Billion in Pork," press release, April 7, 2004, 1; CAGW also pointed out that the nation's public spending deficit had reached $521 billion, and debt was at $7.1 trillion.

2. Richard Bowker, chairman, UK Strategic Rail Authority, speech to National Rail Conference (London, February 11, 2004), 2, www.sra.gov.uk/news/2004/2/nrc_speech (accessed August 27, 2004).

3. Milton and Rose Friedman, *Free to Choose: A Personal Statement* (New York: Harcourt Brace Jovanovich, 1980), 90.

4. U.S. General Accounting Office, *Amtrak's Subsidy Needs Cannot Be Reduced Without Reducing Service,* 48.

5. This is argued well by Wendell Cox in his concurring statement to Amtrak Reform Council, *An Action Plan for the Restructuring and Rationalization of the National Intercity Rail Passenger System,* 65.

6. Wendell Cox, "WorldCom-Class Amtrak," *National Review Online*, July 2, 2002.

7. Henry Hazlitt, *Economics in One Lesson: Fiftieth Anniversary Edition* (San Francisco: Laissez Faire Books, 1996), 86.

8. Personal correspondence with the author, December 27, 2001.

Appendix A: Chronology of Warnings about Amtrak's Financial Condition

1. U.S. General Accounting Office, *Issues Associated With a Possible Amtrak Liquidation*, 1.

2. Phyllis F. Scheinberg, testimony before the Senate Committee on Appropriations, Subcommittee on Transportation, *Outlook for Improving Amtrak's Financial Health*, 105th Cong., 2nd sess., March 24, 1998, 1–2.

3. Senate Committee on Appropriations, Subcommittee on Transportation, *Assessing Amtrak's Future*, 105th Cong., 2nd sess., March 24, 1998, 2.

4. U.S. General Accounting Office, *Financial Performance of Amtrak's Routes*, 2, 5.

5. At the time the states were Alabama, Arkansas, Idaho, Iowa, Kansas, Kentucky, Nebraska, New Hampshire, North Dakota, Tennessee, Utah, West Virginia, and Wyoming. Phyllis F. Scheinberg, "Prospects for Amtrak's Financial Viability," letter to Representative Frank Wolf, B-280160 (Washington, D.C., June 5, 1998), 7.

6. U.S. Department of Transportation, Office of Inspector General, *Summary Report on the Independent Assessment of Amtrak's Financial Needs through Fiscal Year 2002*, TR-1999-127 (Washington, D.C.: Department of Transportation, November 23, 1998), viii.

7. House Appropriations Committee, Subcommittee on Transportation and Related Agencies, *Hearing on FY2000 appropriations for National Railroad Passenger Corporation (Amtrak)*, 106th Cong., 1st sess., March 4, 1999, 2.

8. U.S. General Accounting Office, *Amtrak's Progress in Improving Its Financial Condition Has Been Mixed*, RCED-99-181 (Washington, D.C.: July 1999), 5, 8.

9. U.S. Department of Transportation, Office of Inspector General, *Report on the 1999 Assessment of Amtrak's Financial Needs Through Fiscal Year 2002*, CE-1999-116 (Washington, D.C.: Department of Transportation, July 21, 1999), xxi.

10. U.S. General Accounting Office, *Amtrak Faces Challenges in Improving Its Financial Condition*, GAO/RCED-00-30 (Washington, D.C.: Government Printing Office, October 28, 1999), 8.

11. U.S. General Accounting Office, *Amtrak Needs to Improve Its Accountability for Taxpayer Relief Act Funds*, GAO/RCED/AIMD-00-78 (Washington, D.C.: Government Printing Office, February 2000), 5.

12. U.S. General Accounting Office, *Amtrak Will Continue to Have Difficulty Controlling Its Costs and Meeting Capital Needs*, 23.

13. Ibid., 8.

14. U.S. Department of Transportation, Office of Inspector General, *2000 Assessment of Amtrak's Financial Performance and Requirements*, CR-2000-121 (Washington, D.C.: Department of Transportation, September 19, 2000), iii, viii, xi, 1 and 12, respectively.

15. Phyllis F. Scheinberg, General Accounting Office, testimony before the Senate Committee on Commerce, Science, and Transportation, *Oversight Hearing on Amtrak*, 106th Cong., 1st sess., September 26, 2000, 1, 5.

16. Mark R. Dayton, deputy assistant inspector general, U.S. Department of Transportation, testimony before the New York State Senate Transportation Committee, DOT Inspector General Report No. CC-2001-121, March 9, 2001.

17. Amtrak Reform Council, *Intercity Rail Passenger Service in America*, 4.

18. Phyllis F. Scheinberg, General Accounting Office, testimony before the House Committee on Appropriations, Transportation Appropriations Subcommittee, *Hearing on FY2002 appropriations for Amtrak*, 107th Cong., 2nd sess., March 21, 2001, 5.

19. Kenneth M. Mead, inspector general, U.S. Department of Transportation, testimony before the House Committee on Appropriations, Transportation Appropriations Subcommittee, *Amtrak's Financial Performance and Requirements*, 107th Cong., 1st sess., March 21, 2001, 2–3, 12–13, 15.

20. Kenneth M. Mead, testimony before the House Committee on Transportation and Infrastructure, *Amtrak and High Speed Rail*, 107th Cong., 1st sess., July 25, 2001, 5, 8, and 1, respectively.

21. Laurence Arnold, "Amtrak Plans to Cut Management Jobs," Associated Press, July 27, 2001.

22. Amtrak Reform Council, "Amtrak Reform Council Finds Amtrak Will Not Achieve Self Sufficiency: Reorganization and Liquidation Plans Due," press release, November 9, 2001.

23. U.S. Department of Transportation, Office of the Inspector General, *2001 Assessment of Amtrak's Financial Performance and Requirements*, ii.

24. U.S. Office of Management and Budget, *Budget of the United States Government, Fiscal Year 2003* (Washington, D.C.: Government Printing Office), 260.

25. U.S. General Accounting Office, *Amtrak Needs to Improve Its Decisionmaking Process for Its Route and Service Proposals*, appendix 1, 18–19.

26. Kenneth M. Mead, inspector general, U.S. Department of Transportation, testimony before the Senate Appropriations Committee, Subcommittee on Transportation and Related Agencies, *Amtrak's Financial Condition*, 107th Cong., 2nd sess., June 20, 2002, 2, 4.

27. Linda M. Calborn, U.S. General Accounting Office, letter to Senator John McCain, July 15, 2002, 1–2.

28. U.S. General Accounting Office, *Potential Financial Issues in the Event That Amtrak Undergoes Liquidation*, 6.

29. Kenneth M. Mead, inspector general, U.S. Department of Transportation, testimony before the Senate Committee on Commerce, Science, and Transportation, *Hearing: Amtrak*, 108th Cong., 1st sess., April 29, 2003, 8, 2, respectively.

30. U.S. Congressional Budget Office, *The Past and Future of U.S. Passenger Rail Service*, 15.

31. Kenneth M. Mead, inspector general, U.S. Department of Transportation, testimony before the Senate Commerce, Science, and Transportation Committee, *Hearing: Amtrak*, 108th Cong., 1st sess., October 2, 2003, 1.

Appendix B: Chronology of Acela Express Development

1. David Field, "Leaning closer to implementation, Amtrak gives tilt train a dry run," *Washington Times,* January 28, 1993, 1.

2. Amtrak, untitled press release, ATK-93-24, May 19, 1993.

3. James H. Rubin, "Amtrak Begins Testing High-Speed German Train," Associated Press, October 4, 1993.

4. Amtrak, "Amtrak Announces Six Pre-Qualified High-Speed Train Set Consortiums," press release ATK-93-57, November 3, 1993.

5. Thomas M. Downs, president, Amtrak, testimony before the House Appropriations Committee, Transportation Appropriations Subcommittee, *Appropriations for Amtrak*, 103rd Cong., 2nd sess., March 17, 1994, 20–21.

6. Randolph E. Schmid, "High-Speed Train Group Picked," Associated Press, March 15, 1996.

7. Alice Lipowicz, "Amtrak Eyes Fast Buck From New Trains," *Crains New York Business,* April 22, 1996, 12.

8. David Field, "Amtrak Selected High-Speed-Train Builder," *Washington Times*, March 16, 1996, A13.

9. *Bombardier Corporation v. National Railroad Passenger Corporation*, U.S. District Court for the District of Columbia, CA: 01-2335(RCL), "Bombardier's Memorandum in Opposition to Amtrak's Motion to Dismiss," December 17, 2001, 6.

10. Brian Melley, "High-Speed Rail Faces Challenge as Amtrak's Future is in Jeopardy," Associated Press, April 22, 1997

11. George Warrington, acting president, Amtrak, testimony before the House Appropriations Committee, Transportation Appropriations Subcommittee, *Hearing on FY99 Appropriations for: Federal Railroad Administration; Amtrak*, 105th Cong., 2nd sess., March 11, 1998, 13.

12. Don Phillips, "Amtrak's New Tilt Trains a Bit Too Wide," *Washington Post*, January 7, 1999, F1.

13. Amtrak, "Amtrak Rolls Out 'Acela' Service, High-Speed Trains for Northeast; New Service Will Revolutionize Rail Travel, Continue Amtrak Turnaround," press release, PR Newswire, March 9, 1999.

14. Amtrak, "Acela Express High-Speed Train Makes Washington Debut," press release ATK-99-121, June 29, 1999.

15. Glen Johnson, "Wheel Problems Delay Amtrak's High-Speed Train," Associated Press, August 31, 1999.

16. Glen Johnson, "Even Without Bullet Train, Amtrak Begins Selling Its 'Acela' Service," Associated Press, September 9, 1999.

17. Don Phillips, "High-Speed Rail Meets New Delay," *Washington Post,* February 1, 2000, E1.

18. McKay, "EDC Backed Bombardier Bids."

19. Jane E. Dee, "Bullet Trains Can't Go Full Tilt; State's Rail Conditions Will Slow Acela Express," *Hartford Courant*, May 27, 2000, A1.

20. Joanna Weiss, "3 Hours to NYC? Not So Fast, Amtrak Says," *Boston Globe,* May 31, 2000.

21. Don Phillips, "Amtrak Halts Tests of New Fast Trains," *Washington Post*, June 20, 2000, A14.

22. Amtrak, "Bombardier/Alstom, Amtrak Resume Testing of Acela Express High-Speed Train on Northeast Corridor," press release ATK-00-78, June 30, 2000.

23. *Boston Herald*, "Amtrak Brass Can't Pin Down Start Date for High-Speed Train," July 6, 2000.

24. Don Phillips, "Amtrak Testing of High-Speed Electric Train Is Delayed Again," *Washington Post*, July 22, 2000, A11.

25. Don Phillips, "Amtrak's High-Speed Future," *Washington Post,* September 17, 2000, H01.

26. Laurence Arnold, "Amtrak Speed Train To Debut Dec. 11," Associated Press, October 18, 2000.

27. Laurence Arnold, "Fast Train Begins Service With Washington–Boston Round Trip," Associated Press, December 11, 2000.

28. Daniel Machalaba, "Amtrak Is Set to Christen New High-Speed Acela Train," *Wall Street Journal*, November 15, 2000.

29. Larry Arnold, "Equipment Problem Stops Speed Train," Associated Press, December 12, 2000.

30. Amtrak, "Acela Express Gets Off To Strong Start," press release ATK-01-03, January 11, 2001.

31. Amtrak, "Two More Acela Express Trains Coming," press release ATK-01-34, February 22, 2001.

32. "Amtrak to Begin Weekend Acela Service," *New York Times*, April 29, 2001.

33. Penelope Overton, "Bullet Train Loses Power, Amtrak's Acela Express Experiencing 'A Very Bad Run of Luck,'" *Hartford Courant,* July 13, 2001, B1.

34. Laurence Arnold, "Acela Express Off to Slow Start," Associated Press, August 21, 2002.

35. Penelope Overton, "Bullet Trains Missing Targets," *Hartford Courant,* August 21, 2001.

36. Lewis, "Travelers Use Ground Routes" A14.

37. Kowalczyk and Krasner, "Sudden Drop in Air Travel Strains Rail and Bus Service," A10.

38. Leslie Miller, "Amtrak Adding New High-Speed Trains As Ridership Jumps," Associated Press, September 27, 2001.

39. Raphael Lewis, "Ridership on Acela Express up 40 Percent, Amtrak Officials Say," *Boston Globe,* September 28, 2001, B2.

40. Claire Soares, "Reagan National Airport Reopens After Attacks," Reuters News, October 4, 2001.

41. Tom Ramstack, "Amtrak Limits On-Board Tickets Between Washington, Boston," KRTBN Knight-Ridder Tribune Business News, October 6, 2001.

42. Raphael Lewis, "Shuttle Flights to NYC, D.C. Are Resurgent," *Boston Globe,* November 5, 2001.

43. Amtrak quote is from Laurence Arnold, "Amtrak Sued by Train Manufacturer," Associated Press, November 8, 2001, and paraphrasing of Stangl's comment is from Raphael Lewis, "Acela Manufacturer Hits Amtrak with $200m Suit," *Boston Globe*, November 9, 2001.

44. Laurence Arnold, "Ridership Numbers Contradict Amtrak's Projections After Sept. 11," Associated Press, November 30, 2001.

45. Larry Sandler, "Post-Attack Ridership Levels for Amtrak Don't Rise as Reported," *Milwaukee Journal Sentinel,* November 30, 2001.

46. Laurence Arnold, "Railway, Airline Enter Code-Sharing Partnership," Associated Press, January 17, 2002.

47. Amtrak, "Amtrak Expands Acela Express Service between Washington, New York and Boston," press release ATK-02-015, January 29, 2002.

48. Laurence Arnold, "Private Companies Interested in Parts of Amtrak's Business, Consultant Says," Associated Press, April 11, 2002.

49. Amtrak, "David Gunn Appointed Amtrak President and CEO," press release ATK-02-065, April 26, 2002.

50. Keith L. Alexander, "American Starts Another Shuttle to N.Y., Boston," *Washington Post,* July 31, 2002, E01.

51. Don Phillips, "Acela Rapidly Disappoints, New Amtrak Trains Fast but Unreliable," *Washington Post,* August 6, 2002, E01.

52. Bombardier Inc., "Bombardier Sets The Record Straight Following Media Reports About Its Northeast Corridor Trainsets," press release, August 6, 2002.

53. Don Phillips, "Amtrak Cancels Acela Service on Safety Concerns," *Washington Post,* August 13, 2002.

54. David Stout, "Amtrak Halts Service after New Defects Are Found," *New York Times,* August 15, 2002.

55. Don Phillips, "Fax Fix Has Acela Ready to Run Today," *Washington Post,* August 19, 2002, B01.

56. Associated Press, "Amtrak Suffers Acela Train Setback," August 20, 2002.

57. Tom Ramstack, "Boston, New York Get Acela Restored; Amtrak Express to D.C. Still Limited," *Washington Times,* October 29, 2002.

58. Don Phillips, "Amtrak Sues Maker Of High-Speed Trains," *Washington Post,* November 22, 2002, E01.

59. Laurence Arnold, "Amtrak Acela Still Not at Full Strength," Associated Press, December 10, 2002.

60. Don Phillips, "Upkeep Problems Sideline 9 Acela Runs," *Washington Post,* March 29, 2003, A10.

61. "Amtrak to Cut N.Y.–Bos. Fare," *New York Post,* April 23, 2003.

62. Reitz, "Amtrak Welcomes Shoreline Commuters."

63. John Crawley, "U.S. Airlines Retake Key Business Lost to Amtrak," Reuters, August 10, 2003.

64. Amtrak, "Take Two Round-trips on Acela Express and Bring a Friend on Amtrak . . . on Amtrak," press release ATK-03-139, September 10, 2003.

65. Janice D'Arcy, "Acela: A Poor Track Record," *Hartford Courant,* September 28, 2003.

66. Amtrak, "FY '03 Amtrak Ridership Is Highest Ever," press release ATK-03-170, October 15, 2003.

67. Foss, "Amtrak to Overhaul Acela Express."

68. *Providence News Channel 10,* "Amtrak Modifies Wednesday Service," online transcript, January 27, 2004.

69. Amtrak buried the news about accepting the last Acela Express in June 2003 in a footnote under "Equipment Obligations" in National Railroad Passenger Corporation (Amtrak), *Consolidated Financial Statements,* 8.

70. The 1998 prediction was in Amtrak, untitled press release, ATK-93-24, May 19, 1993. The 1999 forecast was in Thomas M. Downs, president, Amtrak, testimony before the House Appropriations Committee, Transportation Appropriations Subcommittee, *Appropriations for Amtrak,* 103rd Cong., 2nd sess., March 17, 1994, 20–21

71. U.S. General Accounting Office, *Amtrak's Management of Northeast Corridor Improvements Demonstrates Need for Applying Best Practices,* 52–53.

72. Amtrak, "Amtrak and Bombardier/Alstom Consortium Announce Resolution of Legal Claims," press release ATK-04-021, March 17, 2004.

73. Amtrak, "Four New Acela Departures Begin April 26," press release ATK-04-023, March 22, 2004.

Appendix C: The Breadth and Depth
of Worldwide Rail Privatization

1. John van der Burch, "Southern Railway Offers Insight into Privatization," *Vancouver Sun*, November 17, 2003.

2. Gus Welty, "Railroader of the Year: CN's Paul Tellier," *Railway Age*, January 1997, 35–42.

3. Canadian National Railway Company, "CN Announces Three-For-Two Stock Split, and 17 Per Cent Increase in Cash Dividend," press release, January 28, 2004.

4. British Columbia Ministry of Transport, "Private-Sector Investor Sought to Revitalize BC Rail," press release, May 15, 2003.

5. "CN Rail Wins Right to Upgrade B.C. Rail," *Public Works Financing*, November 2003, 28–29.

6. See two stories by Scott Simpson, "CN Buys BC Rail for $1 Billion; Rail Towns Get Jobs, Projects," and "Government Consultant Praises BCR Sale," *Vancouver Sun*, November 26, 2003, and December 18, 2003, respectively.

7. Canadian National, "CN Closes BC Rail Transaction," press release, July 14, 2004, 1.

8. "KCS Maps 'The NAFTA Railroad,'" *Railway Age*, January 1997, 49–51; also Joel Millman, "Group Including Union Pacific Gets Mexican Rail Line," *Wall Street Journal*, June 27, 1997, A10.

9. Rennicke testimony, 115.

10. Grupo TMM, "Grupo TMM, S.A. Reports Fourth-Quarter and Full-Year 2003 Financial Results," press release, February 26, 2004, 1.

11. This is summarized well in "Privatization Mistakes Prejudice Mexican Rail System Operation," *El Economista*, December 9, 2003.

12. Rennicke testimony, 100, 106–107.

13. Jorge H. Kogan and Louis S. Thompson, "Reshaping Argentina's Railways," *Japan Railway and Transport Review*, June 1994, 23.

14. "Eastern Europe Subsidy Woes," *International Railway Journal*, September 2003, 14.

15. "Regionalisation Drive Gathers Pace," *Railway Gazette International*, June 1997, 385–86.

16. "Will DB Make It to the Market?" *Railway Gazette International*, November 2003, 708.

17. Yannick Pasquet, "German Government to Unveil Plans to Privatise Railways in October," Agence France-Presse, July 24, 2003.

18. "'Wise men' Recommend DB Listing," *Railway Gazette International*, July 2004, 385.

19. "Arriva Buys German Operator," *International Railway Journal,* May 2004, 3.

20. "Reforms to Meet the Prospect of Competition on the Tracks," *Railway Gazette International*, October 2003, 645.

21. "Norway Ponders Railroad PPPs," *Public Works Financing*, May 2003, 16–17.

22. "Privatisation Lines for Treasury Assets in 2002," *Privatisation Quarterly* (Warsaw: Ministry of the Treasury, Department of European Integration and Foreign Relations), summary of January–December, 2001, 25.

23. World Bank, "Selection of Consultants for PKP SA to Prepare and Advise on Privatization of PKP Cargo SA," (a "Request for Expressions of Interest" circulated to consulting firms), November 7, 2003.

24. The complex situation in Russia is summarized by Randy Bregman in "How Does Russia's Railway Restructuring Work?" *Railway Age*, October 2003, 48.

25. "Spain to Free Rail Services," *Public Works Financing*, January 2003, 17.

26. David Briginshaw, "Nordic Railways Continue to Evolve," *International Railway Journal*, October 2003, 1.

27. David Briginshaw, "The Pros And Cons of Privatising Maintenance," *International Railway Journal*, February 2004, 24.

28. "Four Contend to Build Tel Aviv Red Line," *Railway Gazette International*, January 2004, 9.

29. World Bank, "Consultancy Services of Financial Advisor to Assist the Privatization of Aqaba Railway Corporation," (a "Request for Expressions of Interest" circulated to consulting firms), March 16, 2004.

30. Summarized from "Latest News" and "Q and A," undated, www.saudirail-expansion.com (accessed April 18, 2004).

31. Ronald D. Utt, "Amtrak's Impending Collapse Offers One-Time Opportunity for Reform," *Heritage Foundation Backgrounder*, No. 1547, May 13, 2002, 9, www.heritage.org/Research/Regulation/BG1547.cfm (accessed August 27, 2004); also "New Melbourne Maintenance Deal," *International Railway Journal*, April 2004, 3.

32. Ian Thomas, "AN Split Up in $95m International Sale," *Australian Financial Review*, August 29, 1997, 1.

33. Michael Byrnes, "Australia Starts Rail Revolution with Privatisation," Reuters, September 20, 1997.

34. Lisa Allen, "Cash Call for Territory Rail Link," *Australian Financial Review*, May 30, 2003, 66.

35. David Briginshaw, "Australia's Missing Link Is Bridged," *International Railway Journal*, March 2004, 52.

36. "Private Sector Kick-Starts Two-Stage Airport Line," *Railway Gazette International*, May 2004, 297–98.

37. "Connex Picked in Auckland," *Railway Gazette International*, January 2004, 9.

38. Francis Small, "Privatisation Benefits Railway and Customers," *International Railway Journal*, August 1997, 34.

39. "Our View: Takeover Bid Spells New Hope for Rail," *New Zealand Herald*, September 9, 2003.

40. "Tranz Rail Rebrands and Takes Over Tranz Scenic," *International Railway Journal*, June 2004, 4.

Appendix D: Legislation Reflecting Reform Attempts

1. HR 1210, 105th Cong., 1st sess. (March 20, 1997).
2. HR 1666, 105th Cong., 1st sess. (May 20, 1997).
3. HR 3591, 107th Cong., 1st sess. (December 20, 2001).
4. S 1958, 107th Cong., 2nd sess. (February 15, 2002).
5. S 1501, 108th Cong., 1st sess. (July 30, 2003).
6. S 2306, 108th Cong., 2nd sess. (April 8, 2004).

Recommended References

Many reports from the U.S. General Accounting Office, the Inspector General of the Department of Transportation, and the Amtrak Reform Council have served as the basis for this book. The reader will have a better sense of the depth of reviews regarding Amtrak by examining the list below. These reports represent a treasure-trove of information. If Congress based decisions on the findings in these reports, Amtrak would have been liquidated some time ago and a system established to induce private operators to take over the busiest train routes. In the belief that current documents are more important than older ones, the reports are listed in reverse chronological order. They are followed by a bibliography of other sources. The first item listed is testimony that presented a comprehensive view of rail privatization around the world. All reports issued by agencies of the U.S. government were published in Washington, D.C., by the Government Printing Office.

Comprehensive Testimony about Worldwide Rail Privatization

William J. Rennicke, vice president, Mercer Management Consulting Inc., testimony before the House Committee on Transportation and Infrastructure, Hearing: Restructuring of America's Intercity Passenger Railroad System, 107th Cong., 2nd sess., April 11, 2002.

Reports from the Amtrak Reform Council

An Action Plan for the Restructuring and Rationalization of the National Intercity Rail Passenger System, February 7, 2002.

251

Intercity Rail Passenger Service in America: Status, Problems, and Options for Reform,
March 19, 2001.
*A Preliminary Assessment of Amtrak: The First Annual Report of the Amtrak Reform
Council,* January 24, 2000.

Reports from the U.S. Department
of Transportation, Office of Inspector General

2001 Assessment of Amtrak's Financial Performance and Requirements. CR-2002-
075, January 24, 2002.
2000 Assessment of Amtrak's Financial Performance and Requirements. CR-2000-
121, September 19, 2000.
Report on the 1999 Assessment of Amtrak's Financial Needs Through Fiscal Year 2002.
CE-1999-116, July 21, 1999.
Independent Assessment of Amtrak's Financial Needs Through Fiscal Year 2002. TR-
1999-027, November 23, 1998.

Reports from the U.S.
General Accounting Office (GAO)

*Amtrak's Management of Northeast Corridor Improvements Demonstrates Need for
Applying Best Practices.* GAO-04-94, February 27, 2004.
*Commuter Rail: Information and Guidance Could Help Facilitate Commuter and
Freight Rail Access Negotiations.* GAO-04-240, January 2004.
Transportation Security: Federal Action Needed to Help Address Security Concerns.
GAO-03-843, June 30, 2003.
Potential Financial Issues in the Event That Amtrak Undergoes Liquidation.
GAO-02-871, September 20, 2002.
*Amtrak Needs to Improve Its Decisionmaking Process for Its Route and Service
Proposals.* GAO-02-398, April 12, 2002.
*Assessing the Benefits of Increased Federal Funding for Amtrak and High-Speed
Passenger Rail Systems.* GAO-01-480T, March 21, 2001.
Decisions on the Future of Amtrak and Intercity Passenger Rail Are Approaching.
T-RCED-00-277, September 26, 2000.
*Amtrak Will Continue to Have Difficulty Controlling Its Costs and Meeting Capital
Needs.* RCED-00-138, May 31, 2000.
Increasing Amtrak's Accountability for Its Taxpayer Relief Act Funds. T-RCED-00-116,
March 15, 2000.
Amtrak Needs to Improve Its Accountability for Taxpayer Relief Act Funds.
RCED/AIMD-00-78, February 29, 2000.

Amtrak Faces Challenges in Improving Its Financial Condition. T-RCED-00-30, October 28, 1999.

Amtrak's Progress in Improving Its Financial Condition Has Been Mixed. RCED-99-181, July 9, 1999.

Amtrak: Contracting Improprieties by Chief Engineer. OSI-99-4R, February 26, 1999.

Prospects for Amtrak's Financial Viability. RCED-98-211R, June 5, 1998.

Financial Performance of Amtrak's Routes. RCED-98-151, May 14, 1998.

Outlook for Improving Amtrak's Financial Health. T-RCED-98-134, March 24, 1998.

Issues Associated With a Possible Amtrak Liquidation. RCED-98-60, March 2, 1998.

Transportation Financing: Challenges in Meeting Long-Term Funding Needs for FAA, Amtrak, and the Nation's Highways. T-RCED-97-151, May 7, 1997.

Amtrak's Financial Crisis Threatens Continued Viability. T-RCED-97-147, April 23, 1997.

The Financial Viability of Amtrak Continues to Be Threatened. T-RCED-97-94, March 13, 1997.

Amtrak's Strategic Business Plan: Progress to Date. RCED-96-187, July 24, 1996.

Northeast Rail Corridor: Information on Users, Funding Sources, and Expenditures. GAO/RCED-96-144, June 27 1996.

Amtrak: Early Progress Made in Implementing Strategic and Business Plan, but Obstacles Remain. T-RCED-95-227, June 16, 1995.

Amtrak: Information on Subsidies in Thruway Bus Operations. RCED-95-138, May 9, 1995.

Amtrak's Northeast Corridor Funding Needs. RCED-95-152R, April 13, 1995.

Amtrak's Northeast Corridor: Information on the Status and Cost of Needed Improvements. RCED-95-151BR, April 13, 1995.

Amtrak: Deteriorated Financial and Operating Conditions Threaten Long-Term Viability. T-RCED-95-142, March 23, 1995.

Amtrak: Issues for Reauthorization. T-RCED-95-132, March 13, 1995.

Amtrak: Deteriorated Financial and Operating Conditions Threaten Long-Term Viability. T-RCED-95-123, March 2, 1995.

Financial and Operating Conditions Threaten Amtrak's Long-Term Viability. RCED-95-71, February 6, 1995.

Amtrak: Deteriorated Financial and Operating Conditions. T-RCED-95-90, January 26, 1995.

Amtrak: Key Decisions Need to Be Made in the Face of Deteriorating Financial Condition. T-RCED-94-186, April 13, 1994.

Amtrak: Deteriorated Financial Condition and Costly Future Challenges. T-RCED-94-145, March 23, 1994.

Amtrak: Financial Condition Has Deteriorated and Future Costs Make Recovery Difficult. T-RCED-94-155, March 17, 1994.

Amtrak Safety: Amtrak Should Implement Minimum Safety Standards for Passenger Cars. RCED-93-196, September 22, 1993.

Amtrak Training: Improvements Needed for Employees Who Inspect and Maintain Rail Equipment. RCED-93-68, December 8, 1992.

Amtrak: Information on Amtrak's Operating Expenses. RCED-92-177FS, April 23, 1992.

Amtrak: Limited Income From the Revenue Enhancement Program. RCED-90-76, February 1, 1990.

Comparison of Amtrak Employee Injury Settlement Costs Under the Federal Employers' Liability Act and State Workers' Compensation Programs. T-RCED-88-49, June 22, 1988.

Amtrak: Auto Train Recovers Costs Required by Law. RCED-87-37, October 7, 1986.

Amtrak: Comparison of Employee Injury Claims Under Federal and State Laws. RCED-86-202, August 11, 1986.

Review of Amtrak's Study of Rail Service Through Oklahoma. RCED-86-140BR, April 14, 1986.

Cost of Amtrak Railroad Operations. RCED-86-127FS, March 27, 1986.

Proposed Amtrak Rail Service Between Philadelphia and Atlantic City. RCED-85-90, August 13, 1985.

Amtrak's Northeast Corridor Trains Operate With a One-Person Locomotive Crew. RCED-85-1, April 18, 1985.

Amtrak's Income Diversification Program: Potential for Increased Earnings and Reduced Federal Financial Support. RCED-84-41, October 14, 1983.

Analysis of Proposal to Reduce Amtrak's Federal Subsidy. CED-81-93, April 9, 1981.

Amtrak's Productivity on Track Rehabilitation Is Lower Than Other Railroads'— Precise Comparison Not Feasible. CED-81-60, March 13, 1981.

GAO Comments on Department of Transportation Study of Amtrak State and Local Taxation. PAD-81-58, January 30, 1981.

Further Improvements Are Needed in Amtrak's Passenger Service Contracts, But They Won't Come Easily. CED-81-35, January 7, 1981.

Alternatives for Eliminating Amtrak's Debt to the Government. PAD-80-45, March 28, 1980.

How Much Should Amtrak Be Reimbursed for Railroad Employees Using Passes to Ride Its Trains? CED-80-83, March 28, 1980.

Amtrak's Inventory and Property Controls Need Strengthening. CED-80-13, November 29, 1979.

Amtrak's Economic Impact on the Intercity Bus Industry. PAD-79-32, January 12, 1979.

Should Amtrak's Highly Unprofitable Routes Be Discontinued? CED-79-3, November 27, 1978.

Amtrak's Subsidy Needs Cannot Be Reduced Without Reducing Service. CED-78-86, May 11, 1978.

Should Amtrak Develop High-Speed Corridor Service Outside the Northeast? CED-78-67, April 5, 1978.

An Analysis of Amtrak's Five Year Plan. PAD-78-51, March 6, 1978.

Quality of Amtrak Rail Passenger Service Still Hampered by Inadequate Maintenance of Equipment. RED-76-113, June 8, 1976.

How Much Federal Subsidy Will Amtrak Need? RED-76-97, April 21, 1976.

Information on Expenditures for Air Travel by Amtrak Personnel in 1973 and Part of 1974. B-175155, August 26, 1974.

Fewer and Fewer Amtrak Trains Arrive on Time—Causes of Delays. B-175155, December 28, 1973.

Amtrak Needs To Improve Train Conditions Through Better Repair and Maintenance. B-175155, June 21, 1973.

Decision by the Amtrak Board of Directors to Bypass the Dallas Fort-Worth [sic], Texas, Area on a Proposed Route Establishing Rail Service Between the United States and Nuevo Laredo, Mexico. B-175155, February 7, 1973.

Bibliography of Other Sources

Fukui, Koichiro. *Japanese National Railways Privatization Study.* Washington, D.C.: World Bank, 1992.

Hilton, George W. *Amtrak: The National Railroad Passenger Corporation.* Washington, D.C.: AEI Press, 1980.

Love, Jean, Wendell Cox, and Stephen Moore. *Amtrak at Twenty-Five: End of the Line for Taxpayer Subsidies.* Policy Analysis No. 266. Washington, D.C.: Cato Institute, December 1996.

Vranich, Joseph, Cornelius Chapman, and Edward L. Hudgins. *A Plan to Liquidate Amtrak.* Policy Analysis No. 425. Washington, D.C.: Cato Institute, February 7, 2002.

Vranich, Joseph, and Edward L. Hudgins. *Help Passenger Rail by Privatizing Amtrak.* Policy Analysis No. 419. Washington, D.C.: Cato Institute, November 1, 2001.

Vranich, Joseph, and Robert W. Poole Jr. *Replacing Amtrak: A Blueprint for Sustainable Passenger Rail Service.* Policy Study 235. Los Angeles: Reason Public Policy Institute, October 1997.

Index

About the Author

Joseph Vranich has had a career in public relations and corporation communications, much of it in the field of transportation.

His work in rail transportation began between 1970 and 1973, when he participated in the campaign to create and expand Amtrak while serving as a regional director and executive director of the National Association of Railroad Passengers. He served as a public affairs spokesman for Amtrak until 1979, when he moved to the Grumman Corporation, contributing to the public relations program of its transit-coach subsidiary, the Flxible Bus Company. Following that he was The Boeing Company's Washington public affairs director, where his involvement with commercial airlines included domestic and international carriers. Between 1989 and 1995 he was vice president, public affairs, and president of the High Speed Rail Association, working for public subsidies to finance Amtrak's Acela Express program while also supporting legislation to induce private financing into passenger rail programs. The association granted him its highest honor, the Distinguished Service Award.

Mr. Vranich's previous books include *Supertrains* (St. Martin's Press, 1991), and *Derailed: What Went Wrong and What to Do About America's Passenger Trains* (St. Martin's, 1997), which argues for an Amtrak liquidation and development of substitute private operators. Following publication of *Derailed,* Vranich was appointed by Congress to the Amtrak Reform Council, where he served from February 1998 to July 2000.

Mr. Vranich earned his BA degree from Slippery Rock University in Pennsylvania and a certificate in an executive development program at the University of Virginia's Colgate Darden Graduate School of Business.